A Bolt from the Blue

of related interest

Counselling and Psychotherapy with Refugees
Richard Blackwell
ISBN 1 84310 316 8

Children, Bereavement and Trauma
Nurturing Resilience
Paul Barnard, Ian Morland and Julie Nagy
ISBN 1 85302 785 5

Music, Music Therapy and Trauma
International Perspectives
Edited by Julie P. Sutton
ISBN 1 84310 027 4

Psychodrama with Trauma Survivors
Acting Out Your Pain
Edited by Peter Felix Kellermann and M.K. Hudgins
ISBN 1 85302 893 2

The Inspiration of Hope in Bereavement Counselling
John R. Cutcliffe
ISBN 1 84310 082 7

Without You – Children and Young People Growing Up
with Loss and its Effects
Tamar Granot
ISBN 1 84310 297 8

A House Next Door to Trauma
Learning from Holocaust Survivors How to Respond to Atrocity
Judith Hassan
ISBN 1 85302 867 3

A Bolt from the Blue

Coping with Disasters and Acute Traumas

Salli Saari

Translated by Annira Silver

Jessica Kingsley Publishers
London and Philadelphia

First published in 2000 in Finnish under the title of *Kuin salama kirkkaalta taivaalta: Kriisit ja niistä selviytyminen* by Kustannusakeyhtiö Otava, Helsinki.

First published in English in 2005
by Jessica Kingsley Publishers
116 Pentonville Road
London N1 9JB, UK
and
400 Market Street, Suite 400
Philadelphia, PA 19106, USA

www.jkp.com

Copyright © Salli Saari 2005
Translation copyright © Annira Silver 2005

Library of Congress Cataloging in Publication Data
Saari, Salli, 1944-
  [Kuin salama kirkkaalta taivaalta. English]
  A bolt from the blue : coping with disasters and acute traumas / Salli Saari ; translated by Annira Silver.--
1st American pbk. ed.
     p. cm.
  Includes bibliographical references and index.
  ISBN 1-84310-313-3 (pbk.)
  1. Psychic trauma--Patients--Rehabilitation. 2. Traumatic neuroses--Patients--Rehabilitation. 3. Post-traumatic stress disorder--Patients--Rehabilitation. 4. Disaster victims--Rehabilitation. 5. Crisis intervention (Mental health services)--Finland. 6. Psychological debriefing. I. Title.
  RC552.P67S2224 2005
  362.196'852106--dc22
                                                                          2004024480

British Library Cataloguing in Publication Data
A CIP catalogue record for this book is available from the British Library

ISBN-13: 978 1 84310 313 4
ISBN-10: 1 84310 313 3

Printed and Bound in Great Britain by
Athenaeum Press, Gateshead, Tyne and Wear

Contents

Preface

The significance of psychological trauma in the evolution of mental health disorders was understood at the beginning of the 1900s. However, almost a hundred years passed before psychology as a science had developed to the stage where one of its aims could be said to be prevention of the development of psychological traumas.

It was not until the 1990s that work on a larger scale was undertaken to promote psychological processing of traumatic experiences. Development of the principles and special methods did not start until the 1980s. However, healthcare and social work professionals, decision-makers and citizens in general could identify with the mode of thinking and action. The operational models of acute crisis work spread quickly in Finland and were widely adopted.

The reason why we can identify with the thinking underlying crisis and disaster psychology is found in our own experiences. Traumatic events are part of life, and we all either have personal experiences of them, or we have been in a position closely to observe other people's struggle to cope. Everybody has experienced the emotions and reactions such events elicit, and the helplessness we feel when confronted by them.

Many of us also have experiences of harmful resolution patterns in which people in such situations often seek refuge, and which our environment also produces and supports. After years and decades, we see how greatly traumatic experiences have influenced our lives.

My training is both in research and as a psychologist working in practical mental health services. In my professional work, the guiding idea throughout my career has been the development of preventive care. I was immediately attracted to disaster-psychological thinking when I heard about it in the early 1990s. I felt that the operational model of acute crisis work was the most effective preventive care possible. It is precisely targeted at people who both feel a great need to receive help, and whose emotional state, along with the demands of their circumstances, produces an increased risk to their mental health. Disaster-psychological work has clearly defined objectives. The method that makes reaching those objectives possible is also known.

The roots of disaster psychology are in the USA and Norway. In Finland, however, the models have developed further. My training as a researcher has predisposed me to approach practical clinical work, too, from a researcher's viewpoint. My natural approach to each clinical event is curiosity. What can I learn from this meeting or situation? Is there some greater truth or significant revelation behind this experience? I set out to test this question, and in this way my own modes of thinking and operating evolve constantly.

Many of the concepts and experiences I have introduced in this book originate from situations which have occurred by chance, after which I have set out clinically to investigate the gained experience. In terms of development, it is a good thing that in clinical work one can never fully influence the circumstances and situations in which one operates. This is particularly true of acute crisis work. Thus, one may become involved in situations which one might otherwise try to avoid. They often produce new experiences and help to advance the field.

I have attempted to describe this process in my book. That is why I use many practical examples. This has its own problems, as crisis work is governed by strict rules of confidentiality. Wherever it is possible to identify an event or persons, I have requested their permission to publish the text.

Although every traumatic event and experience is individual and unique, they contain many common features. I know that many readers will feel that I am describing an event that happened to them. This feeling betrays the general laws governing traumatic events and the way we experience them.

When I set out to write my book, I worried in case I had nothing new to say on the subject. I understood that several good books had been published on the topic. But I was surprised to find that a large part of the thinking and experience underlying acute crisis work is such that it has not been presented in written form. The thinking and modes of operating are so new that they have only been passed on verbally at training courses. Many of the topics outlined in this book are in written form for the first time.

I use relatively few references in my exposition. This does not mean that I have invented everything I describe. Naturally, it is based on all the knowledge passed on in books, research papers and lectures and other educational opportunities by researchers and experts in the field. I have set out to test the applicability of this knowledge and experience in practical situations, and to develop it further on that basis.

How far this developmental work has advanced in Finland only became clear to me during the last couple of years, as discussion sprang up on the efficacy and outcome of acute crisis work, and the psychological debriefing method in particular. I was shocked by the primitiveness of the intervention methods employed in research, its mechanistic application, and the oversimplification and flaws of the whole thinking, when compared with practical reality. However, these factors also motivated me to write this book.

I am grateful to all the people with whom I have been permitted to walk a little stretch of life's path at a time when, for them, it has contained great suffering and pain, but also the experience of coping with that pain and being able to continue living. You have all taught me a vast amount, and I have endeavoured to pass on that experience, to enable us better to help and support those who must endure shocking experiences in the future.

I am thankful to all the hundreds of counsellors engaged in crisis work, with whom I have been able to share experiences and learn. Through this shared learning, my knowledge and experience have increased greatly in a way that is not otherwise possible within one human lifetime.

I also extend my gratitude to my employer, the Helsinki University Students' Health Service, which has given me the opportunity of widening my experience over and above what would have been possible within my customary job description. I have been granted leave of absence from my routine tasks, in order to undertake external training and supervisory assignments, whenever I have requested it. The encouraging attitude of my colleagues and superiors has had a great bearing on my ability to continue self-development by responding to challenges, even when they have seemed difficult. Naturally, equally important have been the colleagues who have met the challenges with me, and friends and family, who provide an outlet for relaxation alongside and after work.

Acknowledgement

The translation of this book has kindly been sponsored by Finnair.

1

Background

Almost 20 years ago, a young woman was killed in a road accident on her way to work. The accident happened on the morning of Maundy Thursday, before eight o'clock. The woman died instantly. She was married with two children, a nine-year-old son and a seven-year-old daughter.

When the boy, Risto, started university, he sought help from the psychological services. The reason was his problem with his studies: he was unable to concentrate on them. In addition, he had difficulties with close relationships. He was very angry and aggressive towards almost everybody.

When filling in his patient card, he drew a line through 'mother's age and occupation'. I have occasionally seen a line through the father's details, but never the mother's. I was surprised to hear that the line signified that his mother had died when he was nine years old. Yet, that line was an excellent reflection of his psychological experience. He could not recall a single memory image of his mother. When I asked him what his mother looked like, he replied that he had seen a couple of photos of her, which enabled him to describe her looks. He could access nothing from his own memory.

How is it possible that memory images can disappear so totally? After all, Risto was already nine when his mother died. He told me of his memories after his mother's death. He remembered how his father and his mother's parents wiped the tears from their eyes, embarrassed, and hurriedly changed the subject when the children were present. After the time when his father told him about his mother's death, he never talked to adults about his mother and her death. The one exception was his teacher, who hugged him. They cried together, when he returned to school after the Easter holiday.

Later, during psychotherapy, it became clear that the relationship between mother and son had been very close. The loss was too great for Risto to bear and to handle. The only way of coping was to block his mother totally from his mind, to deny the painful memories and mental images.

Risto became a model pupil at school, high-achieving and well-behaved. During puberty and later youth his hatred and bitterness began to erupt. He systematically bullied his younger sister, felt intellectually superior to his peers, used a great deal of alcohol and experimented with drugs.

After matriculation from school, the emptiness and hopelessness of his life, his bitterness and anger made Risto seek psychotherapy. Our paths crossed when I had just become interested in disaster psychology and the possibility that psychological trauma may be preventable. I was deeply affected by Risto's experiences and their impact on his personality. I felt a strong need to set out, together with him, to investigate the evolution of a psychological trauma, how it influences the course of a life and the development of a personality. I was also intrigued by how this damage could be repaired. That was the beginning of our collaboration which was to last for years.

First, we tried to access Risto's blocked memory images of his mother. We worked through details and experiences associated with her death. I encouraged Risto to visit his mother's grave. He had not been there since the funeral. He did make this visit. But talking to his father or to his grandparents about his mother and her death seemed impossible. After many months of systematic work, memory images of his mother started to come to him. He remembered going skiing with her; he had images of his mother cooking dinner, returning from shopping, and memories of being on holiday. To begin with, his mother had no face, only a figure.

At the same time, we had been working through how the trauma caused by the sudden loss of his mother had affected Risto's behaviour and his life. That Risto understood the sudden loss of his mother to be the root cause of his many problems was not sufficient to resolve them. What was required was more in-depth analysis, working through and re-experiencing. The thought that he had spent almost half his life living with his mother was cataclysmic. He had a great deal of sound foundation upon which to build, even though the impact of his mother's sudden death and his inability to cope with it psychologically had been powerful. Risto felt that he was different from other people. Something quite essential was missing from him, and he had been forced to find a way of coping with this shortcoming alone, which made him bitter and angry.

The psychological trauma experienced by Risto manifested in an interesting way in his behaviour. He did everything possible to ensure failure in various test situations. He was conscious of this himself, but could not influence his actions. The same situation was repeated endlessly. Yet, he was extremely gifted. This had mostly saved him from failure, but he was very aware that he would have succeeded better and more easily without this behaviour pattern. My interpretation was that Risto was unable to accept his mother's death, which was why he acted in such a way that the psychological injury caused by this traumatic event was revealed in his performance.

Another of Risto's problems was his inability to concentrate. He felt that while he was focusing on one thing, other things might be happening simultaneously around him which could significantly affect him and his life. Risto's mother was killed before eight o'clock in the morning. Risto spent the day at school, and the afternoon with his friends. He felt good, the Easter holiday had begun. At five in the afternoon, Risto was about to go out again, when he met his father on the stairs. He called to his father: "Hi, I'm going out. Mom's not home yet." His father asked Risto to come inside because he had something important to tell him. "Can't it wait?" asked Risto. "No," said his father. Once indoors, his father had told him that his mother had died.

I am convinced that the fact that Risto learned of his mother's death only hours later played a decisive role in the evolution of his difficulties in concentration.

Many of Risto's problems have been alleviated with therapy; some still remain. However, his experiences provide an excellent example of the powerful impact of psychological trauma on a person's life and behaviour.

Why, then, did Risto develop a psychological trauma? Is the development of a trauma unavoidable in such situations? Could it have been prevented, and how? These questions are addressed in the subsequent chapters of this book.

History of the concept of psychological trauma: return to Freud

Sigmund Freud introduced the concept of trauma to psychology. He extended the concept of trauma (injury, wound) to phenomena of the mind. A trauma is defined as a powerful event in a person's life to which the individual is unable to respond appropriately, and which has a powerful, sudden and enduring effect on him. A trauma is characterized by a flood of extremely strong stimuli that exceed the individual's tolerance threshold, his ability to control his feeling of agitation and to process it.

The concept of trauma was originally used in medicine and surgery. There, it denotes an injury caused by extraneous violence, and the effects of such an injury on the organism as a whole. When the concept was adopted by psychoanalysis, three features central to the concept were also transferred into psychological thinking: the idea of a violent shock, the idea of an injury, and the idea of its impact on the whole system.

Freud defined a psychological trauma as an experience where, in a short space of time, the mind is forced to receive such a flood of stimuli that it is too powerful to be processed in the customary way, resulting in permanent malfunctioning in the way energy works (Freud 1916–1917). Intolerable stimulation can result from a single, extremely strong stimulus, or the combined effects of several separate stimuli.

Later, Freud (1920) described the phenomenon as the relationship between an organism and its environment: a shield or a barrier protects a living being from external stimuli. It allows penetration of only those stimuli that the mind is capable of tolerating. If this threshold is exceeded, a trauma is formed. Then, the function of the protective system is to reach a state of equilibrium by every possible means, by reducing the intensity of the state of stimulation, and thus producing the state prescribed by the pleasure principle (see Freud 1916–17).

In the early years of psychoanalysis (1890–1897), theoretical understanding of the origin of neuroses was based on earlier traumatic experiences. Effective treatment was possible by purging and working through the traumatic experience. Later, Freud emphasized the role of internal sexual stimuli in the evolution of psychological traumas. According to drive theory, invisible internal factors produce a state of tension which exceeds the tolerance threshold of the mind, and which is therefore blocked. These theories have sometimes been seen as competing explanatory models, although Freud himself deemed them to be complementary.

A salient feature of Freud's trauma theory is repetition compulsion, by which is meant the individual's tendency to make similar unsatisfactory choices, to repeat behaviour patterns brought about by the trauma. The model also includes problems caused by endogenous anxiety originating from the trauma. Endogenous anxiety refers to situations where an individual becomes extremely anxious without any obvious reason.

The origin and evolution of disaster psychology

Psychologists and psychiatrists became interested in the reactions of human beings to extreme situations during World War II. Subsequently, a great deal of research has been published on both immediate and long-term reactions to shocking situations. The effects of natural catastrophes (earthquakes, volcanic eruptions and floods) on people have been studied. In addition, studies were carried out on the effects on people of various accidents (traffic accidents, explosions, accidents at work, fires and drownings), as well as on the consequences of violent acts. As well as the objects of the studies, the methods used also varied. In some studies, the immediate effects were studied; in others, duration of the effects was monitored over months or years.

Central to these studies was the desire to find out how people react in different situations. The aspiration to influence these reactions by offering help and support to accident victims or people who have experienced a shock was transformed to formulation of systematic operational methods as late as the 1980s. In this sense, disaster psychology is a very new science.

The development of operational models and special methods originated in the USA. These models were adopted very quickly in Norway, and it became the centre of disaster-psychological know-how in Europe. The reason was the number of accidents on oil rigs which presented a great challenge to those taking part in the rescue effort.

The first major accident in Finland, after which attention was focused on victims' psychological reactions and coping, was the explosion at Lapua explosives works in the 1970s. The psychological counselling carried out at that time was pioneering in nature. The procedures and methods employed were those available at the time. The working models and methods of modern disaster psychology were developed many years later.

Disaster-psychological thinking reached Finland from Norway at the beginning of the 1990s. The first large-scale training opportunity, headed by the Norwegian disaster psychologist Atle Dyregrov, was held in 1991 in Helsinki. The occasion became the incentive for implementation of this kind of work in Finland. The Finnish Psychological Association appointed a working party, consisting of members who were psychologists at the National Railways, Finnair, the Armed Services, the Police and the Finnish Red Cross, among others. Its remit was to come up with a proposal on how the disaster-psychological operational model should be organized in Finland.

The working party proposed a two-tier organization: a national specialized group for major accidents, and local crisis groups, attached to health centres, to deal with everyday traumatic situations. The task of the working party was completed when a national psychologists' major disaster preparedness group was founded, in conjunction with the Finnish Red Cross, and became operational on 1 April 1993.

The first local crisis group was set up in 1990 at Pietarsaari. During the previous summer, Krister Andersson, the local health centre psychologist, had attended Atle Dyregrov's disaster psychology course, organized as part of the Congress of Scandinavian Psychologists in Iceland. On returning home, he assembled a group of human relationships professionals (psychologists, social workers, church pastoral workers, healthcare workers and nurses), trained them, and organized the group's operation. His pioneering work was later recognized with an award from the Ministry of Social Affairs and Health.

From Pietarsaari, the operating model continued to spread. By 1998, Finland had a comprehensive network of local crisis groups.

Although Norway is the leading country in Europe when it comes to disaster-psychological expertise, Finland holds that position in comprehensive coverage and systematic organization of the work. No other service has been adopted as swiftly in Finland as the work carried out by crisis groups.

The Nordic countries are frontrunners in Europe in disaster-psychological counselling. All Nordic countries have a special system in place for the organization of psycho-social services and support for major accident victims immediately after the accident. Of other European countries, the Netherlands is well prepared for this work. In the great majority of European countries, this preparedness is only just being constructed.

What is unique to Finland is that so-called everyday traumatic events and situations are included under the umbrella of special preparedness (Finnish Ministry of Social Affairs and Health 1998). This speeds up access to help and makes preventive work possible. Even Norway does not have a similar network of local crisis groups for everyday traumatic situations. In other countries, victims are usually directed to either public health and mental health services, private service centres, or centres maintained by various organizations (e.g. rape victim support centres or torture victim support groups).

2

Acute Traumatic Events and Situations

Disasters, major accidents and exceptional societal situations

In international literature, a disaster is defined as an accident where the number of dead exceeds one hundred. The sinking of MS Estonia thus fulfils the criteria of a disaster. With regard to healthcare services, a disaster is often defined as an event where customary assistance and care organization and resources are insufficient, or where the number of injured exceeds the capacity of normal facilities. In a small town, a serious accident involving a bus full of passengers already fulfils the criteria of a disaster in terms of medical care.

In Finland, a major accident is customarily defined as an accident where:

- there are a number of dead

- there are scores of injured

- a number of people are in mortal danger, but good luck, favourable circumstances or other positive factors prevent lives being lost: 'near-miss' situations

- great financial losses are incurred (e.g. factory fires).

Major accidents are relatively rare. In the ten years between 1988 and 1998, there were 17 incidents that might be defined as major accidents in Finland. About 60 people perished in them and approximately 160 were injured.

Disasters or major accidents are classified as centrifugal and centripetal accidents. The effects of centrifugal accidents and disasters reverberate widely around the country. Such accidents are usually traffic accidents (train, bus and shipping accidents), where the victims come from around the country and sometimes around the world, and where the families and immediate circles of those killed or injured are all in their own home communities. Thus, crisis assistance is needed in numerous localities. In centrifugal accidents, nationwide co-ordination of psycho-social crisis work, effective communication with crisis groups, and a comprehensive network of local crisis groups are essential requirements of effective assistance. Most major accidents are centrifugal accidents.

A centripetal accident or disaster affects a geographically delineated area and its inhabitants. Such accidents or disasters are various natural catastrophes (floods, tornadoes, earthquakes and volcanic eruptions), explosions, and accidents involving chemical or radiation leaks. Fires are often also characteristically centripetal accidents. Examples of centripetal accidents are the Gothenburg disco fire and the Bhopal Union Carbide disaster.

In a centripetal accident or disaster, the demands of crisis work are different from those in a centrifugal accident. Suddenly, there are large numbers of people in the locality in need of psychological help. In such situations, local crisis resources are insufficient and outside assistance is required.

Peacetime states of disruption may be other special situations containing the danger of a catastrophe or social disaster. Such situations may be, for example, the threat of spreading of a dangerous contagious disease epidemic, or a sudden, uncontrolled flood of asylum seekers or refugees.

Deliberately caused danger situations and threats, such as terrorist attacks and hostage situations, are included in peacetime states of disruption. They also include certain long-term threats which do not fulfil the criteria of a tense international situation, threat of war, or an economic crisis, and consequently do not occasion declarations of states of emergency.

Distinguishing features of a traumatic event

Recognition of catastrophes, major disasters and societal disasters or special situations is generally easy. The less severe and more limited the event, the harder it is to decide whether acute crisis work should be activated.

A fundamental feature of disaster-psychological thinking is that the external event is held to be the variable to initiate activity. Work activated on the basis of disaster psychology is at its best when the starting point is what happened, and not the psychological or physical reactions of people. The distinguishing features of a traumatic event are:

- unpredictability of the event or situation
- uncontrollability of the event, inability to influence it by one's actions
- the nature of the event being such that it tests and changes values and priorities
- everything changes.

Unpredictability of the event or situation

The event takes place unexpectedly, like a bolt from the blue. We are unable to prepare psychologically for it. The significance of advance preparation is evident in occupations where the work consists of responding to emergencies. Such tasks form part of the work of, for example, the police, rescue personnel and doctors. During the few minutes between receiving the call and arriving at the scene, these workers are able to prepare themselves psychologically for the impending situation, and this shows in their behaviour and the way they perceive the situation. The shock is greater if there is no chance to prepare for it in advance.

People have great reserves of various resources which become available in extreme situations. The ability to prepare for a shocking event in advance is one of them. This so-called 'psyching up' can be used in preparing for particularly demanding and dangerous situations. Sportsmen use it before an important sporting event, but those engaged in crisis situations can also anticipate the imminent task by going over its demands, content and salient features in advance.

Alexander and Wells (1991) studied the after-effects experienced by police officers following a major accident. The disaster was a fire in the dormitory wing of an oil rig, which resulted in the sinking of the whole wing. One hundred and sixty-seven people lost their lives. The sunken dormitory wing was raised intact from the sea bed several months after the accident. The task of the police was to go through it, find the bodies, tidy them up, and have them identified. Seventy-three bodies were found in the dormitory wing.

In selecting police officers for the task, preference was given to those with previous experience of identification of bodies. In addition, the officers were prepared for the task by going over anticipated shocking situations and their own reactions to these situations. Another aim was to create a good team spirit and wide-ranging mutual support between team members. At the end of each day's work, a thorough psychological debriefing session was organized for everybody.

The work took months. The officers taking part had undergone a thorough health check before they were informed of their special assignment. This check was repeated at completion of the work, and again a few months after the end of the assignment. The result was that in this group of officers, absenteeism rates remained at the same level as before the assignment, as did their depression rate. Cases of anxiety actually decreased during and after the assignment, demonstrating the importance of careful preparation and anticipation of the task.

Uncontrollability of the event, inability to influence it by one's actions

Often, a traumatic event is characteristically such that we cannot influence what happens by our own behaviour or actions. We just happen to be in a certain place at a certain time, and this coincidence makes us party to the event. Generally, however, we do not perceive these situations in that way:

> A seven-year-old little boy was killed in a road accident. He had set off cycling with his friend to a nearby shop, and rode into the road from a car park surrounded by a high hedge. Just as one of the boys came out into the road, the firm's delivery truck happened to be driving by on its usual round. The driver did not even have time to see the boy. He only saw something blue, which later turned out to be the boy's bicycle helmet, and then he felt a bump, when his rear wheel went over something. He did have time to comprehend that there was a person under the wheel. Yet the sight was shocking when he went to see what had happened. The rear wheel of the truck had run over the boy's skull.
>
> A couple of days later, when the driver was going through the event at the psychological debriefing session arranged for him and his family, he said that he usually called in for coffee at a café which was just before the accident spot. That day, he missed out the coffee break, thinking that he would get home ten minutes earlier. If he had stuck to his normal routine, the boy would be alive.
>
> Less than an hour later he returned to the same theme. He said that on the day of the accident, a load of vegetables off the ship was late, and he set off on his round ten minutes later than usual. If the shipment had arrived on time, nothing would have happened.

The driver's way of analysing the course of traumatic events afterwards is very typical of us. We have an inbuilt deterministic way of thinking and perceiving events in terms of cause and effect. We see such connections even when they do not exist.

When something very shocking has taken place, we begin to search for preceding situations, where, had we acted differently, we could have prevented the whole episode. Such wisdom after the event and 'what if' thinking are a salient part of processing a traumatic event. It is impossible to accept the fact that we cannot always influence the course of events. It is easier to endure feelings of guilt than to lose the sense of being in control.

Mostly, such events are sums of many coincidences. However, it is difficult to accept the significance of coincidence in life. Many of us would rather believe in fate, a higher force, or seek refuge in religious explanations, than accept the importance of coincidence in the course of our lives.

Life also contains shocking events for which we are responsible. Some traumatic events (murders, rapes, assaults, robberies, etc.) are consequences of deliberate acts.

The nature of the event being such that it tests and changes values and priorities
Values in life generally change in three ways:

1. *We become more aware of our vulnerability.* Every day, we read in the papers and hear on TV about various accidents and acts of violence, but believe that they do not concern us. We live in a kind of delusion of inviolability. Then, when something shocking does happen to us or those close to us, we suddenly become aware of our own vulnerability. Taken to extremes, it is a consciousness that anything can happen at any moment. It is impossible to live in such a reality.

   I remember a woman student who had lost her partner in a fire. They had lived together for six years. This young woman spent at least six months pondering the question: "What is the point in my studying for my exam or preparing for a seminar, when anything can happen at any moment?"

   Psychologists have recently discussed the question of the reality of the world view of those who are mentally 'sound' and those who are depressed. It is known that people suffering from depression perceive the world and living as threatening. Conversely, the 'sound' pay no attention to these risks and dangers; they ignore them. Mental health is characterized by living in a kind of delusion of inviolability. When something very shocking happens, we become conscious of our own violability in a moment. But very soon we begin to process this feeling of vulnerability out of our system, and gradually, it does become weaker. In a few months, it has almost disappeared, provided that no new event takes place which would cause it to be renewed. Many successive traumatic experiences are capable of destroying the sense of inviolability totally or for a long time.

2. *Our world view and outlook on life change.* Everyone has some kind of a view of the world, life and its purpose. For some people it is clear, for others less defined, but it is part of the nature of traumatic events that they render our world view and outlook on life questionable.

   Generally, we think that our country is a relatively safe place to live where, in the main, justice prevails. When an innocent person is killed, our previous assumptions are grossly upset. Traumatic events also bring about a crisis in our outlook on life. We are forced to reassess our ideas and thinking about the world and the course of life. At the time of the sinking of MS Estonia, "Where was God when the Estonia sank?" became a catchphrase. We are able to preserve our former view only through a mental struggle. The world view and outlook on life of many people change as a consequence of traumatic experiences.

3. *Our values and priorities change.* Traumatic events also bring about a change in life values: work, career, status, money and property lose their importance and the value of family and interpersonal relationships is heightened.

   A Finnish survivor of the Estonia disaster publicly expressed how, after the accident, he wanted to concentrate on his family, to devote more time to it, and significantly to reduce the time spent working. In the Jokela train accident, the victims included a young family, the father of which was just about to fulfil his life's dream in the field of research. After the accident, he felt that the dream had lost a greater part of its importance. What now felt important were the family and his little son.

Everything changes

The life change brought about by a traumatic event forces us to embark on a very demanding process of adaptation. All human resources of strength are required for coping with this task. Often, the person is functioning at the limit of his resources; sometimes his resources are insufficient.

In a traumatic crisis everything happens quickly and violently. Thus, we are unable to control either what happens to us externally or our own inner reactions. Our typical feelings are: I can't take this; I won't be able to cope. That is why we need external support and help.

At the time of traumatic events, we are forced to face many psychologically challenging adaptation tasks. These tasks do not only concern the people at the centre of events, but also people around them at quite a wide radius. Consciousness of one's vulnerability, insecurity, and questioning about fulfilment of justice in life occupy the thoughts of many people. Even a single traumatic event has wide-reaching consequences.

Everyday traumatic events

Above, I have discussed characteristics of a traumatic event which facilitate identification of such situations. It is often thought that such events are very rare and that only a few people are forced to face them. This is certainly true of major disasters and catastrophes, but so-called everyday traumatic events touch very many people every year. Table 2.1 shows the number, or an estimate, of ordinary everyday traumatic events. The figures are based on most recent available statistics.

Table 2.1 Approximate annual number of acute traumatic incidents in the UK

Deaths in road accidents	3500
Serious injuries in road accidents	33,700
Deaths at work	600
Serious injuries at work	52,900
Deaths assigned to homicide (England and Wales)	2700
Victims of serious violence	38,000
Deaths by drowning	500
Suicides	4500
Sudden death syndrome (young people)	400
Accidental deaths at home	4000

The accidental or violent death of a loved one is one of the most shocking traumatic events in a human life. Every year, more than 16,000 people die under such circumstances in the UK. Approximately 4500 people annually commit suicide in the UK. Every day, about 12 people kill themselves. Suicide is always a traumatic event for the family and close friends. It is even more shocking that in recent years suicides have increased particularly among younger age groups and even children.

There is no precise information on the number of attempted suicides in the UK. The estimated annual number is approximately 140,000 in England and Wales alone, based on information from the mental health charity, Mind. Not all attempted suicides are such that the disaster-psychological approach is suitable for dealing with the reactions they evoke. Yet in many situations it offers valuable help in addressing the reactions of the person who attempted suicide and his family, and in their recovery. Such treatment also helps prevent future attempts.

A young woman attempted suicide by jumping from the balcony of an apartment block. She was in a coma for days and her condition was critical; she was close to death several times during this period. She had no lower limb or head injuries, but she had very serious internal injuries and one of her arms was totally crushed.

Everyone around her was at a loss and very shocked. Nobody could have imagined that she would attempt suicide. Debriefing sessions were organized for her family and closest friends. At that stage, she was still in a critical condition, and it was not known whether she would survive. During the debriefing sessions, all alternatives were thoroughly discussed, with the thoughts and feelings they elicited: that she would die, that she would survive but be very disabled, and that she would recover from her suicide attempt.

The woman survived and made a full recovery. I visited her in intensive care a couple of times a week, when she began to recall her attempt and details associated with it. When she was released from hospital, I made home visits twice a week. When she was sufficiently recovered, she started to attend my clinic. At first, she was sorry that she had not succeeded in her attempt, but gradually her zest for life returned and she began to discover new significant things in her life. A couple of years after our collaboration ended, she sent me a photograph of herself with her two-month-old baby. Later, I received a note accompanied by a wedding photo. Sometimes a suicide attempt can be the beginning of a new life.

About 3500 people annually are killed in road accidents in Britain. The number injured is approximately 33,700. A couple of theses have recently sparked off debate in Finland on the lack of psychological support for accident victims. The reasons are twofold. Generally, those seriously injured in road accidents are treated in large hospitals, where there are no facilities for sufficient psychological services for accident victims. The help offered by crisis groups is usually centred on the days following the accident, and in many municipalities it is restricted only to accidents where people were killed. Furthermore, this assistance provides an appropriate service for the victim's family, but it is well known that physical injuries delay the victim's psychological processing of the event. The psychological processing of the injured and his family proceed at different rates, making the timing of shared sessions difficult. Often, the amount of psychological support needed by the injured person is incorrectly estimated.

The most shocking traumatic events are cases of homicide, of which approximately 2700 are estimated to happen each year in England and Wales alone. They often shake large communities. They also shake the general public, owing to the widespread publicity they receive. About 18,000 people become victims of serious wounding or acts endangering life every year. In reality, this number is probably much greater, if personal experience is used as the criterion. Victims of violence number approximately 38,000 people annually in the UK.

According to statistical sources, violence is clearly on the increase. This means an additional challenge for crisis work, as research shows that violent acts which are directed from person to person have the most severe psychological impact. Violent situations cause extremely powerful reactions in victims.

In the UK, about 500 people drown each year, depending on the warmth of the summer. If the summer is warm and a lot of people spend time on the water, there are more cases of drowning than in cool summers. Relatively few people are killed in house fires, but the loss of one's home is always a very traumatic experience. The number of people killed in accidents at work is around 600, those severely injured number approximately 53,000. An accident at work always has a widespread shock effect on the work community, and requires special treatment.

A death does not need to be accidental or violent to deeply affect the family, friends and other close social groups. Sudden natural deaths, too, where a perfectly healthy person suddenly dies, cause great shock to people close to the deceased. Naturally, the age of the deceased has a bearing on how shocking the event is perceived to be. There is a difference in a 70-year-old healthy grandmother dying in her home and a 20-year-old young person, let alone a child. The younger the deceased person, the more unexpected and shocking the death.

> A young man of 25 went to settle his small daughter to sleep in the evening. He lay down to rest on his own bed, at the side of the child's wooden cot. The man's mother was visiting and wondered why her son was so long in the bedroom. She went to see what was keeping him. She saw that her son had dropped off to sleep and thought that she would let him rest a while before waking him up.
>
> After about 15 minutes, the mother went to wake her son, but however hard she shook him, she could not wake him. She called an ambulance and the paramedics tried to revive the man in vain. The son had died while settling his daughter to sleep.

Typical causes of death in such sudden natural deaths are heart attacks and strokes, and cot deaths form their own special group. Every year, there are about 400 sudden natural deaths of young adults.

Some everyday traumatic events are so-called 'near-miss' situations. If the situation causes such a great threat or risk to people that they believe they are going to die, the psychological reactions elicited are usually so strong that their systematic treatment is necessary.

Every year, approximately 300,000 sudden traumatic events take place in the UK. As each of them affects a number of people, it can be estimated that about one person in twenty in the UK experiences a traumatic event each year.

A characteristic of the disaster-psychological model is that the event or situation is first identified as fulfilling the criteria of a traumatic event. Then, steps are taken to plan for the services required. It is not always easy to decide whether an event fulfils the criteria of a traumatic event. On many occasions, crisis workers must first assess the nature of the event, and then, based on its particular features, the suitability of the disaster-psychological model, or whether some other model of service and support would be more effective and appropriate.

It is often thought that psycho-social support is only necessary in connection with major disasters. People's reactions and their need for support are similar in everyday traumatic events. A shocking event is equally trauma-tizing for an individual, whether it touches ten or a thousand people. Often, a single event can be even more traumatic.

Major disasters are rare and they affect relatively few people. The importance of psycho-social support and services is most apparent in practice in preventive work carried out in everyday traumatic situations. The work carried out in connection with major disasters is the most visible in the media.

3

Traumatic Events and Psychological Victims

Considering the psychological aspect in defining victims

Victims of an accident are usually defined as those who were killed or injured. This is, indeed, the case from a purely medical viewpoint. When the human psyche is taken into consideration, the concept of a 'victim' is seen in an entirely new light. In the psychological sense, victims are all the people who are deeply shocked by the event and who suffer a psychological trauma.

Both in defining the victims of a traumatic event or situation and in understanding the psychological reactions of these victims, it is important to note this psychological law: we do not react only to what really happened, but also to a mental image of what might have happened.

> For example, the impression conveyed by the newspapers of the shipwreck of the Sally Albatross was quite different from that of the people involved in the accident. We read in the papers that there was no danger. The rescue operation went extremely well. Nobody was killed or injured.
>
> Instead, we heard both from passengers and crew how threatening and frightening the situation was, how thoughts of the sinking of the Titanic were triggered (at the time, the film had not yet been thought of) and how a mental image forced itself on them – that this is now my fate, too.
>
> Many people who were involved told us that they themselves and more particularly their loved ones had difficulty in understanding the intensity of the reactions elicited by the accident. It was only when they received a letter from the shipping company, explaining the psychological law that we react psychologically also to what might have happened, that they felt better.

I will quote another example of this law and its significance.

A young woman came out of the library into the street in a city centre, at around six o'clock in the evening. She had time to take a few steps, when a man attacked her from behind, tearing her clothes off her, at the same time dragging her towards a van parked at the roadside. From the corner of her eye, the woman saw that two other men were leaning against the van, calling encouragement to the third man.

The woman managed to wrench herself free and escape. She ran straight to the nearest police station to report the incident. Although her breathing had returned to normal after running, as soon as she was recounting the event, she began to hyperventilate violently. She was able to utter only a syllable at a time. She was shaking all over. The police barely managed to find out what had happened to her. After she had made her statement, the police took the woman to hospital, where she spent the night.

The woman could not process this traumatic experience, although she was offered the opportunity. She said that she did not want to discuss it, she just wanted to forget. As soon as she began to think of the incident, the earlier reactions returned. She did, however, manage to describe her mental image of what the situation could have led to. She saw in her imagination how the man succeeds in dragging her into the van, they drive her to a quiet spot, and then the men each take turns in raping her and finally kill her.

In reality, of course, hardly anything had time to happen. Her powerful reaction is understandable, once we know her mental image of what could have happened.

The power of the psyche is reflected in an incident told by an experienced health centre doctor many years ago.

He was working as a health centre practitioner on the western coast of Finland. At the time, young people were in the habit of driving around on the frozen sea on sunny spring days. One Sunday morning, four young people, two boys and two girls, went off for a drive. On their way out to open sea, they spotted a line in the ice, showing a crack, but took no notice of it. On their return, the break was already slightly open but, driving over it at speed, they cleared it easily.

By six o'clock in the evening, the same crack was six metres wide. When one of the girls heard this, such intense symptoms were triggered that she was forced to seek help at the health centre. Merely the knowledge that she had been in mortal danger triggered these reactions, even though she had been safe for hours.

A traumatic event or situation has a multifaceted psychological impact on people. It is possible to become a psychological victim from a number of perspectives.

Perspectives in defining victims of a traumatic event

Those involved in the incident

Everyone involved in a traumatic incident usually receives some kind of a psychological trauma. Psychological victims are:

- the physically injured and their families
- the physically uninjured and their families.

Those who have experienced the loss of a loved one

All those people and social groups who have suddenly lost a person close to them are victims of the event in the psychological sense. Such people are:

- spouse
- children
- grandparents
- other relatives
- friends
- colleagues
- school friends
- members of leisure activity groups, etc.

Rescue personnel and helpers

Members of certain occupations are in the course of their work continually exposed to danger and threat to their safety, physical and psychological pain, and shocking events and sights, as they help victims and carry out their duties. Such occupations are those of, for example:

- rescue personnel
- police
- doctors and nurses involved in acute medicine
- social workers involved in acute work
- various crisis workers
- photographers
- journalists.

Eyewitnesses and bystanders

In accidents and violent or other traumatic situations, there are often people present who see and hear the event. They, too, are victims of the traumatic event, because they are forced to witness a shocking event as bystanders. One does not need to be involved in the incident in order to receive a psychological trauma.

The intensity of a developing psychological trauma is affected by at least two factors: identification with the actual victim of the event and the event itself, and whether the person is an eyewitness voluntarily, out of curiosity or unavoidably. The importance of identification is illustrated by the following example:

> In a densely populated urban area where a lot of families with children lived, a mother was about to go out in the family car. She placed one child in a child safety seat in the front, strapped in, and the five-year-old sister went on the back seat. However, the car would not start, and the mother decided to get the buggy from the garage so they could set off on foot. The children stayed in the car.
>
> While the mother was in the garage, the car exploded in flames. The five-year-old managed to get out from the back seat on her own. The other child was burned to death in the car.

This incident evoked great emotion and reactions widely within the whole community, not only among those who knew the family and the children, but in people who were total strangers. In general, reactions are always intense if the victim is a child. In this situation, however, an additional factor was that all of us who have, or have had, small children, have acted like that mother. The thought that it could quite easily have happened to me makes the event particularly psychologically poignant.

We can end up as eyewitnesses of a shocking event in many ways. We may be the first to arrive on the scene after an accident, or we may just happen to be there when something shocking happens. We might also see a crowd gathered around something, and go along out of curiosity.

Five passenger ferries, carrying about 8000 passengers in all, took part in the rescue effort at the Estonia disaster. Although the passengers were able to control what they saw to a degree, they certainly could not shut out their awareness of what had happened, and the fact that they were at the scene of a disaster. In such a situation, we are usually unable to make a free decision about whether we want to see the consequences of an accident or not. Our eyes tend to lock on to it. We are compelled to look, even if we do not want to.

At Christmas 1996, there was a fire in an apartment in a large block in a Finnish city. A 13-year-old girl was trapped by the fire on a balcony, and was finally forced to jump from the balcony in a panic, to escape the fire and the heat. The situation evolved over several minutes, during which the girl was calling for help.

A large number of people were at the scene. Some of them had been evacuated from the burning building, some had come from neighbouring buildings, and some witnessed the event from their own window or balcony. Many described the event: "I knew that I should have looked away, but I couldn't".

Causes of a traumatic incident

Although traumatic events are often accidents, sums of several coincidences, there are also events that are clearly caused by some person or persons. Mostly, these situations are accidental in nature, not caused consciously or deliberately, such as many traffic accidents, but the person who caused the incident is clearly identifiable. In some situations, the act itself may be conscious and deliberate.

Usually, the protagonist of the act, the person who caused the event, is also deeply shocked by it. He, too, and his loved ones, receives a psychological trauma.

A young taxi driver knocked a nine-year-old girl over on a pedestrian crossing. The taxi was not speeding. For some reason, the driver did not see the girl, but hit her. The girl was taken into hospital, where she was found to have sustained only slight injuries and was released immediately.

After a couple of days, a very anxious and tearful man arrived at the police station. He had enormous guilt feelings about the accident. He wanted to contact the girl and her parents and ease his anguish that way. The investigating officer asked the girl's parents if they would allow the taxi driver to get in touch with them, talk to them, and see that the girl was all right. The girl's father refused. His attitude was to "let him suffer".

When the taxi driver attended another interview with the police after a few weeks, he was even more anxious and said that it was almost impossible for him to continue as a taxi driver. He was clearly becoming incapable of work without psychological help.

In crisis work, the causer of an incident or situation and his family are often forgotten, even though the event may cause them a psychological trauma that is at least as serious as those of the other victims.

Sometimes, the protagonist is arrested by the police, in the police station or in prison. These people are then thought to be out of reach of psychological support and services. This is not necessarily the case. It is often possible to give them, too, psychological crisis care. In such cases, the police will be present at the sessions. Exceptions are cases where crisis care is not possible for investigative reasons.

Hidden victims

Many traumatic events produce hidden victims. They are people who should have been, for example, on a train, bus or plane that crashed, or in a restaurant when there was a shooting incident. A hidden victim, even though he was not present, often reacts partially in similar ways to those who were there.

Direct and indirect victims

A distinction often made when defining psychological victims of a traumatic event is that of direct and indirect victims.

Direct (primary) victims are:

- the deceased
- those physically or psychologically injured
- others directly involved in the incident.

Indirect (secondary) victims are:

- those who have lost family or loved ones
- family and loved ones of injured survivors
- colleagues and friends of the deceased and injured
- outsiders who witnessed the incident or its consequences
- professional and volunteer helpers who participated in the rescue, treatment and investigative effort
- others who participated in victim support and care
- those who suffered financial losses due to the incident
- those who were evacuated because of the threat, without other losses
- family and loved ones of the helpers
- others whose mental balance was adversely affected by the incident
- people who might have been involved in the incident (e.g. those who cancelled a fateful journey).

Taking the psychological perspective into account in defining victims places fresh demands on crisis work. First, the number of victims is multiplied. For each medical victim (dead or injured), there are, at a conservative estimate, 10–30 psychological victims. Sometimes only one person is killed or injured, but there are hundreds of psychological victims. For example, a few years ago, there was an accident in a Finnish town, when a schoolgirl bent down to pick up some candy from the ground during a carnival parade and was run over by a truck. This is an example of a situation where the incident has a shocking effect on hundreds of people.

A second special consideration in crisis work, when the psychological aspect is taken into account in defining the victims of an incident, is the geographical location of the victims. Medical victims are always located at the scene of the incident. Conversely, the psychological victims are often scattered around the country, even the world. They are at their homes, work, school and daycare. This fact places demands of a different kind on crisis preparedness, co-ordination of crisis work and communication.

4

Processing a Traumatic Experience

Our reactions after a traumatic experience reveal clearly uniform characteristics. Many people react in a certain way, although there are individual differences, too. Time and again in crisis work, I have marvelled at people's ability to cope. We humans have huge resources of strength which are triggered in extreme situations. Often, a person over whose coping I have had serious doubts has successfully overcome an experience he initially perceived as unbearable, and regained his zest for living.

We human beings have many inbuilt, very appropriate reaction and processing models that help us cope with tragic experiences. They are triggered automatically, assist the progress of the coping process and increase its efficiency. Often a problem is only created by our conscious attempts to interfere with this process, and thus prevent the processing of the experience.

However, not all automatic reactions aid or enhance the processing of a traumatic experience. Over the years, we may have adopted ways of coping which, on the contrary, prevent or hinder the process.

The concepts usually referred to in disaster psychology are 'immediate reactions' and 'after-effects' or 'long-term reactions' (e.g. Dyregrov 1994). In my view, a more accurate picture of the psychological process following the experience, its different stages, and its progress is gained by applying Cullberg's (1991) distinction of four stages of crisis processing to coping with acute traumatic experiences. I have applied this description to many situations where people who have suffered various traumatic experiences have commented on how relevant it is to their experience.

Psychological shock

Shock reactions

When we learn about something shocking, or when something very shocking happens to us, our first reaction is psychological shock. What we have heard or experienced does not feel real. Although we may be involved in what happened, it may feel like a movie.

Psychological shock is a case of our minds protecting us from knowledge and experience that it cannot take in and endure. Earlier, when discussing the characteristics of a traumatic event, I referred to its most important feature: unpredictability. It takes place suddenly, without prior warning, and it is not possible to prepare oneself for it in advance. In psychological shock, the mind is taking time out.

In psychological shock, a larger part of the brain's capacity than usual is in use (Dyregrov 1994). The senses, too, open up to receive perceptions, and they impinge directly on the brain, without the usual selectivity and editing. That is why the sensory perceptions and mental images created are extremely powerful, detailed and clear. They are so strong that the brain may later reproduce the perceptions, so-called 'flashbacks'. Flashbacks are powerful, intrusive sensory perceptions, created in a state of shock, and they frequently occur after a shocking traumatic situation. They can occur within any sensory modality. The most common are visual perceptions, but auditory, smell, taste and touch perceptions occur, too. Sometimes, a flashback is associated with movement, such as sudden movements after train crashes. A vision of a burning body, the expression of a drowning child, a car coming towards you, the smell of smoke in fires, the smell of cordite in shooting incidents, the taste of blood in a resuscitation situation, and the feeling of coldness of skin are typical sensory perceptions turned into flashbacks.

A person in a state of shock is also powerfully affected by people he encounters and by what they say. A contact lasting a few minutes is so important that the person will remember it for the rest of his life. Especially in major accident situations or when the rescue is prolonged and difficult, an enduring friendship often develops between rescuer and rescued. The words a person in shock hears from rescue workers, police or medical personnel are very significant words. They usually create the ambience for the entire event.

> A two-year-old little girl had drowned. Her mother found her and immediately attempted to revive the girl. Soon other people with resuscitation skills arrived, and the mother was relieved from this task.
>
> Later, the ambulance paramedics and police arrived. The mother found unexpectedly that her home was full of strangers and she had nothing to do,

having been forbidden to go where her daughter was being resuscitated. So, to alleviate her anxiety, she decided to make coffee.

When the coffee was made, there was a dilemma as to who would drink it with the mother, as everyone was very busy. An older police officer settled quietly at the kitchen table with the mother. There they discussed the mother's anguish and her fears that she had resuscitated her daughter incorrectly. The officer consoled the mother and said that she had almost certainly done everything she could to save her child.

Later, the mother said that that conversation with the policeman at the kitchen table was a huge consolation to her.

Here is another example of the importance of frontline helpers' words at the shock stage:

A housewife had been to do the shopping at the mall with her two children and was on her way home. She was driving along the shopping mall perimeter road, when suddenly a 13-year-old girl ran in front of the car. The car hit the girl, who was thrown into the road.

An ambulance and the police had been called, but they had not yet arrived. The girl was lying in the road unconscious, but she was still alive. People had gathered around.

A police patrol happened on the scene, but not in response to the call. The police officers stopped their car and came to see what had happened. According to the driver, the officer first on the scene said: "What's going on here, then? Oh yes, someone's been knocked down. Well, it happens." The driver who had knocked the girl down was very offended by the officer's nonchalant tone. The first words of the second officer were: "Tell us at once how much over the speed limit you were."

Both of these utterances by police officers affected the tone of the already shocking event in the driver's mind. She repeatedly went over them in her head and talked about them at every opportunity. Those words materially contributed to her already traumatic experience.

With these examples, I want to emphasize the importance of the actions and behaviour of frontline helpers in traumatic situations. Their calming, security-inducing and encouraging demeanour has an enormous impact on a person in psychological shock. Their approach and words give the incident its tone. It may be positive, supportive of the experience, but it can also be negative, adding to the pain and anxiety.

We are not aware of everything that happens at the scene of an accident or incident. Our perceptual field contracts and becomes like a tunnel, leaving some events completely outside our attention, but what we do take in, we perceive with great accuracy, clarity and detail.

Although our perceptions in a state of shock are detailed and accurate, our concept of time changes. Often, people talk of 'subjective time', meaning how long the time span seemed to be. For example, if we have to wait for the police or an ambulance, time can seem very long. Conversely, if there is much to do, the time may seem very short.

> In early summer, in the small hours, an apartment in a small block caught fire in a city suburb. Some neighbours were woken by the fire, alerted the fire brigade, and then woke the residents of the building and evacuated them to the yard. There they stood and waited for the fire service to arrive. The interval seemed like an eternity, and when the fire brigade finally came, the residents said: "You must have come from out of town, it took you so long." The residents estimated that the fire service took at least 45 minutes to arrive; in reality, it was at the scene seven minutes after the alarm was raised.

Psychological shock is a survival technique. Everything serves this goal. One of the phenomena associated with psychological shock is so-called supermemory. Many people who have been involved in a car accident, where, for example, an oncoming vehicle is approaching on their side of the road and there is nothing they can do, describe their ability to review their entire life during those few seconds before impact, as if they were watching a video.

Many professionals, too, who face tough situations in the course of their work, have experiences of supermemory associated with psychological shock.

> At about five o'clock on the day before a public holiday, a bomb was thrown into the garden of a police drug squad officer. He happened to be home alone, and he heard in his bathroom that someone had gone through the gate in the back yard. He thought that his wife and children were coming in that way and went outside to meet them. He saw movement behind the fence and thought that the children were hiding from him, and set off to walk towards the gate. He had taken a few steps, when he wondered what the devil the smouldering thing at his feet was.
>
> He picked up the smoking lump and thought that it looked like a bomb: a hand grenade with a burning fuse attached. He reached out, picked up some pruning shears off the living room window ledge a metre away, cut the fuse and threw the lump onto the lawn. Then he went inside, took his jacket, his official issue weapon, put on his shoes, and ran 100 metres in one direction and 50 metres in the opposite direction, thinking he would catch the villains. When he was 50 metres away in the other direction, the first thought that came to him was that his house was unoccupied, doors wide

open, anybody could enter and do anything. Then he rushed to call the police.

This is how this experienced policeman described his actions. It is perhaps worth mentioning that the grenade would have exploded in 5–7 seconds. His friends at work commented on hearing this description, "It's a good job it happened to just this chap, as he is so level-headed. If it had been me, the grenade would have exploded, no problem. I wouldn't have been able to do a thing." My response was: "I don't believe it. I'm sure that if the incident had taken place at your home, each of you would have acted just as efficiently."

One of the effects of psychological shock is that we are able to access all the experience and knowledge we have amassed during our lives. This is again proof of the brain's ultra-efficient functioning in shock. We recall everything we have learned in training, practice and experience. Our survival and preservation of functioning is also served by the fact that, in shock, we usually have no feelings. The more shocking the experience, the more likely our emotions are to vanish.

Let us return to the example where the seven-year-old boy was run over by a truck. As this situation developed, it turned out that someone at the scene knew the driver. He knew that the man lived nearby, called his wife at home and asked her to come to support her husband. The wife came, but she was so shocked by the incident that she withdrew to some bushes, where she wept profusely.

The dead boy's mother also arrived at the scene. She walked up and down the road, pushing the boy's bike, looking calm but distracted. The truck driver's wife told me that her eyes met the mother's. For a moment, she thought that now the mother was coming over to comfort her.

The absence of emotion in the shock stage is an often surprising phenomenon. Frequently, the person who has experienced the greatest shock directs the traffic, takes care of and comforts others, contacts the rescue services, etc. I recall a situation where a brother had just learned of his sister's suicide. When neighbours and friends called round to offer their sympathy, the brother, a clergyman, patted everyone's shoulder saying, "Try and cope."

Often, we have a guilty conscience afterwards over this lack of emotion. How can it be possible that I feel nothing, although my child or sister has died? For this reason, it is important to recognize the psychological shock reaction, to enable us to understand our own and others' feelings.

As well as the absence of emotion, psychological shock also brings about an absence of the sensation of pain.

A young man, a keen rock climber, fell 18 metres, when the anchorage of his safety rope gave way. He broke his femur, one of his wrists was crushed, and he had facial injuries which bled profusely.

The accident happened in a spot six kilometres from the nearest road. It was more than 20 degrees below zero. One of his climbing friends set off to get help. The other stayed with him to await rescue.

Due to the low temperature, however, they began to get cold, and they reckoned that they would freeze to death before help could reach them. So, they set off walking. The injured man walked three kilometres across country on a broken femur, before help arrived.

Men who have been to war tell of such acts. They seem impossible, but they reflect the power of psychological shock and its expediency. All the reactions support survival.

Although our actions in shock are very appropriate in many ways, our ability to make decisions is impaired. Decision-making in general is difficult, and when we are forced to make decisions, they do not always appear to be very sensible in hindsight. Yet, there is often a certain purpose in these decisions, however amusing after the event.

One of the passengers involved in a train crash was a woman of about 50. Her sleeping compartment was in one of the coaches most badly damaged. She was awake when the coach began to wobble, shudder and lurch about. It came to a halt almost on its side so that the door was at an angle above her. In the crash, the wall of the carriage formed a wedge which protruded about half a metre into the carriage.

When the coach stopped, the woman first felt herself to see if she was all right. When she found no physical injuries, she tried to open the sleeping compartment door, but it was stuck. So, she tried to find a position where she could sit and wait for help. Further up, she heard a child crying and people calling for help.

While sitting there, it occurred to her that perhaps she ought to get dressed. She was only wearing a nightdress. She found her shoes and put them on, but all her clothes were stuck under the wedge. While searching for her clothes, she found her bag which was also wedged fast, but in it she found an unbroken bottle of wine, a packet of butter, a packet of yeast, and a bag of chopped nuts and some spices. These she placed inside a headscarf, forming a bundle. She was holding this bundle when she was rescued from the carriage.

She was taken to a waiting bus. The other people in the bus were fully dressed, 'as if they'd been to a party'. In the bus, she began to feel sick and she felt weepy, but thought, 'It's no good losing face now', so she controlled herself.

There was an announcement on the bus that at their destination, the station, they should contact the crisis centre. The woman looked around in the station concourse, in her nightie and clutching her bundle. She could see no sign of a crisis centre. She stopped an official and asked about the crisis centre. The official asked: "What crisis centre? Has there been an accident?" A woman passing by gave her a phone card, so she could call the friend she was on the way to visit.

The bottle of wine was, of course, a gift to her friend, but why had she brought along the packets of butter, yeast and spices? She said that she had intended to bake some really nice *pulla* (Finnish sweet bread) for her friend to enjoy with coffee. She left her purse, all her money and her spectacles on the train, among other things.

Usually, we endeavour to finish what we were doing. If we are involved in an accident on the way to work and escape with minor physical injuries, our first thought is getting to work on time. At work, we then discuss the incident.

In such situations, the task of other people is to make decisions on behalf of the person in shock. Generally, people in a state of shock are very grateful for help received in a decision-making situation, and follow instructions meekly. This inability to make decisions is often confused with freezing. However, the great majority of people retain their functionality in a state of shock. They only need instructions.

Above, I have described the psychological shock reaction extensively. The majority of people act and behave in a shock situation in the way I have described. About 20 per cent either panic and become hysterical or freeze and become apathetic. If people assess the accident or danger situation to be one where the chances of rescue are slight, but that it is possible, the number of people panicking is increased. Such a situation is, for example, a fire among a large crowd of people. If the situation is assessed to be such that there is no chance of being saved, the number of people freezing increases.

Often the concepts of shock and panic are used as synonyms. In fact, only very few people in psychological shock will panic. The number may seem large, because panicking people are very visible and audible.

A person in a state of panic cannot hear speech or understand its content. When calming a panicking person, it is essential to securely and physically hold him, move him aside, and offer calm, even verbal reassurance. Panic can easily 'catch on' to other people present, which is why it is necessary to remove the person in a state of panic.

Freezing can be so severe that the legs give way. Consequently, a frozen person is unable to move or take care of himself. Others must take care of him.

Often, a different picture of people's reactions in a state of shock is drawn. This is because many studies on the subject have focused on the preservation of perfect ability to function and make judgements. Consequently, the scale is designed to recognize all intervening variables, when the nature of the scale and perspective will affect the results. The shock stage generally lasts from a few hours to 24 hours. In some very extreme events, it may last longer.

Evacuations

In evacuation situations, it is important to understand how people react and function in a state of psychological shock. A large number of people must be compelled to act in a controlled manner and according to instructions. As a matter of fact, psychological shock facilitates the management of evacuations. It puts people into a regressed state: childlike needs take precedence. One such need is the need for and confidence in authority. So, people in shock need an external authority to tell them what they should do.

In shock, everything is aimed at survival. Shock guarantees good functionality both psychologically (no emotions) and physically (physiological reactions). Particular attention must be paid to the narrowing of perceptions which may impair absorption of information.

Also, basic needs become paramount. Worry over loved ones, family members and particularly children is more powerful than the need for obeying instructions and advice. Sometimes, it even supersedes the need for one's own survival. This should be taken into account in instructions.

In evacuation situations, it is essential that official communication of information is fast and instils confidence. In a well-managed evacuation, panic does not arise, but people stay calm and obey authority.

If information is delayed or it is unreliable, the person in charge loses his credibility and his position of authority. People will create their own theories on the event, and then the situation can no longer be brought under control.

Often, professionals, whose jobs demand ability to direct and manage evacuations at times of disaster, worry about their own ability to function. They, too, react to an emergency situation by entering psychological shock. In such cases, the shock affects those responsible for rescue operations by making them act particularly efficiently and with a cool head. They are able to apply everything that training, experience and practice have imprinted in their minds.

Psychological shock and disassociation

Disassociation is a psychological phenomenon associated with psychological shock. In disassociation, the self is removed outside the person, so that events happening to one may be as if observed from the outside. Disassociation is typical in extremely traumatic and prolonged situations, such as rape and other long-lasting violent situations.

Disassociation protects the self. A terrifying situation is easier to endure if one feels that it is not happening to oneself, but only to one's body. Thus, in the shock stage, disassociation is a reaction model which protects the self and personality. On the other hand, disassociation hinders processing of a traumatic experience. It produces contradictory memory images. It is difficult to process the experience when the individual is detached from his own sensations.

> A young woman sought help at the clinic for her anxiety attacks, which were reminiscent of a panic disorder. The attacks had started at her summer cottage, while she had been watching a programme on murders on television. She had been compelled to leave the cottage, and found it impossible to walk in the country, although she was a nature lover.
>
> When we were exploring her recent past, she recalled an experience which in her view was insignificant. She had been working abroad, and one night, around midnight, she had been walking home from work. She noticed that two men were following her, and started running. The men also set off running, caught up with her, and pushed her onto the pavement. They grabbed her handbag, but she hung on to it so tightly that she was lifted off the ground, as the robbers tried to get the bag from her. Finally, she gave in and let go, at which the men fled with the bag. Fairly soon the police arrived at the scene, and the robbers were caught. The woman went home and tried not to think about the incident. A couple of days later her holiday began, she returned to Finland and forgot the experience.
>
> I had a suspicion that the violent robbery incident and the anxiety attacks were connected. We worked through the violent robbery, which the victim clearly belittled. At the end of an hour-and-a-half therapy session, she said: "At last, I understand now that this robbery happened to me. In fact, what happened was awful. It makes me very sad that something like this happened to me."

This is an example of the effects of disassociation and its significance in processing a traumatic experience. The use of disassociation can also spread to other situations which somehow resemble the original situation.

The original situation in which disassociation occurred was one of sexual abuse. The victim became the object of sexual abuse at the age of 12 by a boy three years older. In this situation, the girl froze, did not fight back, did not scream. It was as if she was outside herself, observing what was happening to her.

Later, in situations where she should defend herself, the same thing happens to her. She feels helpless, freezes, and cannot get a word out of her mouth. She removes herself outside her body, and watches her own helpless feelings and behaviour like a bystander.

The reaction stage

A typical characteristic of the shock stage is often a great conflict between outward behaviour and functioning, and the mental chaos underneath or in the background. Gradually, the psychological chaos takes precedence. Transition from the shock stage to the reaction stage is gradual. During the shock stage, something like reaction spikes begin to occur, when emotions surge powerfully to the surface for a moment, to be hidden again in a distant and emotionless state.

The precondition of transition to the reaction stage is that the danger and threatening situation have passed. In addition, one must feel safe. One's own home represents the safest place for most people, and that is why the transition to the reaction stage is often only completed at home.

While a psychological shock protects our minds from information which we are unable to absorb, in the reaction stage we become conscious of what happened and of its impact on our own lives.

Along with consciousness, emotions come, too. The reaction stage is often quite an emotional turmoil. People weep a lot, but when they are asked the reason, they are unable to name it. At intervals, feelings of relief surface that it could have been even worse. Sadness, despair, a sense of emptiness, anxiety, self-accusations and guilt feelings are typical.

Some of us concentrate on apportioning blame. Then, the most prominent emotion is anger and aggression which is directed at some outside person or organization. Focusing on accusation and apportioning blame in fact protects one from all processes taking place within oneself. It is a kind of defence mechanism which protects one from one's own difficult emotions.

A 13-year-old girl cyclist was run over by a car. She took a left turn into a side road, and did not notice an oncoming vehicle. The car collided with the girl and she was killed.

The crossroads where this accident happened had already been deemed to be dangerous, and a campaign for an underpass had been started.

Preliminary plans for building the underpass were in existence, but the final decision was lacking.

All the emotions of the girl's family and close relations were directed at searching for the guilty party in the accident. When the driver of the car could not be blamed, the guilty party was found in the highways authority that had not ensured sufficient road safety.

The girl's family members and relatives were unable to grieve properly for the loss of the girl, owing to their rage. The anger directed at external officials entirely prevented them from processing the loss.

We may also feel anger, rage and aggression that merge to become part of an emotional turmoil, in which case their aim is not the apportioning of blame. Fear is also almost always present in a traumatic experience. Fear for loved ones is generally the primary reason for fear.

A twenty-year-old son found his mother dead in her apartment. He had heard nothing from her for a couple of days, so he became concerned and went over to see if everything was OK. The mother had taken an overdose of pills, and the son found her sitting on the sofa in the sitting room.

The boy's girlfriend was waiting for him in the car. When they got home, the girlfriend felt a compelling need to call her own parents, to make sure they were all right. The girl was extremely ashamed of this powerful emotion. She felt that she should have concentrated on comforting her boyfriend.

Fears may also be focused on the self. For example, if someone has committed suicide or acted violently while mentally unbalanced, we may begin to fear that the same thing could happen to us – that we could commit suicide too. Fears characteristic of the reaction stage are often very powerful and irrational: however one tries to talk sense into oneself, it does not help.

An occupational health practitioner sent a message to a crisis worker about the need for psychological debriefing for the staff of a children's daycare centre. The staff had learned that morning that one of the children at their nursery had died a couple of weeks before. The child's father had murdered both the mother and child.

The doctor herself had a child the same age. However she tried to convince herself that her child was in no danger at his nursery, the doctor was unable to suppress her fear, but was compelled to leave her office in the middle of the working day and collect her child. The daycare centre staff, too, reported a great need to supervise their children more closely than before, even though some of the children were much older.

Traumatic experiences often also elicit embarrassment. This seems incredible to outsiders. At its mildest, the embarrassment attaches to meeting people after a traumatic experience. It is hard to go to work or school and see all the acquaintances and half-acquaintances there. One is afraid that tears will come, or that one cannot cope with seeing familiar people.

Colleagues and friends, too, may feel embarrassed and helpless when meeting a person to whom something very tragic has happened. They are unsure as to how they should relate to him. Should they broach the subject, or should they act as if nothing has happened?

A family that had suffered the loss of their child through cot death said that the hardest thing after the event was that it was always they themselves who had to broach the subject. People did not have the courage to address it. Thus, a person who has experienced a shocking event should be approached by expressing that you know what has happened, and offering your sympathy. If you want to help him, tell him that, too. "I heard that your child has died. If there is any way I can help you, please don't hesitate to get in touch." If you offer someone help, you must really mean it.

Many traumatic experiences, for example the suicide of a family member, becoming a victim of a violent incident, or rape, may even bring about severe shame. Shame is an irrational emotion that cannot be controlled by common sense. However one decides that the incident was not one's fault, the shame will not dissipate.

In such situations, the shame may affect the person's willingness to talk about the experience. The shame may supersede the need for sharing. Then, the victim may shut herself in her home and her own world. She may avoid all contacts and isolate herself. Among people, she may behave normally, pretend that everything is fine, encapsulating her terrible experience in her mind and trying with all her might to forget it. Often, forgetting is not possible, and the event continues to trouble the mind. Occasionally it is possible to forget, but then the memory will often remind the victim of its existence through unexplained emotions, psychological disorders, etc. Shame will decrease through talking. Confronting a difficult experience, working through and discussing it will gradually diminish the shame.

Powerful somatic reactions are also characteristic of the reaction stage. Physical reactions generally begin with trembling which at first is clearly visible, and may later continue as so-called inner trembling. The sensation of trembling is continuous, but it is not externally visible. Inner trembling can continue for around 48 hours after the traumatic event.

The home of a single mother was burgled. The family lived in a first-floor apartment, and the burglars got in by throwing a rock through the glazed balcony door. None of the family members was home at the time. The burglars took only jewellery and silver. While searching for valuables, they had made a bit of a mess.

The mother described her state of mind after the burglary as a feeling that her innermost being had been stolen, leaving her only with the shell. She described her physical state as one of inner trembling. She could feel the trembling throughout her body, and this sensation had persisted for 48 hours.

Other typical somatic problems are vomiting, nausea, cardiac symptoms (a feeling of a weight in the chest, a tight band across the chest, palpitations, racing pulse), muscle pains due to tension, dizziness, and an oppressive fatigue that does not pass with resting. Some people sleep a lot, but the majority have difficulty sleeping. They are afraid to close their eyes and allow sleep to come, or sleep is spasmodic. They may drop off to sleep, but are startled awake immediately, feeling that they are in the middle of the traumatic event again.

Today, we human beings are afraid of powerful emotions. For this reason, we often seek tranquillizing medication to control these frightening feelings. The emotions of the reaction stage, like emotions in general, serve a purpose. With their help, we are reacting the experience out of our system. If the emotions are suppressed, those feelings and experiences remain inside us. So, it is best to try to endure those emotions, to let them come and prevail. A good slogan to adopt is: use people, not pills.

Similarly, with sleeping pills, a good rule is to wait three nights. If on the third night you are still awake, it may be best to have a few good nights with the aid of sleeping tablets, and then try to manage to sleep without them.

Our natural balance should not be lightly interfered with. We can easily become psychologically dependent on sleeping tablets and dare not try to sleep without them, because sleeplessness is frightening. It is best to try to manage without sleeping tablets. Typically, everyone spends the first night awake. The second night might be no better, but on the third night, one is usually so tired that sleep will come.

The shipwreck of MS Estonia was deeply shocking for the crews of other car ferries, too. Five car ferries took part in the rescue effort at the scene, and their crews saw and experienced the terrible moments of that night, morning and the following day.

One of the car ferries had two women among its personnel. Both had been doing the same job for years, and they held the same position on the ship. During the night of the disaster, one of them worked in the first aid group, helping those rescued from the sea: warming them, dressing their wounds and caring for them. The other woman's task was identification of people pulled from the sea. However, rescue from the car ferry was almost impossible.

Both continued their usual work on board ship for a good three days and nights after the disaster, before they were off-duty. One of the women phoned the Finnish Red Cross psychologists' helpline from the ship. She said that she did not want to talk on board the ship. However, she asked to be contacted, once she was off-duty and back at her home.

On Saturday, her day off, I called her at the appointed time. She cried a great deal, and recounted her experiences in giving first aid to the rescued. She reported that from the morning of the accident, the faces of those saved had passed before her eyes, as if on video, and she could hear them talking. When she looked in the mirror, she saw one of the saved looking back at her. She was able to describe her feelings thoroughly and vividly. After we had talked for some time, and she had become a little calmer, I checked that she was not alone, and arranged an appointment for a debriefing session for the following day.

On the evening of the same day, the psychologists' helpline received a call from the other crew member on the same ship. She had arrived home and, as soon as she had closed the door, collapsed in tears in the hall. She had wept there for at least an hour, then moved to the sofa and called the helpline.

She had thought that her family would be home, but the house was empty when she got in. She found it very difficult to describe her emotions on the telephone. The only mental image she spoke about was one of events of the night of the disaster on the second deck of the Estonia, with the cheapest cabins, therefore generally occupied by families with children. She was very anxious, and we agreed that she should attend the same session as her colleague.

The first woman arrived at the debriefing session, the second did not. At the session, the woman described her experiences in great detail. During the morning of the disaster, between three and nine o'clock, she had personally cared for five of six rescued people. She had warmed them with her own body, listened to their rescue experiences, their horrific experiences during the hours of the night. They had told her their entire life stories.

She had totally immersed herself in her work, giving her all. At nine, someone came to tell her that she was required at her usual duties. She was not able to say a personal goodbye to her charges. Some were asleep, to others she just gave a communal wave. She left to do her usual job, and then the images of those rescued began to pass before her eyes.

She was still experiencing these clear hallucinations, which could be called flashbacks, when she arrived at the debriefing session. She addressed her reactions, emotions and thoughts really deeply and with feeling, and gradually she began to feel better. The flashbacks stopped, the weight in her chest and the anxiety eased, but the sadness remained. After a four-hour session, she left to go home, feeling greatly relieved.

At the end of the session, I asked her how she felt about returning to work in a week's time. She replied that she could not imagine a week's time. Thus we agreed that I would call her on the Friday, and we would discuss returning to work then. When I rang her on the Friday, she said that she was feeling reasonably well, and would report for duty as normal.

The next time I heard from her was on the day before Christmas Eve of the same year. The anxiety had returned. She was thinking how miserable Christmas would be for those rescued from the Estonia. She was particularly worried about one Swedish man who was one of the last to be saved, and who was in a very bad way at the time of rescue.

She had received the contact details (addresses and phone numbers) of most of her charges. I encouraged her to call this man and ask him how he was. She called and spoke to him. The man said that he was doing pretty well. He had been attending psychotherapy for three months after the disaster, but then it had started to feel futile. When the woman commented on how hard the Christmas of those rescued would be, the man had interjected: "Would it have been better, then, if we had all drowned?" After this, the woman no longer worried about the man.

We met again after Twelfth Night. She was still anxious, repeatedly waking in the night to find herself on all fours on the floor, looking for her charges. I assumed that the return of the reactions was connected with the fact that she had been unable to say goodbye to the people who had become so important to her. I advised her to write a farewell letter to each of them, saying in the letter what she would now like to say to them, and then to put the letters away in a drawer. She acted on my advice, and it helped. After four weeks, I received a card from her: "Life is worth living again," she wrote.

I contacted her myself on the first anniversary of the disaster. She was doing fine. On the second anniversary, she rang me. She was still doing fine. On the third anniversary, there was a similar storm to that on the night of the disaster. It brought the events of that night back to her, but she got over them quite soon.

In spite of her extremely severe symptoms and reactions, she did not take even a day off work because of feelings connected with the disaster. Neither had she used medication in the period after the disaster.

I called the second woman on the evening of the debriefing session. She said that she had not attended because her children and grandchildren had come to see her. When I called, she was extremely anxious, breathing hard and unevenly. She thought she would die. I talked to her for a while, managed to calm her a little, and advised her to go and see her doctor in the morning. When I tried to reach her in the following weeks, the family always said that she was asleep. She had been prescribed strong sedatives and sleeping tablets. After four months' sick leave, she tried to return to work, attended intermittently, and is now retired on incapacity benefit.

These two women differed from each other in their ability to cope with their difficult experiences and the emotions elicited by them. I am certain that the second woman would have been greatly helped by being present and observing how her colleague coped with her own emotions. In many ways, their experiences and feelings were similar.

The reaction stage generally lasts from two to four days. The powerful emotions connected with it are often difficult to endure. However, the most difficult phase passes surprisingly quickly. In the reaction stage one's feelings and reactions are not always under control, which is perceived as frightening. A person may believe that he is going mad. However, such feelings are appropriate, and they have a purpose.

The Estonia disaster taught me that human beings are so flexible that the reaction stage can be postponed. Before, I believed that the reaction stage comes automatically after a certain time from the event, and if there is no space for it, the entire process is disrupted. My experiences with crews after the sinking of the Estonia showed, however, that employees were capable of continuing their work on board ship for several days after the disaster. They said that they were weepier and more irritable than usual, but did manage to carry out their duties. When they finally got home, the reactions came with great force. This ability to postpone the reaction stage posed a new problem. Many crew members, and especially their families, were surprised at the severity of the reactions, as a week had already passed since the accident. Only on receiving an explanation that their reactions had been 'on hold' until the homecoming did they understand the situation to be normal.

Nevertheless, the reaction stage cannot be postponed to an indeterminate time in the future. Postponement only works in circumstances where one knows that if one can manage until a certain time, then one will have the space to feel and to react. This usually means a few days.

The working through and processing stage

The reaction stage is followed by the working through and processing stage. In this stage, the process of coping with a traumatic experience changes in nature. While generally people in the shock and reaction stages are willing to talk about their experiences, on moving on to the working through and processing stage, they no longer want to discuss it. They say that they do not have the energy to talk any more. The fact is that the human mind begins to close up after the first three days from a traumatic event. The processing of the experience, of course, does not stop. It turns inwards and continues in our own minds.

The coping process now slows down. In the shock and reaction stages, the process moves forward quickly. Each day is different from the day before. Now progress is not easily discernible. The days are alike, weeks follow one another. The purpose of the working through and processing stage is, particularly in cases of the loss of a loved one, parting with the lost person, grief. Grieving is a long process, and at the beginning it feels as if it will never end.

Initially, the loss and the events connected with it are in one's thoughts all the time. At some point, a moment comes when the thoughts are occupied by something entirely different. Usually, that moment is identifiable afterwards. Gradually, such moments, when the loss is not foremost in the mind, become more frequent. By monitoring the number of those moments, we can see the progress of our own grieving process. By pointing out the increased frequency of these moments, one can offer proof to a person in deep grief that progress is taking place, although the person himself feels that he will never recover from his grief.

Strong emotions do not disappear during the stage of working through and processing. Anything can remind one vividly of the lost loved one, and then the powerful longing, sadness and grief erupt again. For example, a young woman who lost her husband in an accident said that shopping was particularly difficult. Every item on the supermarket shelves reminded her of her husband. "He hated that; I'd always have to get him that; he loved that; he used to enjoy that on special occasions" were typical of her thoughts while doing the shopping.

People who have experienced the loss of a loved one often talk of good days and bad days during this stage. Bad days are those when the loss and the emotions associated with it are very much on the surface and fill the thoughts. Good days are the ones when those emotions recede to the background.

Particularly in violent situations and accidents where the person was present himself, the principal purpose of the working through and processing stage is addressing fears and traumas. Fears are very persistent and can dominate life, and working through them is difficult.

In a training session, a social worker who had endured a violent incident recalled her experiences. In the course of her job, she had to make decisions on benefits, and a male client was not happy with his decision. He arrived at the social services office without an appointment and asked to see the social worker responsible for the decision.

He was informed that he could not be seen without an appointment, but because his behaviour was very demanding and threatening, the social worker responsible for the case was called. The man immediately grabbed the social worker by the lapels and lifted her up against a wall. The other workers slunk into their offices to call help. The situation continued to be threatening for several minutes before the police arrived at the scene.

Once the situation had been resolved, her colleagues agreed that the social worker who had been the target of violence should not continue on duty, but that it would be best for her to go home. She lived alone, and could not really settle down to doing anything, wandering about restlessly. The night passed without sleep.

The next day, she arrived at work and was about to start receiving her clients, when her colleagues decided that she was not fit to work. They arranged for her to see her supervisor, giving her the opportunity to tell her about the incident. She was referred to an occupational doctor and sent on sick leave. Four years went by before she returned to work.

She said that she could not be alone at all. She moved in with her sister in another town, and slept on the floor behind the sofa, with her back against the wall. She was comforted by the feeling that nobody could sneak up on her from behind, and she could see, under the sofa, if someone was in the room.

Eventually, she sought help from psychotherapy. She tried a number of forms of therapy, and each one offered some alleviation of her fear. After four years, she was able to return to work.

However, this did not mean that all her fears had passed. She said that she still could not wear tops that are pulled on over the head. She could not tolerate the moment when she loses visual contact with her surroundings.

The social worker's experience dates back 20 years. At that time, we had no idea of crisis- or disaster-psychological knowledge and means of helping that we have today.

So, in the working through and processing stage, the processing of a traumatic experience is turned inwards. It takes place in our minds either consciously or subconsciously. We may feel as if we are not actively thinking about the experience at all, but nevertheless, its processing is ongoing. This shows in a number of ways in our behaviour and actions.

Typical symptoms of the working through and processing stage are difficulties in memory and attention. A part of our attention is directed at the processing of the traumatic experience. Consequently, we only have the use of part of our usual attention, which means that it lets us down more often than usual. The result is that we do not remember things and find it hard to concentrate for long.

> A young man had lost his younger brother in a road accident, in which he was uninjured himself. After a few weeks, when he was working through his feelings at the clinic, the conversation repeatedly followed the same path. I asked him a question, he answered it, and finally he asked: "What was the question again?"

The following is another example of inability to concentrate:

> I saw some crew members of the Sally Albatross about three weeks after the shipwreck. They told me that if they were doing something very interesting, they managed to concentrate for about 15 minutes. Then the concentration disintegrated and had to be re-focused.

The resources demanded by processing a traumatic experience can also be seen in interpersonal relations. A typical sign is the disappearance of our customary resilience, resulting in our tempers being easily lost. This is discharged as atypical fits of rage, as we dissipate our fury both on quite external targets such as bus drivers and supermarket checkout staff, and on loved ones such as our spouse and children.

> Above, I have recalled a lorry driver who ran over a seven-year-old little boy. I saw him and his family four weeks after the accident. The night before, he had had such a furious row with his employer that he did not know whether he had walked out or been dismissed.
>
> He also told me that the Sunday before, he had become so infuriated by his elderly mother that he had left her house slamming doors behind him. A similar event had not taken place for 25 years.

As this irritability may continue for several weeks, sometimes even months, it stretches close relationships to the limit. The spouse or partner may well think that the person's character has completely changed. This is not the case, however, and the irritability caused by processing the traumatic experience will disappear in time.

Another characteristic often seen in the working through and processing stage is the desire to be left alone, and to process the experience alone in one's mind. In many cases, working through alone is beneficial. Many people reinforce it by listening to music, reading books or poetry, or by writing themselves.

Working through a trauma may be apparent in that the person is not psychologically present, even though he is physically there. People close to him may find this hurtful. In the working through and processing stage, a person may also almost totally withdraw from relationships and other attachments. He does not contact anyone or want to be committed to anything. From here, the road to depression is very short.

The working through and processing stage and going to work

In the working through stage, the efforts of an ordinary working day may seem very hard, even insurmountable. However, return to work relatively soon after a traumatic experience is desirable. If a loved one has died, it is good to stay off work until the funeral. If the traumatic experience was, for example, being a target of violence, and sick leave is not necessary because of physical injuries, it is best to return to work as soon as possible.

Nevertheless, this does not mean that the person is fully fit for work. It is beneficial if the working arrangements can be flexible, so that after a traumatic experience, the employee might work shorter hours, or his workload could be reduced. If the duties include demanding client contacts, their number should be reduced.

> There were only two principal employees at a workplace. One of them became a victim of violence at work. A man came into the office, asked for the other employee, and as he was unavailable, smashed his fist into the face of the employee on duty.
>
> The doctor signed both employees off work for two weeks. I met them on the fourth day after the incident, and at the end of our meeting, I discussed their return to work. I suggested they go to work the very next day, meeting up in town first and then going to the workplace together. That way, going to work was made as safe as possible.
>
> My advice was: "Recognize the fear in yourselves, give yourselves permission to be afraid, but don't let the fear rule your actions or behaviour." I suggested they stay at work on that day, without actually needing to do any work. The next day would be much easier.

Prompt return to work is justified by the fact that work is in many ways therapeutic after a traumatic experience. Such an experience produces a feeling that everything is one's life is changing. Work brings a sense of continuity, relationships with colleagues afford social support, and work normalizes life.

Unfortunately, the nature of work is often such that it is very difficult to allow for flexibility. It is easier for the work organization if the employee is on full sick leave. This prolongs sickness absence and hinders the return to work.

Creating a future perspective

The creation of a perspective of the future requires that three conditions are simultaneously fulfilled:

1. The future must be perceived as predictable, at least to a degree.

2. The future must be perceived, at least to a degree, as such that one can influence it.

3. The future must hold at least something hopeful.

When a person has experienced a traumatic event, none of these conditions is fulfilled. This is why he does not have the ability to picture the future. He only lives in this moment and in the past.

In the shock stage, and even during the reaction stage, it is difficult to picture even tomorrow. When trying to arrange a meeting for the following day with people who are in shock, they utter, confused: "Tomorrow? I can't think of tomorrow."

Let us return to the example of the two members of ship's personnel and their reactions after the Estonia shipwreck. When I asked one of them four days after the accident about returning to work after a week, she could not visualize the future that far.

It is important to be aware that the perspective of the future is missing after traumatic events, because it affects the possibilities of offering consolation. Usually, everything that is comforting is in the future, and consoling is based on the tenet that time will pass. When there is no future, there is no consolation.

By observing the extent of the future perspective, it is also possible to draw inferences on the progress of the recovery process. Gradually, after a traumatic experience, people are able to picture a few days, at some point a week ahead. When the person who has experienced a shocking event is planning his summer vacation in three months' time, the recovery is already well advanced.

The reorientation stage

Traumatic events usually bring about many changes in one's life. Through the acceptance of what has happened begins the process of adjustment to the changes caused by the event. Through letting go and grieving, space is made for the new. The development happens gradually, often unnoticed.

At first, we must force ourselves to be interested in things and people. Often, we comply because our friends and relatives demand it and we want to please them. Gradually, our own interest in life grows.

Letting go is hard. Often, people have a need to cling to the grief, and there is no desire to continue their own life. Letting go often happens through concrete actions. Gradually, we are ready to clear the lost loved one's clothes out of the closet. Gradually, objects that were part of his everyday life are moved aside, and the space is occupied by the things of those living.

A loss also means emptiness. Many people describe their feelings after the death of a spouse by saying that it feels as if half of themselves is gone. At first, there is a need to nurture this emptiness, and to resist filling the empty space. We are unwilling to accept what has happened. We just want to nurture the memory of the lost one.

Sometimes, people who have lost a loved one want to get everything over with very quickly. The funeral is organized promptly, and the things of the deceased, including photographs, are disposed of immediately after the traumatic event. This is an attempt to block or deny the loss. The idea is to forget the event quickly, an attempt not to think about what happened. Facing it seems to cause too much anxiety. Risto, described at the beginning of this book, acted this way when he lost his mother.

At the start of the process of coping with a trauma, the reorientation stage seems so distant and unattainable that it is not even worth talking about. It becomes topical and worth addressing only towards the end of the working through and processing stage.

Yet, even when the person concerned continually and repeatedly states that he will never get over such a loss and grief, or such an experience, at some point the process moves on to reorientation, a new life. The opportunity of witnessing these people's slow, painful but increasing recovery gives us faith in human beings' incredible reserves of strength, enabling them to cope with even unbelievably difficult situations, and their ability to begin a new life.

Above, I have described mainly the customary, normal working through process of a traumatic event. Naturally, there are individual differences. Not everyone has the reactions described above, and some people manifest many other kinds of additional reactions. Some get over their experiences more quickly; for others it takes longer. Some people's reactions and emotions are very powerful; others' are less so. However, the process follows a pattern in that the stages described above are recognizable.

The desirable end result is that the traumatic experience becomes a conscious and restful part of the self: I have experienced such an event; it is a part of me. One can either think or not think about the event. It is not always on one's mind, preoccupying it completely, as was the case at the start of the process. It is possible to think about the event and experience and to confront it without strong feelings of anxiety or fear. Thus, the aim is that the experience is not blocked or denied, but processed and worked through.

Factors affecting working through a traumatic experience

In the case of the two ship's employees who had experienced the Estonia disaster we found that their capacity to cope with their shocking experiences was different. People's ability to work through and process traumatic experiences varies. These abilities are affected by our personal histories and the experiences they contain.

> I was very struck by what the commanding officer of a military garrison said during a seminar, the subject of which was 'What I learned from the Estonia incident', and which was held three and a half months after the accident, in December 1994.
>
> The officer said that one of the most difficult tasks he faced after the accident was selection of the men who were to receive the bodies of the victims that had been plucked from the sea or from life rafts by helicopters. Their duties included tidying up and tagging the bodies, and safe keeping of their personal effects. Their task was concluded by placing the bodies in temporary coffins.
>
> He tried to choose men who he thought would endure anything, so-called macho men. While watching the men work, however, he observed that he had made mistaken choices, of men who wept or vomited while working, and talked a great deal about their work and the experiences it entailed to colleagues, family, and also at the psychological debriefing session.
>
> In December, having now followed up how these men, ordered to carry out the task, had coped with the experience, the commandant said that he should have selected the men quite differently. In fact, the men he had decided were 'mistakes' had come through much better than the so-called macho men. It seems that what is considered to be weakness is in this situation strength, and what is deemed to be strength is weakness.

Thus, the crux of the matter is that we have learned to face up to difficulties and losses, to tolerate and recognize the reactions elicited by them, and to process the feelings and thoughts evoked by them. If our lives are full of difficult traumatic experiences, it is likely that we have not had sufficient resources and capacity to process all of them. A very traumatic past generally impacts on the development of the personality adversely. Even one difficult unresolved traumatic experience may be enough for the personality to become disordered.

If, on the other hand, we have never encountered difficulties or losses in our personal histories, we have not learned how to face them, cope with them and get over them. In particular, coping is affected by the way we have learned to relate to frustrations and losses as children or in our youth. This we generally acquire from our parents and other significant adults. The crucial difference is: do we learn to confront difficulties and deal with them, or do we learn to sidestep difficulties, avoid them, block and reject the reactions, thoughts and feelings caused by them.

Our individual ability to deal with traumatic events is also affected by the level of our self-esteem and self-confidence. If we are confident, we believe that we will overcome difficult experiences; on the contrary, we perceive them as challenges. If we have no self-confidence and do not believe that we can cope with the experience, we give up more readily. Difficulties are perceived as causes of pressure, as paralysing.

It seems that there are gender differences in reactions to traumatic events and the ability to cope with traumatic experiences. Research (Gleser, Green and Winget 1981; Lindeman et al. 1996) shows that women react more powerfully and display more symptoms of different kinds than men, but in the long term women are capable of coping with their traumatic experiences better than men. Men suffer from prolonged breakdowns more than women.

On the other hand, the picture formed in practical work differs somewhat from research results. Many crisis workers have agreed with my experience that men are capable of deep emotions after traumatic events, and are also capable of thoroughly processing their experiences.

Men's methods of coping with their shocking experiences are possibly only partially different from those of women. Women characteristically talk and share experiences with family, relatives and friends. Men tend to discharge their experience more in action and solitary thought.

Social support is of paramount importance in coping with a traumatic event. This is shown very clearly also by research. A good, extensive social network is the best comfort to one who has been through a traumatic experience. People living alone and lonely people who do not have such a safety net form a clear at-risk group. They develop long-lasting disorders more frequently than the norm, as a result of traumatic experiences that have remained unprocessed.

It is important that the social network is activated after a traumatic event. Friends, relatives, colleagues should proactively and spontaneously contact the person or family that has experienced a great shock. In this situation, even contacts from distant friends are a comfort.

It is important that friends and relatives offer their support as time goes on, too. During the weeks and months following a traumatic experience, the need for social contacts is enormous. Many people say that they felt that friends and relations had tired of them, and their going on and on about their experience. That is why a number of contacts are necessary, to share the burden equally.

Previous traumatic experiences are another clear risk factor in effective processing of the experience. A new traumatic experience will bring back all earlier experiences, and once again, they all must be addressed and processed. This is particularly true when they have remained unresolved.

> A woman's partner died violently at his workplace. They had been together for 25 years. From her previous marriage, the woman had three children, the youngest of whom was four weeks old when the children's father was drowned. He was 27 at the time. Thus, the mother's partner had become father to the family's children.
>
> When the death of the mother's partner was being worked through, the drowning of her first husband was continuously brought up. The mother and children were obviously processing the traumatic event of 25 years ago at the same time as they worked through the death of the partner.

As a general rule, the new event will activate old experiences especially if the traumatic events resemble each other. Conversely, they may be so dissimilar that an outsider finds it difficult to understand them. Sometimes it seems that a new traumatic event activates all previous traumatic events.

Sometimes, the previous traumatic event has been totally blocked so that there is no conscious recollection of it. Then, the intensity of the reactions to a new traumatic experience comes as a surprise. This force partially springs from the earlier experience.

At the time of the Estonia disaster, many psychotherapists reported that clients had addressed their own earlier traumatic experiences during therapy. Such a huge disaster was perceived by almost everyone as so shocking that it reactivated earlier traumatic experiences.

> One therapist recalled a client who told her that the disaster had brought on an attack of quite incomprehensibly intense anxiety. The anxiety included difficulty in breathing, a feeling of choking.
>
> The therapist made the interpretation that this was a case of some earlier traumatic experience, one that she had completely blocked, and therefore did not remember. The patient had discussed her sensation with her mother, who told her that she had almost drowned at the age of two.

Processing several traumatic experiences simultaneously ties up more resources than processing one. The process usually takes longer, and one's own resources are not always sufficient to cope with the situation, so professional help is required.

Processing a traumatic experience demands circumstances conducive to it. There must be time and opportunities for feelings and thoughts, and for their expression and processing. Sometimes, extraneous circumstances prevent processing. Even if a friend is killed in war, there is no opportunity to begin the grieving process. One must remain functional and carry on.

> In an accident at work, a young man was killed and another seriously injured. The dead man had a family of three small children, aged three, eighteen months, and four weeks. They had only recently moved into the area, and had not yet got to know people there. The grandparents and other relatives lived a long distance away from them. In this situation, the mother had no space for her own pain and grief, because she had to invest all her energy and time into taking care of the children.

Circumstantial factors preventing the processing of a traumatic experience can also be subjective, not appreciated by outsiders as the kind of factors that really would prevent taking the time and space required for processing the experience. However, for the person concerned the situation may be such that he cannot see any other possibility.

> An ambitious young girl was preparing for her baccalaureate exams when her father was killed in a road accident. Her exams were a week away when news of the death came. The girl shut the whole event out of her mind and invested all her time and energy in preparing for her exams. After they were over, she embarked at full steam on preparations for the university entrance examination.
>
> She gained excellent grades and was accepted on the course of her choice. In the autumn, she began her studies, and the following spring, when the anniversary of her father's death approached, she made an appointment with the psychologist. The reason she gave was that at the time of her father's death she had not had the opportunity of dealing with her loss and the emotions elicited by it; she now wanted help in this process.

5

Breakdowns in Processing Traumatic Experiences

The process of coping with a traumatic experience described above is rather prone to breaking down. I view such breakdowns as fixations of the process at some stage, in which it becomes stuck and is no longer progressing. Fixation can happen at any stage, but the consequences are different at different stages.

Fixation in the shock stage

When the processing of a traumatic experience becomes fixated in the shock stage, no psychological processing takes place. The experience is blocked from the mind or denied altogether. It is too anxiety-inducing or frightening to face or to cope with. It descends into the subconscious, and the person may even forget completely that he has ever had the traumatic experience.

The denial or blocking can be total, in which case the entire event is forgotten, or it can be partial, so that the actual event is remembered but the individual is absolutely incapable of processing it. This is what happened in the case of Risto in relation to his mother's death, at the beginning of this book. In such cases, the event becomes somehow encapsulated within the mind, and a psychological trauma is created.

Psychological traumas can, of course, come about in many other ways, too. However, sudden traumatic events place an individual at particularly great risk of developing a psychological trauma.

Many years ago, a health centre psychologist in charge of a local crisis group contacted me, saying that a kind of dispute of principle had arisen within his town. A six-year-old girl had lost her mother in a fire, when the family's house burned down. The mother was the child's single parent.

The girl's next of kin, her mother's mother, the girl's grandmother, could not face the loss, but used large quantities of tranquillizing medication, and was constantly in a drugged haze. Her opinion was that the girl should not be allowed to attend her mother's funeral.

The girl attended kindergarten, and the staff were amazed at how well she had got over the event. She was as happy and active as ever. Her behaviour had not changed at all. The kindergarten staff agreed with the grandmother that it was not a good idea for the girl to go to her mother's funeral. The consultant psychologist of the kindergarten thought so, too.

The leader of the crisis group was worried by the situation, so he wanted to consult, to hear a second opinion on how the situation should be approached. His opinion was that the mother's death had not yet even become real for the girl, and that every effort should be directed to helping her face the truth. Otherwise, great difficulties might be expected later on.

I asked the psychologist if he had seen the mother's body, thinking that the mother had been burned in the fire. The psychologist said that he had, and that she had died of carbon monoxide poisoning and had no visible injuries. She looked like an angel, very peaceful and pretty.

We agreed that he should do everything possible for the girl to be given the opportunity of saying goodbye to her mother; to see her body, and, if possible, also to touch her, to give her the sensation that her mother was cold. We took it for granted that the girl must be allowed to attend the funeral.

I recalled this case at a training session attended by members of the crisis group in question. One of them came over to chat to me after the session. She said that she recognized the case and that the girl had attended therapy with her for a year after her mother's death. Our instructions had been heeded, and the therapy was mainly to support the girl in processing the loss of her mother, and settling in her new foster home. The therapist told me that the girl was fine and had recovered well from the loss of her mother.

There is nothing wrong as such in forgetting tragic events. The problem is just that this 'forgetting' causes constant difficulties and problems in later life. An unprocessed experience insidiously affects all our decisions, choices and relationships. The consequence may be poor choices, or behaviour that repeatedly harms relationships, such as violence and jealousy. We do not always even notice the impact of the experience, or we know it, but nevertheless are unable to act any differently.

A young woman was the victim of her boyfriend's violence nine years before. He hit her, so that she fell to the floor injuring her mouth and teeth.

She tried to get help when the boyfriend hit her again, and the woman's face caught on the corner of a cabinet. Even then, he prevented her from calling a taxi and seeking medical help. Gradually, the situation calmed down, the woman managed to call a taxi and got to hospital. All this she was forced to do alone. The boyfriend did not help her in any way.

This experience remained totally unprocessed both between them and in the girl's mind. However, the violence was never repeated. But nine years later, when the girl became the victim of a new traumatic event, the violent experience was reactivated.

When this violence and the psychological trauma it had caused were addressed and the different emotions associated with it worked through, the girl realized how greatly this single event had influenced her life, through the choices she had made. She saw how everything in her actions after that experience was aimed at increasing her sense of security. Her choice of career, choices regarding her studies, jobs, friends, were all directed to this end. When this need was no longer there, she realized that she could choose differently, freely. She was very sad about the nine lost years, but happy with her newfound freedom.

The function of psychological shock is to protect the mind from information and experiences that it is unable to absorb. Fixation in the shock stage reflects the idea that the event is so horrific that we are incapable of accepting that the information is true. This mental struggle may continue for months.

A woman who lost both of her children in an accident described this struggle very well. She was able to absorb the information that her children had died, but no emotions of any kind were attached to it. She returned to work on the third day after the children had died, and managed her work without difficulty. She had been to see her dead children and was able to tell me about it quite calmly, without emotion. Her ability to function remained for months, and no emotions surfaced.

Yet, the woman wanted to stay in contact with me, because she had a feeling that the situation might not remain as tranquil. She described her psychological state: "It feels as if my mind is like a fortress in the middle of a stormy sea. Huge waves are continuously beating its walls and testing its strength, and I'm constantly afraid that it will collapse."

While the struggle between psychological shock and transition to the reaction stage continues, encapsulation of the traumatic experience has not taken place either. Generally, encapsulation brings with it a kind of artificial peace. Psychological shock can continue in some cases for months, in a kind of active state.

Fixation in the reaction stage, Post-Traumatic Stress Disorder

The process of coping with a traumatic experience may also become fixated in the reaction stage. In such a case, powerful reactions and symptoms fail to lessen over time and instead remain 'switched on'. This is a Post-Traumatic Stress Disorder (PTSD). PTSD was included in the international diagnostic classification (DSM III) in 1987 and its definition was modified in 2000 (DSM IV).

The definition contains six classes of criteria:

First, that an extraordinarily powerful event has taken place, posing a serious threat to one's life or physical inviolability or to one's children, spouse, other relatives or friends. The event may also have been, for example, the sight of a seriously injured or dead person as a result of an accident or an act of violence, or a catastrophe causing the sudden destruction of one's home or entire community. The event must have been experienced as very horrifying or frightening, or created a sense of helplessness.

Second, that the event is continuously re-lived, for example in recurring nightmares, hallucinations or intrusive memories, or that severe mental and physical agitation results from events symbolizing or reminiscent of the incident (for example, anniversaries).

The third criterion is that there is continuing avoidance of thoughts and feelings associated with the event, or activities and situations which trigger memories of the trauma. There may also be difficulty remembering parts of the experience. There must also be less emotional sensitivity and expression, for example, an inability to feel love. There may be feelings of alienation from other people, disregard for important functions (for example, young children may lose skills already learned, such as toilet skills or speech), or less expectations for the future (for example, a child may not believe that he will have a job, get married, have children or live to an old age). If at least three of the above symptoms are present, the criterion is deemed to be fulfilled.

The fourth class of criteria concerns heightened physiological activity as if the body were being prepared for fight or flight. This may manifest in poor concentration, sleep disturbances (problems in dropping off and waking), rage or irritability, or excessive alertness (perpetually prepared to meet with a catastrophe or looking for signs of one). Physiological reactions to situations resembling the traumatic event may be sensitized, for example a child who has lost her family in a fire may react with intense fear and terror (manifested as crying, screaming or freezing) to a cigarette being lit or a fire alarm. When at least two of these conditions are present, the criterion is considered fulfilled.

The symptoms of the second, third and fourth criteria must be present for at least one month. Finally, the symptoms must be severe enough to interfere with work or social activities for PTSD to be diagnosed.

PTSD may present as acute, when the symptoms continue as severe or increasingly severe for over a month, or delayed, when the symptoms only emerge about six months after the traumatic event.

PTSD is the only diagnosis in psychiatric disorder classification where an external event and its characteristics are set as conditions of diagnosis. In that sense, its inclusion in the classification of disorders is historic.

Usually, PTSD is easily identified and connected to the original traumatic event. However, occasionally the symptoms emerge after a delay of several months, and the actual root cause of the disorder is not identified, but treatment is directed only at the symptoms.

As a rule, treatment of the symptoms is futile. Producing a lasting improvement requires identification of the original experience causing the symptoms, and defusing of the thoughts and feelings associated with it.

A man who held an executive position was coming home around eight o'clock one evening. Suddenly, he was attacked by three men who assaulted him by beating and kicking him until he was in a very bad way. Then they disappeared. The man was in hospital for a week, and returned to work after a couple of weeks. The assault turned out to be an act of revenge for a decision he had been forced to make at work.

His employers provided him with security guards who also guarded his home for several weeks. In spite of this, the man and his wife felt worse with each passing day. They were constantly fearful and could not sleep or eat properly. They lost their ability to concentrate, and the husband no longer managed to cope with his duties at work. He took sick leave, but that did not help. The malaise of the couple began to manifest in their quarrelling and inability to tolerate the partner and his or her pain.

Untreated or with inappropriate treatment, PTSD can result in temporary or permanent incapacity for work.

Some years ago, there was a plane crash in Northern Finland, killing four of the nine passengers. At that time, there was no provision of psychological help for the survivors, so they had to cope with their shocking experience alone. One passenger said that she had been on sick leave for two weeks after the accident, and then tried to return to work. She could not manage her duties, because she was unable to concentrate and because she felt incredibly fatigued. She was signed off sick for another week, and after that for yet another. She still did not feel able to work, but the doctor refused to sign her off again. So, she took unpaid leave of absence which lasted seven months.

She was not offered any psychological help at any stage, but had to cope on her own. On some days, she did not get out of bed at all, and had no energy to do anything. About six months after the accident, she said that she just woke up one morning feeling energetic and well. Her recovery had begun. After a couple of months, she was able to return to her job.

I have already touched on long-term incapacity for work caused by a traumatic experience, in the case of the social worker who became the victim of violence. The internationally best-known example of the subject is the experience of Jeffrey Mitchell himself, the developer of the disaster-psychological model and its principal methods. His prior training was as a fireman and ambulance driver, and he worked for several years in those duties. He was forced to give up his career because of a very shocking and traumatic event. He could no longer continue as a fireman and started studying psychology. He is now a professor of psychology.

We have seen that PTSD can cause such a difficult situation that the individual is no longer able continue in the job with which the experience is associated. Untreated, it may even force a change in career.

Denial of the truth

A traumatic event is almost always accompanied by an attempt to deny it. However, a part of a healthy coping process is that the event gradually becomes real. The victim understands that what happened cannot be undone. He must accept it and continue living. One just has to try to adapt to what has happened, however unjust the event seems. This is called facing or confronting the truth. It does not always happen. Then, the person is fixated in accusation and seeking to apportion blame, believing that if those responsible are prosecuted, they will feel better themselves.

These events are usually such that a police investigation and consideration of prosecution are carried out as a matter of routine. Such traumatic events are accidents, violent situations, and cases of medical negligence, where someone dies or is permanently disabled.

When there is no psychological acceptance of the truth, the result is bitterness and anger. Some want to be actively involved in the situation, when the perceived injustice is channelled into dissatisfaction with the police investigation and consideration of charges. They demand further police investigations, and may bring a private prosecution. When they fail to get a result that is perceived to be just, they go to the appeal court and high court, if at all possible. They write to Members of Parliament, send complaints to the Parliamentary Ombudsman and the Attorney General, appeal to ministers and the President, and never feel that they are receiving justice.

This process can take years. All resources, time, energy, and available cash are channelled into this 'fight for justice'. Social support is channelled to support only this process. Connections are severed with friends and relatives who disagree.

In a psychological sense, a traumatic experience can be influenced right at the start of the processing. Without psychological processing, there is no adaptation either. The traumatic event retains its freshness, even if years have passed. One's own life is put on hold.

There are many examples of such fixations. The Suzy Lamplugh murder, the Hanratty hanging and many medical negligence trials are good examples. The discussion in Sweden on the raising of MS Estonia, too, contains the same characteristics. The debate and fighting are focused on the question of whether the Estonia should be raised from the seabed, or whether the bodies should be removed from the wreck. Yet, the fighting contains features which relate to the perception of injustice concerning the whole accident and an inability to accept that such a disaster with its terrible consequences has happened. In fact, the dispute is channelled into fighting against the Swedish government which decided that the victims will not be removed.

It is worrying to note how even the activities of the relatives' groups formed after the accident have focused only on the debate over removing the victims. Here, too, social support has been harnessed to support the fixation of processing the traumatic event, and not to promote processing and helping adaptation and getting a hold of living again.

A father who had lost his son during his national service contacted me after reading a piece of mine in *Helsingin Sanomat*, the daily newspaper. The son had had the 'flu, and had returned to his barracks a little under the weather. In the small hours, he had been ordered to transport officers to another location, and on the return journey had apparently dropped off to sleep and collided with a juggernaut. He was killed in the accident.

A police investigation was conducted, and no charges were brought. However, the parents felt that the garrison, and specifically the person who had ordered their son to drive, were responsible for the accident and its consequences. They sent a request for an investigation to the headquarters, and embarked on a litigation process over their son's death. They have published a book on this process.

They complained about the prosecution being blocked and the subsequent decisions to the Parliamentary Ombudsman; they made a complaint to the National Authority for Medicolegal Affairs; a question was directed at the Defence Minister during parliamentary question time; they wrote to President Ahtisaari and Mrs Ahtisaari, and felt that they received justice from nowhere. On the contrary, they felt that their belief in Finnish crime investigation and the judicial system had been trashed. On the anniversary of their son's death each year, they publish a leaflet detailing the latest developments in the judicial process. It is now over four years since the accident. (Alavuotunki 1995)

The experience described above is very typical. People set out to seek justice in the courts for an event which is *perceived* to be unjust. Various officials of the judiciary and the police investigate whether the law has been broken. Not everything that is perceived as unjust is regulated by law. This is why these judicial processes are generally felt to be extremely frustrating, and people are almost always very dissatisfied with the end result.

These cases are also frustrating for officials of the judiciary and the police. Usually, experienced investigators and officials see immediately that the whole process is futile, but it is their duty to see it through. Thus, a lot of resources are wasted on work with no prospect of results, work which in fact helps nobody – on the contrary, it produces huge stresses and suffering for many people over several years.

In a psychological sense, an unjust experience, which a person is unable to work through and convert to even partial acceptability, gives rise to anger and bitterness. These emotions destroy a person from within in a certain way, causing serious damage to his or her personality and life.

Fixation in grieving

As well as being a traumatic experience, the sudden death of a person close to us usually brings about long-lasting grieving. Processing the traumatic event is a prerequisite for success in working through grief. If the traumatic experiences associated with the loss are not processed, no space will be found for the grief.

Another essential factor in working through grief is that the person who has experienced the loss faces up to reality. Often, having lost someone close to us, we want to deny the truth. We expect the dead person to return home soon, we may see him in a crowd, or feel that he is present in our home. Hovering between the truth and wishful thinking may continue for weeks or months. Many fight ferociously against acceptance of the truth. However, the progress of grieving is conditional on acceptance of the loss.

Reminiscing is a typical part of grieving. Various vivid memories pass through the mind. They may cause pain, but they can also bring relief. Although the loved one is gone, the memories remain. The memories may be elective to begin with, so that only positive memories are recalled, making the loss even more painful. But gradually the memories become more inclusive. Quarrels, unpleasant characteristics and difficulties faced with the deceased are recalled, too. Looking through photographs and reminiscing with a close person are good ways of advancing the grieving process.

An essential part of grieving is giving up a shared future; letting go of all plans and projects made together, such as holiday plans. It is as if life has stopped. This is particularly hard when there are lots of plans for the future, and they affect central areas of life.

> A young couple was preparing for a life together. Their first house was being built, and it was to be finished for Christmas. They had lived in temporary accommodation for a long time, concentrating on planning their new home. They were looking forward to marriage, their own home, a family, a shared future.
>
> A few days before their moving date, the man died suddenly. His partner was left alone. She found it almost impossible to believe that her partner had died. She lost everything when she lost their shared future. She felt that she had nothing left, in spite of moving into the new house for Christmas.

It is often said that grief is a very selfish emotion. A large part of grieving consists of thoughts such as "What will happen to me now?" and "I have lost so much that I will never get over this loss". Grief contains self-pity, worry over oneself and how one is going to cope. Often, grief is also accompanied by anger and rage. We are angry with the deceased for leaving and abandoning us. We are furious that he left without taking care of anything, and now we are left to suffer and manage alone. The deceased is seen as a traitor.

Grief also contains powerful longing and pain. We want to hold on to what we have lost. Often, people want to wear something that belonged to the deceased, like a sweater, T-shirt or pyjamas that still have his smell.

Holding on to the deceased can lead to unwillingness to give up the grief, too. We want to linger in it, because letting it go would be like abandoning the lost person himself. When people become fixated in grieving, this is often what is really happening. Letting go of the grief and continuing one's own life are seen as forsaking the lost loved one. That is why letting go of the loss is so hard.

Processing the sudden death of a loved one is especially difficult. In such cases, it is not possible gradually to prepare for his departure, to make one's feelings known, to clear up misunderstandings, to say everything one wants to say. One is forced to do all this work alone in one's own mind, or with friends and relatives, but it is never the same as addressing important issues face-to-face with the dying person.

An ambivalent relationship with the deceased is a risk factor in working through the grieving process (Parkes 1990). Other similar risk factors are great dependence on the deceased and low self-esteem. People who are active in several areas of living cope with grief better than passive people (Hersberger and Walsh 1990). For example, working mothers recover from the death of a child better than stay-at-home mothers (Dyregrov and Matthiesen 1991).

> A young mother was on maternity leave when her husband was killed in an accident. They had three children, the eldest of whom was eight and the youngest four weeks old.
>
> A few months after the husband's death, the mother wanted to cut short her maternity leave and return to work. She felt that it would be easier for her to cope with her grief, if she had other things to think about. Returning to work clearly helped her and aided her recovery from her severe loss.

At first, the grieving process is maintained by various concrete tasks: ordering the burial plot, choosing the coffin, composing the obituary, and preparations for the funeral maintain activity. The real grief is often encountered only after the funeral.

Many concrete tasks reflect the progress of grieving and make it tangible. Sorting out the estate of the deceased, packing away his things and clothes are part of grieving and letting go. That is why it is best if those close to the deceased do these jobs themselves when it feels right and possible.

Often, friends and relatives actively keep in touch and provide support at the early stages of grieving, but relatively soon one may encounter expectations of 'bucking up' and getting on with one's own life.

People immersed in grief need support. They need people who may be called even in the middle of the night, if the pain and anxiety become overwhelming. They need people around them who can put up with their crying and despair, and do not make demands of 'bucking up' or recovery. The grieving process is usually longer and slower than we outsiders imagine.

Often, both the person who has experienced the loss and his support persons may lose faith that the process is moving forward. It does not look as if any progress is being made. The grieving person just feels awful all the time. In such cases, two measures may be used to reflect progress that has taken place.

I have mentioned both phenomena before, in connection with the progress of the coping process of a trauma. The first concerns the length of the future perspective. At first, a person who has lost a loved one cannot even conceive of the next day. After a few months, he can perhaps conceptualize next week. When he is making plans several months ahead, recovery is already pretty well advanced. The progress is so slow that it is only worth repeating the assessment every other month. A longer interval between assessments produces a clearer result.

Another good indicator is the number and duration of moments when the thoughts are not filled with the loss or grief. As the process advances, the number of such moments increases. In this respect, too, progress is slow, and certainly not straightforward. Some very difficult periods may still occur.

Grieving places great demands on interpersonal relations. Generally, those immersed in their grief feel that they should keep it internalized, and avoid expressing it. It is particularly difficult to endure the fact that grieving takes so long. This may lead to avoidance of others and isolation. On the other hand, we may feel under pressure to perform, feeling that we are not coping in the way those around us expect. We may also feel under pressure in the other direction: we may feel that we are not grieving enough or in the right way.

The progress of the grieving process is also often revealed in dreams:

> A young woman lost her husband in an accident, in the middle of a particularly idyllic phase in their family life. A few weeks after her husband's death, she had a very vivid dream, in which her husband returned home as usual after a day at work.
>
> A few months later, she dreamt that her husband was leaving on a long journey. In her next dream of him, the husband came home dirty and covered in soot, with his clothes torn, and she wondered and worried what had happened to him.
>
> Seven or eight months after the husband's death the woman had a dream in which the husband returned home, but she knew that he was dead and had to tell him: "You can't just come back like this because you are dead." She was very anxious in the dream about having to tell her husband that he was dead.

Above, I have described the progress of the grieving process. At some point of the process, the person who has suffered the loss must let go of what he has lost and also of the grief, and continue his own life. We must learn to live *with* the grief, and not *immersed* in it, as Atle Dyregrov (1994) put it.

Criminal and antisocial behavior

Inability to process traumatic experiences may also be channelled into criminal and antisocial behaviour.

> A quite large electrical contracting company started receiving frequent nuisance calls. They came to the switchboard, the CEO's direct line and his mobile. The phone rang and nothing was said, but the line stayed open. The calls came in such numbers that the firm's business activities were affected and the matter was reported to the police.

The police investigation revealed that the calls came from call boxes in a very wide area. This indicated that there were several callers. However, they made no further progress in spite of assigning a number of officers to the case.

Quite by chance, they discovered that a very similar case had been the subject of a police investigation a few years earlier in another town. A business in the same sector received similar nuisance calls. The police finally abandoned attempts to solve the crime, and gradually the nuisance calls stopped.

By studying common factors between these two businesses, the police spotted that the previous firm had had an employee who had applied for a job in the firm now receiving the nuisance calls. The police traced the man and arrested him. When questioned, he admitted both crimes.

As for a motive, he said that he had worked for the previous firm for a long time. However, he was dismissed in a way that he perceived to be demeaning, crude, and offensive to his self-esteem. Just a month before the dismissal, his father had died.

The man had suffered ill-health, had undergone medical investigations, and been diagnosed with an occupational illness. He had claimed for reimbursement of his sickness and living expenses from the National Health Service. A couple of weeks before the nuisance calls began, his application had been refused. He was forced to seek employment.

He had applied for a job at the contractors, where the director had said in a very disdainful tone: "You'd probably not be safe on a ladder." He had felt that the director's attitude insulted his worth as a human being. The following day, he started making the nuisance calls. He bought phone cards and used them to call from call boxes. He sold the used cards to collectors.

The man started calling at eight o'clock in the morning, had a half-hour break at half past nine, and again from twelve o'clock to one o'clock. Then he carried on phoning again until four o'clock. He visited different telephone booths to avoid being caught.

When questioned, he broke down completely and threatened suicide. The investigating police directed him to mental health services which he gratefully accepted.

This is an example of how a traumatic event can lead to bitterness, a need for revenge and through this into criminal activity. In such cases, it is rarely a question of a single isolated traumatic event, but several experiences which the person is unable to process. These unresolved traumatic experiences lead to powerful feelings of bitterness and anger that begin to dominate actions and behaviour. They may be directed at either outsiders or oneself.

A salient part of this experience is the feeling that one's psyche is breaking down and of loss of self-worth. What remains is the ability to use power and an indifference to oneself: nothing matters. The perpetrators of many horrific and seemingly mindless acts of violence have later said that their embitterment and anger were the result of numerous traumatic experiences.

6

Long-term Consequences
of Traumatic Experiences

Let us briefly review research results on long-term consequences of traumatic events, when people have received no specific psycho-social support, but tried to overcome their experience with the help of friends, relatives and other social networks.

There are quite a number of studies on the consequences of traumatic events. They vary in respect of the nature of traumatic event, research methods applied, and follow-up interval.

If a psychological trauma has developed, the effects of the traumatic event only manifest several years later, and even then on a subconscious level. Such consequences have been left completely outside the scope of these studies. Neither have I found any studies on the sense of injustice caused by a traumatic event, and its channelling into litigation. This would be a very interesting and important area of research.

The studies focus on persistent presentation of PTSD-type psychological and somatic symptoms. However, the problem with many studies is the short follow-up interval. Normal psychological processing of a shocking traumatic event can often take six months. If the event has had a significant impact on the individual's life (for instance, a prolonged and difficult physical recovery process, permanent disability, loss of a loved person), normal recovery can take years. For this reason, many of the studies only look at symptoms associated with the processing of a traumatic event. Very few studies found long-term consequences that remained after this normal processing had ended, or effects that reflected fixation or failure of the process.

There are, however, a few such studies. Gleser *et al.* (1981) studied the consequences of a sudden flood disaster. The accident was caused by the bursting of a dam. Massive amounts of water quickly covered a large area. The researchers found that 80 per cent of the adults rescued from the disaster were still suffering from psychological problems more than two years later. Four to five years after the accident, a third of the men and a quarter of the women were suffering from significant psychological problems. The same research group carried out a further follow-up 14 years after the event: the results showed that the victims were still suffering from more symptoms associated with PTSD than the control group which had not experienced a catastrophe (Green *et al.* 1990).

In 1983, 28 people died in Australian bush fires, and hundreds were injured. Research (McFarlane 1990) showed that 42 per cent of the victims suffered mental health problems, as measured by the General Health Questionnaire (GHQ). The percentage was significantly greater than among the general population, and the same result was found also after a long interval.

Long-term effects of traumatic events are also evident in interpersonal relationships and capacity for work. In 1990, there was a fire on the car ferry Scandinavian Star, killing 159 people. A study (Elklit, Andersen and Aretander 1995) showed that after three and a half years, 43 per cent of those rescued had changed jobs, and 39 per cent were having work or family problems.

MS Herald of Free Enterprise was shipwrecked in the English Channel in 1987, and 196 of the 545 people on board lost their lives. Forty-two members of the crew were saved. Two years after the disaster, only two of them had returned to work at sea. Survivors of the disaster had severe problems in their relationships and in getting on with living again. They also suffered various persistent symptoms of PTSD (Johnston 1993; Yule, Williams and Joseph 1997).

Some occupations expose people to certain kinds of traumatic events. Train drivers are repeatedly forced to experience potential suicides jumping in front of trains. Theorell *et al.* (1992) studied drivers' absences from work during the year following such a traumatic event. These drivers were absent from work 24 per cent more frequently than other drivers.

To summarize the research, it is evident that if people are left to process their traumatic experiences without professional psychological support, about 30–40 per cent are unable to do so. As a consequence, they suffer symptoms of PTSD, increased absences from work, problems in relationships and in settling down in their jobs. Clinical experience also supports this conclusion. Raphael (1986) reached the same conclusion, having reviewed accident investigations carried out using systematic measures. He found that 30–40 per cent of affected people present with symptoms within a year of the traumatic event. After two years, there is a slight drop, but many people are still at the same stage.

It is generally thought that time will heal. With time, reactions and symptoms are diminished, especially within the first six months of the traumatic event, while the normal processing of the trauma is ongoing. Research seems to show that once this normal processing is over, spontaneous recovery is only slight or nonexistent. So, in this sense, the adage 'time heals all wounds' is inaccurate.

Holen (1990) conducted a thorough longitudinal study of the consequences of the Alexander Kielland oil rig accident. In its course, Holen interviewed all but one of the Norwegians who were saved. He took particular care in forming the control group. It corresponded perfectly on the criteria of age, marital status, and time of employment on the oil rig. Before the accident, no differences were found between these two groups in number of sickness absences or accident-proneness. The two groups were followed up for the next nine years. There were very marked differences between the groups in the average annual number of sickness absences, and they remained constant for eight years. In the group of workers who had experienced the disaster, sick leaves were significantly longer, and they had about four times as many sickness absences as the control group. The rescued also had eight times more psychiatric diagnoses than the control group. They were also more accident-prone than those in the control group.

At a Stockholm conference of Scandinavian psychologists in 1996, Dagfinn Winje presented the results of a study of 28 children and 36 parents who had lost a sibling or child in a bus accident in Norway in 1988. The bus was transporting a class of Swedish children on a school trip, when it crashed on a mountainside. The children were aged 11 to 12. Twenty-one people were killed, the majority of them children, but their teacher and a few parents were among them.

The children and parents who had lost loved ones were interviewed one, three and five years after the accident. Both the children and the majority of the adults had obvious symptoms and problems a year after the accident. A large proportion of the adults still had severe symptoms five years after the accident, whereas the children's symptoms were clearly reduced three years after the incident. Thus, the children recovered better than the adults.

7

Measures to Prevent Traumatization

Are preventive measures necessary?

In the previous chapter, I reviewed research evidence showing that about 30–40 per cent of people who have endured a traumatic experience are unable to process it relying on their usual social network and their own personal resources. The consequence is often a Post-Traumatic Stress Disorder or some of its symptoms. Considering that PTSD is only one of the manifestations of breakdown in processing a traumatic experience, the above figures must be regarded as alarming.

Those involved in mental health work are very aware of the significance of psychological traumas as causes of and contributing factors to psychological disorders. Unprocessed traumatic experiences are both predisposing factors and triggers for many psychological disorders. However, these experiences are often so totally denied or blocked that their connection with the disorder only emerges in the course of long-term psychotherapy. The person himself cannot necessarily associate or even remember past traumatic events at all, let alone appreciate their significance.

Psychological traumatization may also become channelled into somatic malaise. Recent research results confirm the contribution of psychological factors in the development of somatic illnesses and recovery from them. Many doctors, who can see the backgrounds to their patients' illnesses, report that the onset of illness was preceded by a severe traumatic experience which the patient did not have the resources to process. Sometimes the interval between the traumatic experience and onset of illness is only a few months, but it can be years.

I have described in the preceding chapters how inability to accept a traumatic event and to adapt to the situation sometimes leads to years of frustrating litigation, causing many people much mental suffering, and at the same time increasing public costs.

Criminal and antisocial behaviour, too, frequently results from unprocessed psychological traumas. People suppress difficult feelings and thoughts caused by the traumatic experience or attempt to distance themselves from it, often by using intoxicants. It is quite common for serious alcohol or drug dependency to be triggered by a traumatic experience, the associated emotions and reactions of which cannot be processed or endured. They erupt as violence towards others and the person himself.

Much less severe reactions also reflect on a person's functioning and the course of his life. Psychological traumas tend to ruin lives by causing incorrect and inappropriate life choices and solutions. Psychological traumas are like inner invisible chains, preventing functional and sound choices and solutions, and forcing one to choose inappropriately again and again.

The above phenomena naturally also affect our capacity for work. Traumatic experiences increase sickness absences, and also temporary or permanent incapacity for work. They increase demands on healthcare and social services, as well as medication costs.

This worrying outlook, describing the manifold and wide-ranging long-term consequences of the after-effects of traumatic experiences, made experts in the field of disaster psychology wonder how it might be possible to facilitate the processing of traumatic experiences. This would prevent both human suffering and social costs caused by the disrupted process. These costs are so huge that if acute crisis work succeeds in preventing the development of even a few psychological traumas, the work will have paid for itself.

The foundations and principles of acute crisis work
Timing of interventions is important

The principles of crisis work carried out after traumatic events derive from the main characteristics of the processing of traumatic experiences. One of the key psychological laws in this coping process is that our minds begin to close up three days after the traumatic event. During the first three days, the mind is open, and the person who has experienced a shock is willing to talk about his experiences. Furthermore, a traumatic experience is so powerful that it impels us to process it in our minds in the early stages. This is why action should be taken immediately after the shocking event.

Acute crisis work aims to exploit the mind's natural way of processing a traumatic event. Thus, the idea is to help the victim to process his experience systematically and profoundly at the stage when he is processing it naturally. Crisis work augments and directs the normal, automatic processing.

Proactive offering of support and services

By and large, victims of a traumatic incident are in a state of severe shock for several days after the event. Very few will seek professional help at this stage, and very few have the strength to do so. Experience in crisis work has shown that if we wait for victims to seek out crisis services spontaneously, the majority will do so after about a month. By then, the processing of the experience has already been disrupted, and there is no longer scope or opportunity to take preventive action.

For this reason, with reference to traumatic crises, the nature of crisis work is proactive and seeking. Acute crisis services must be organized in such a way that they come to the victim of a traumatic event. By this I mean that these services and psycho-social support are proactively offered to the victim, and their own initiative in the matter is not awaited. Usually, the so-called frontline helpers (police, rescue personnel, emergency room staff) ask victims for permission to alert the crisis group, and the crisis group duty officer then contacts the victims.

Alerting the crisis group is also the duty of management in workplaces, and, for example, headmasters in schools. They are responsible for the welfare of their charges, and thus also for organizing help for them. It can also be done by a neighbour, friend or colleague, if others have not thought, remembered or known how to contact the crisis group.

In principle, it is the duty of local crisis groups actively to offer help, even when no official contact by any outsider has been received. The fundamental principle of disaster psychology is that those affected by the event are actively offered help. This seems very hard for crisis workers. We are so firmly accustomed to expect that the victim himself should seek help. Only then can support be given. It seems to be almost impossible to get rid of this learned practice.

At best, the principle that everyone should seek help himself is based on respecting individual privacy. On the other hand, proactively offering help is a part of caring and looking after people. In the case of traumatic events it is justifiable for the culture of caring and taking care to take precedence over the culture of respecting privacy.

Confidentiality and data protection are regulations and practices which often hinder proactive offering of services. These regulations were designed to protect people from issues that may be harmful to them. They often prevent effective services in other areas, too, and not only in crisis work. People often refer to these practices when they want to be sure that nothing is done wrongly. However, it is also wrong that people suffering great anguish are not given help because of some formality. In these situations, too, one would hope that the culture of caring would override rigid caution.

The 1998 report of the Finnish Ministry of Social Affairs and Health recommends that the crisis group duty officer and director, and leaders of defusing and debriefing sessions, should have the right of access to necessary information on the incident from official bodies. Thus, an offer of appropriate services must not be prevented by lack of communication between officials.

On countless occasions, I have personally telephoned a family, workplace or student community, having learned of a shocking event that has befallen them. Making contact is just as difficult every time. Many minutes are spent gathering my thoughts and rehearsing my words. My heart beats fast when I pick up the receiver and dial the number. I cannot recall the words I planned to use, but must open the conversation with spontaneous words. Not once have I been received with hostility or aggression. Not once have I been asked how I knew about the horror that happened to them. Not once has anyone said: "Why are you calling me? I have enough problems already." On the contrary, people are grateful for the contact and the caring. People say that it is wonderful that such an organization exists, that they are actively taken care of like this. Such caring brings comfort and creates a feeling of security.

Very rarely, the reception may be standoffish or aggressive. In such cases, it is often a question of prejudice against healthcare or social work officials based on previous experiences, bad experiences of services, or fear of openly discussing a difficult experience, when people are accustomed to a culture of keeping their private lives quiet and secret. Crisis workers should not be put off by such experiences either. Often, it is not a case of aggression towards the crisis worker or crisis work, but something else. The contact person just becomes the target of displaced aggression. Naturally, it is difficult for the worker to get over such experiences. But these isolated cases of negative or aggressive attitudes to this work must not be allowed to prevent others from receiving appropriate treatment.

No needs assessment based on victims' behaviour

Effective prevention demands that local crisis groups are notified of traumatic events in their area as methodically as possible. The crisis group should always be contacted when some incident that fulfils the criteria of a traumatic event occurs in the locality. Frontline helpers and supervisors should not carry out a needs assessment on the basis of the victims' behaviour. The only criterion should be the traumatic nature of the event.

This is important, because psychological shock usually guarantees a calm and sensible approach to the event. Frontline helpers come into contact with victims precisely at the time when they are in psychological shock.

Consequently, a needs assessment based on victims' behaviour is misleading. The majority of those needing help will not be reached if a needs assessment is based on their behaviour. Frontline helpers seem to find this impossible to understand.

On the other hand, it is easy to imagine why frontline helpers find it difficult not to trust their own judgement. It is much easier to tell a person about the work of the crisis group and request permission to contact it if he is alarmed, shaken and overwhelmed by emotion, rather than if he is viewing the situation calmly and quietly. This situation is usually the only time when these helpers are in contact with the victims. They have no experience of how a quiet and calm victim becomes anguished and anxious when the event begins to become real to him, and he moves into the reaction stage.

However, we must remember that frontline helpers (police and rescue workers) have their own specific tasks at the scene. Informing victims about the operation of the crisis group and alerting it must always remain secondary to their actual professional duties. Furthermore, the work is hampered by lack of time. A new emergency is waiting. That is why it is quite understandable that alerting the crisis group may be forgotten.

In its Memorandum, the Finnish Ministry of Social Affairs and Health recommended that in 'clear-cut' situations, emergency centres should also directly notify the crisis group. Such situations are at least suicides, serious accidents, drownings, serious fires and grave acts of violence. The idea is absolutely not that the crisis group duty officer should rush off to the scene. This way, however, more accurate communication is assured, so that the crisis group is at least notified of all serious traumatic incidents in the locality. The task of the crisis group duty officer is to assess what action is necessary in each situation.

In 1998, the Ministry gave emergency centres directions on alerting local crisis groups (Finnish Ministry of Social Affairs and Health 1998a). The directions state that contrary to normal emergency centre procedure, the client is not questioned about his need for psycho-social support, but the response is assessed by the alerted authorities, most often the crisis centre duty officer. At the time of writing, this directive has only been implemented in exceptional circumstances.

Nordic people firmly believe that it is honourable and heroic to cope alone, without outside help. But it is obstinate and cowardly rather than honourable to refuse professional help after a traumatic experience. Yet this idea is very deeply embedded. That is why it is vital that the question of outside professional help is broached in the right way. For example, it is best to say first: "We have a crisis group of professional people here in our town, and usually when such incidents happen, we inform the group and they will then contact you. I hope that you have no objection." Most people will refuse if they are asked: "How about it? Do you need professional help?"

Having been notified of the incident, the crisis group must acquire the necessary information on the incident and everybody affected by it, ascertain the action required, and encourage and motivate the victims to accept the help offered. This entails communicating to the victims what the aims of the help are, why it is offered, and why it is important that the help is accepted. At the same time, general information is given on why crisis work is carried out and what its main principles and objectives are. The aim is that victims have sufficient information of the course of the processing of a traumatic experience, and how the services can help them.

It is important that victims understand what they are refusing. It is a great pity if their refusal is based on an erroneous impression of the nature of the services or of how honourable it is to cope alone.

Effective prevention of the development of psychological traumas demands, as well as systematic alerting of crisis groups of traumatic events, also as full participation as possible in the psychological interventions deemed to be necessary.

All affected parties must be included

Crisis interventions should be organized in such a way that subjective need assessment is also avoided. It is essential that everyone affected by a traumatic event takes part in interventions. By subjective need assessment, I mean asking oneself: "Do I need outside help to cope with my experience? Are my reactions and feelings more severe than those of others, and do I therefore need more help? Am I somehow weaker than others?" In such a situation, the norm can easily become that there must be a good reason to participate in crisis intervention. The criterion becomes the idea that only the weakest and those with severe reactions need help, and crisis intervention is intended only for them.

In order to avoid subjective need assessment, the services should be organized in such a way that it is taken absolutely for granted that everyone affected will participate. The basic assumption should be that of course everyone will take part. It is a pity if someone cannot attend. Much of the effectiveness of prevention is lost if the threshold for participation in crisis intervention is raised high because of subjective need assessment.

Continued availability of support

After a shocking experience, our state of mind often feels unpredictable and frightening. We feel that we never know what will happen in our minds next, and how we are going to feel the next moment. This is why it is important that psychological support is always available during the first few days following a traumatic event.

My own solution to this principle is that during the first contact, often initiated within a few hours of the incident, I give all my contact details – including my home and mobile telephone numbers – and say that I may be called at any time of day or night.

This is really inexpensive support. People call extremely rarely. Yet I know that those numbers by the telephone and permission to call at a moment of distress are very important in bringing a sense of security. If they were not available, the distress is likely to grow to such proportions that one would have to make contact.

The same principle appears to be at work in other situations, too. I mentioned it at a training seminar for dentists. One said that as long as he kept his home telephone number private, patients called him constantly in the evenings and at weekends. When he had the number printed on the appointment card, the calls stopped.

Family members together

When something very shocking happens, such as a sudden death in the family, it is important that the news is communicated as quickly as possible to all family members, including children.

> A local crisis group member called to consult me on appropriate action in a situation where the 16-year-old son of a family had committed suicide by hanging himself at home before nine o'clock in the morning. He was found by his eight-year-old sister.
>
> The incident was immediately reported to the crisis group. By then, the mother and father had managed to get home, but the other two children were at school. The question was, should they be collected from school, to let them know immediately what had happened, or should the parents wait for them to come home after school?
>
> My advice was that one of the parents should collect the children from school and tell them immediately what had happened.
>
> This was done. The father collected the children, and also informed the headmaster at the same time.
>
> Later, it emerged that the family consisted of two children and two foster children. These two were siblings. One of them had committed suicide; the other was at school.

If the news of the death of a very close person is delayed, it is often perceived as hurtful. The hurt is associated with feelings of worthlessness. Am I such a worthless person that I do not need to be told, even though a person who is very important and close to me has died? Even the order in which the news is imparted to family members, relatives or friends, can invoke feelings of hurt. Why was that person, who is not so close, told before me? For this reason, those who are entrusted with passing on the news should think carefully about the order in which it is done.

Another reason why news of the tragedy should be received as soon as possible is that feelings of guilt invariably arise concerning the interval between the moment of death and when the news is received. We have guilty thoughts of having spent that time as usual, even having a good time, although a person dear to us was dead. The guilt is particularly strong if that interval was spent enjoying ourselves or partying.

It is crucial that victims of a traumatic event are not left alone after the incident. It is natural to gather the family together and invite close relatives and friends round. But they are not always in the same town. Sometimes it feels impossible to tell friends what has happened.

A young woman became the victim of attempted murder at her home. Her boyfriend strangled her so violently and for so long that she was almost unconscious. The woman called the police and reported the offence.

The next day, the woman visited a psychologist's clinic, where the course of events was worked through, and the thoughts, feelings and other reactions caused by the incident thoroughly discussed. The focus was on fear and how it is possible to cope with it.

The woman was very ashamed of what had happened. For that reason, she had not told anyone about the incident. At the clinic, this feeling of shame and overcoming it were also discussed in detail. They stressed that she had to tell a friend what had happened because it was impossible for her to spend the next night alone in her home.

But she did not follow the instructions. She thought that she would manage the night alone. In the middle of the night, however, she was so overwhelmed with fear that she had to call the police. They took her to a psychiatric hospital where she spent the night. The trip to hospital would surely have been unnecessary had she overcome her feelings of shame and sought the help and support of her friends.

Supporting the unity of natural groups

If a group has experienced a traumatic event together, this experience should be addressed with the whole group.

At the sinking of MS Estonia, 38 survivors were taken to Finland on car ferries. They were first taken to hospital, and their physical injuries were treated. Afterwards, they were all gathered together in a hotel which was carefully kept secret from the media, to give them the opportunity to recover from their shocking experience undisturbed. During the evening, their physical needs were attended to. They were offered food and given necessary clothing, items of personal hygiene, etc. They were also given the opportunity to contact their families, and to discuss their experiences among themselves.

For the evening and night, a doctor and four psychologists had been summoned, who between them spoke five languages.

The next day, psychological debriefing sessions were carried out in language groups. During the afternoon, most people were returned to their families.

In this way, an effort was made to maximize the available social support and an opportunity of sharing their experiences with various people was provided. Discussing an event with people who have themselves experienced the same moments of terror and struggle is indeed quite different. On the other hand, it is also important that the survivors' loved ones can share their experiences.

Thus, the aim of disaster-psychological work is maximization of social support received by victims. That is why it is important that people who have together experienced something very shocking discuss their experiences as a group. This should not happen at the expense of family, relatives and friends. The need to get to one's family is very strong after traumatic events. This need must be respected, and efforts made to fulfil it as soon as possible.

A 16-year-old boy lost all his immediate family in the Estonia disaster. Both his parents were among the dead, as well as his girlfriend. His uncle, who was now his closest relative, rang the hotel from Sweden, saying that he had booked plane tickets for the boy and his friend. The departure time was in half an hour. The psychologist taking the call said that it was impossible for the boy to make that flight, but the uncle would not hear any arguments.

The boy had not yet been interviewed by the police at the time of the call. They carried out a swift interview and took him to the airport in the police car. The flight had already closed and the plane was taxiing towards the runway. When he heard that the boys were at the airport, the captain turned back to pick them up, and they got to Stockholm on the flight the uncle had booked.

This basic human need to be with one's family as soon as possible is not always respected. For example, the US citizens who had been hostages for over a year after the occupation of the US Embassy in Iran were first taken to Germany for a week. The plan was that they would first receive psychological support there, and the opportunity of discussing their experiences together. Only after a week did they have the opportunity of meeting their families. This arrangement attracted much criticism afterwards. Experience has shown that the opportunity for discussing experiences with the group must be arranged very quickly after the traumatic event, so that it does not delay the victims getting to be with their families.

Supporting coping

The most salient feature of the disaster-psychological approach is that it is based on supporting normal, healthy people in abnormal situations. The work is directed at ordinary people who have just been forced to experience something very shocking. In this respect, the difference from catastrophe psychiatry is clear. The latter is interested in people's abnormal reactions in catastrophic situations. The reactions of victims are studied to find possible signs of a psychiatric disorder. Crisis work based on disaster psychology does not pathologize reactions or people.

The basis of disaster-psychological work is always supporting victims' coping. This demands a high degree of professional skill from the workers. They must constantly assess the victims' ability to cope. This varies from one task to another and from one moment to the next. The victim must be given responsibility, and he must be encouraged to do for himself all he can and has the energy to do, but the support person must also identify what the victim is unable to do, and assume the responsibility.

Managing everyday chores or challenges demanded by a particular situation brings strength and self-confidence to those who have lost a loved one or become victims of violence. This opportunity of achieving a feeling of coping and increasing self-worth should not be denied them by unnecessary coddling.

8

Psycho-social Support and Services after Traumatic Events

Crisis work is community work

Acute preventive crisis work after traumatic events is always social or community work. Its aim is to process the traumatic experience in all the communities affected by it.

> In a small town in Finland, two young people were killed in a road accident. Their car skidded in icy conditions and collided with an oncoming truck. Both teenagers died in the ambulance on the way to hospital.
>
> The local crisis group conducted the psychological aftercare of the incident with great skill. Ten psychological debriefing sessions in all were carried out in the town. First, separate sessions were organized for the families of both victims and for the truck driver and his family. At the sessions for the victims' families, no precise information was available on how the accident happened. Information was only available from when the call was taken at the emergency centre. Consequently, another session was arranged for both families of the victims which the truck driver also attended.
>
> The accident happened near a playing field. Five young people were playing on the field; they heard the crash and went to see what had happened. They were the first on the scene. A special session was arranged for them.
>
> One of the dead youngsters had still been at school. His classmates and teachers had their own sessions. The youngsters' friends were gathered together for a session. In addition, debriefing sessions were organized for the attendant ambulance crew and police officers, as well as for staff at the hospital emergency room.

The aim of crisis work is to control the reactions in a community caused by a traumatic event. If the community is not equipped to address an incident that has shocked the whole community sufficiently comprehensively and quickly, the emotions elicited by it will drift around uncontrollably in people's minds. People reinforce each other's fears and anger, which can easily acquire quite un-controllable proportions. Appropriate processing and information will calm, provide tools for controlling emotions, and keep people in touch with reality and everyday life. The community will recover more quickly and suffer less damage from the traumatic incident. Such situations are typically suicides and accidental deaths of young people, deaths by violence, rapes, and sexual abuse of children.

Acute crisis work in major disasters

Disaster-psychological modes of intervention vary according to the nature of the incident and the number of victims. The greater the number of psychological victims, and the more geographically widespread they are, the more diverse the interventions that are required.

Mapping the incident

When notification of a shocking event is received by the crisis group or crisis worker, a phase of active information gathering follows. They must ascertain what exactly has happened: how many are dead and how many injured? Were people involved who were not injured, and how many? Where did the dead and injured come from? Where are the injured now? Where do the people who were involved but not injured or killed come from? Where are they now?

What was the rescue like? Did it involve dangerous situations? Were the rescuers exposed to shocking sensory perceptions or experiences? How many people took part in the rescue effort, and how long did it take? Which communities are affected by the incident? Are there reference groups that are shocked by the event?

Such information forms the basis of an assessment of the action to be taken, the order in which it should be taken, the human resources required, and where these resources may be found.

Organizing a telephone helpline

When an accident or other, more far-reaching traumatic event takes place, the need for information is enormous. In fact, the accident does not need to be very wide-ranging for it to touch a large number of people.

In June 1991, there was an accident in Finland, when an amphibious armoured personnel carrier sank. It happened during a military exercise involving about 1000 men. On that fateful Saturday, the exercise included a waterway crossing; the troops had to cross a lake four kilometres wide in the personnel carriers.

Some of the troops had already crossed, while the rest prepared to follow. Then it was found that one of the vehicles had developed an electrical fault which rendered it useless. The third vehicle in line moved to first position, as it contained the lowest number of men, and took most of the men from the first, broken-down carrier. When the amphibious vehicle set out on the crossing, it contained 14 men, exceeding the weight limit by a few men.

The accident happened at five past eight in the evening. The first vehicle in line was halfway across the lake, when it sank to the bottom stern first. Seven soldiers inside the vehicle drowned; another seven riding on top were saved.

News of this accident was made public in the ten o'clock news. It was reported that seven men had drowned. The names of the victims could not be published, as the next of kin had not yet been notified.

Many thousands of homes were worried. Is my husband, our son, my boyfriend among the dead? There was no way of getting information. At that time, no telephone service was immediately organized that people could call and use to express their anxiety. They could do nothing but wait.

The instructions given to the soldiers on the exercise were that they should call their families as soon as they could get to a phone. However, they were deep in the forest, and it took many of them a long time to reach a phone. At that time, mobile phones were not yet commonly used. The last family was delivered the tragic news on the Sunday morning. After that, the names of the victims were published. (Finnish Ministry of Justice 1992: major accident investigation report no. 2/1991)

Today, activating the telephone helpline is the first consideration after a major accident. The functions of the telephone service are dissemination of information, gathering information about people who may have been involved, and psychological support of anxious people. Volunteers from, for example, the Red Cross are often used to man the phones. After the sinking of MS Estonia, the telephone service was organised by Turku Police and manned by its personnel.

Researcher Pertti Raittila interviewed personnel who had run the helpline after they had finished their shifts. They had four lines and took almost 10,000 calls over four days. The Estonia disaster was an international incident, placing great demands on the telephone personnel's language skills.

The phone lines were overloaded. When people could not get through to the official helpline, they called every possible place where they thought information might be available. The telephonists said that most stress was caused by lack of sufficient time to talk to callers. The pressure to answer new calls was so great that almost every call had to be interrupted. This showed that capacity was inadequate, particularly on the first day.

Our experiences of organizing emergency telephone lines after major accidents raise these main principles:

1. At least for the first 12 hours, a sufficient number of lines must be provided for the helpline to ensure that all callers get through. A telephone constantly bleeping with an engaged signal exceeds the tolerance threshold of anxious and distressed people.

2. The telephone system should be such that the public needs to be given only one telephone number, which is manned by a number of staff. The system will always find a free line.

3. The telephonists must have adequate prior training for such tasks. They should also have precise instructions regarding information and advice they may give.

4. A record of the calls must be kept, and if something is promised during a call, for example that the caller will be contacted later, the promise must always be kept. Giving an impression of security and trust is particularly important.

5. It is best to organize the telephone service in two tiers, so that staff who concentrate purely on providing information are separate. If the caller needs support and conversation, the call is directed to experienced professionals.

6. The welfare of the telephonists must be considered. They must be provided with sufficient breaks. About four hours a day of this kind of work should be the maximum.

Round-the-clock psychological support

Major accidents touch large numbers of people. However, in most cases rescue and support organizations have no information on everyone affected. For example, in the case of train accidents no records exist as to who may have been on the train. Consequently, even efficiently and proactively seeking action will not succeed in reaching all the victims. On this basis, for example, the Finnish

Red Cross (FRC) always immediately establishes a psychologists' helpline after major disasters, enabling people to call 24 hours a day.

At the MS Estonia shipwreck, the FRC psychologists' helpline was originally set up for ferry crews and staff. At the scene of the disaster alone there were five car ferries with about 1000 personnel. Off-duty personnel at home, about 1000 people, were also victims.

However, the number was inadvertently released by the media to the general public. Consequently, its function was extended to other kinds of needs, too, which turned out to be only to the good. Thus, the psychologists were contacted also by many groups of passengers who were travelling on the ferries that participated in the rescue effort. The psychologist assessed the group's needs during the call and, when necessary, organized help in the group's home town by contacting the local crisis groups and passing any follow-up actions to them. Such assignments were numerous.

Families that had been passengers also called to ask for help. They were dealt with in the same way, that is, help was organized for them through their own local crisis groups. In other words, the psychologists' helpline was not used purely for providing talking help. Assessments of need for follow-up support were also made, and the task passed on to local groups. In this way, numerous debriefing sessions were organized all around Finland.

One essential helpline function was psychological counselling and advice on various questions. The helpline was called by parents who had a family cruise booked in a few days. Should it be cancelled or should they go regardless? We have to travel by ferry next week and the children are frightened. What should we do?

Schoolteachers contacted us for advice on how they should address the disaster at school to reassure pupils. People suffering from anxiety owing to the disaster called to talk about their anxiety and to ask where they should go for help. Some asked for written materials they knew had been distributed to passengers at the ship terminal but which for some reason they had not received. Some wanted to pass on feedback on the written material, etc.

The FRC psychologists' telephone helpline has proved its workability and usefulness in a number of major accidents. Consequently, it has become standard practice in major accidents, activated if the incident is large enough for such a service to be deemed necessary. The primary objective of the activity is separately identified for each incident.

The helplines are answered by experts in disaster psychology. Experience has also shown that the majority of calls received require expertise and special know-how. Sometimes, the psychological support services for victims are combined with the telephone service. However, my own experience is that they are two separate forms of service, and it is impossible to amalgamate them. It would undermine the quality of service and cause clear gaps in it.

Setting up a crisis centre

At major accidents, it is often necessary to set up a crisis centre where people involved in the accident but without physical injury are gathered. The centre is also open for families and friends of the injured or dead, as well as everyone shocked by the accident, and those who were at the scene or travelling to it. If a crisis centre is set up, the telephone service intended for imparting information may also be attached to it.

In order to provide support for the victims, the crisis centre should be staffed by both professional members of the crisis group and volunteer helpers. The volunteers must be trained for this task and always work under the supervision of crisis group members.

It is essential that the number of volunteers is in proportion to those requiring help. I have seen situations where six or seven volunteer helpers stood around one victim. This kind of situation hardly helps the victim.

A passenger on an train that had an accident described her visit to the crisis centre:

A small, slight woman carefully opened the door, fastened with a safety chain, to a wooden building. I sat in the warm room and had a cup of tea. I could see the station and the tracks through the window.

Two crisis workers came to the table. They didn't let me meet other victims, although I asked them to. I would have liked to talk to some other people who were in the accident. It was now quiet in the crisis centre, but during the afternoon, many victims and their families had visited the building. There were many small rooms where everyone had their own conversations.

I went over the day's events again and again. What if I had picked another carriage? I thought. It felt luxurious that in the middle of the night, two people were there for my feelings and grief. I asked them about their employment and overtime payments; I felt awkward about their attention. They were kind, but not cloyingly warm and empathic. They looked me straight in the eye, and asked only a few questions. They were silent if I was silent.

I joked about the little gingerbread house, where frightened and lonely travellers of the night sought refuge. I ate three jam doughnuts and drank numerous cups of tea. I craved more sweet things, but they ran out of doughnuts. (Jokinen 1999, p.14)

It is vital that the crisis centre is set up sufficiently quickly after the accident. For fast action to be possible, advance plans must also include a detailed plan for the crisis centre – where it will be set up, how it will be staffed, who will lead and organize its activities, where the necessary equipment (telephones, faxes, photocopiers, etc.) will be obtained.

Group meetings

If the number of people affected by a traumatic event is large, group meetings are a good method of efficient communication of information about the event and its consequences, and the effects of such incidents on people. Generally, the focus of group meetings is on imparting information in such a form that it calms people and equips them to process their own experiences and reactions.

In Finland, group meetings have been utilized for two different purposes. They have been organized immediately after a traumatic event, when they were used to impart information on what happened, how it all happened, and how to carry on from here. Sometimes, a moment of remembrance is held at this meeting, if the event was, for example, the death of a colleague. Sometimes, a group meeting is followed by psychological defusing or debriefing sessions in smaller groups.

An example of utilizing a meeting for this purpose:

A teacher was the victim of a violent attack at school. A pupil pushed him to the ground and then threatened him with a knife. The situation was resolved without physical injury. Once psychological first aid had been arranged for the teacher who had been attacked, and the perpetrator, the headmaster called a meeting of the whole staff. He explained what had happened and suggested that all teachers should tell their pupils at the next lesson, and use the period to discuss the incident. At the same time, he announced that he was organizing a psychological debriefing session for the whole staff the following day, and hoped that everyone would attend.

At the sinking of MS Estonia, group meetings were also arranged on the ships that had taken part in rescue efforts. Their content varied depending on how close the event itself was. If only a few hours had passed, the meeting acquired more of an air of imparting information. The staff were told what had happened, what the overall situation was, the role of their particular ship in the rescue effort, what would happen next, etc. In addition, the staff was thanked for their part in the rescue work.

The longer the interval from the disaster itself, the more prominent were psychological factors at group meetings. Psychologists told the meetings how people usually react after accidents, how one should approach these reactions, and what kind of help is available.

Other kinds of group meetings were arranged in cases of various fires, siege situations, shootings, etc., where large numbers of people were evacuated from their homes because of the danger, but the threat to them was relatively minor. In these situations, too, a part of the meeting was used to inform about various issues, a part to discuss people's own experiences, psychological and somatic reactions, thoughts and feelings, and the remaining time to tell people about common reactions, instructions on how they should be approached, and how to cope with them. Sometimes, these occasions have been called debriefing sessions, but they do not, in fact, fulfil all the criteria of psychological debriefing.

Producing and distributing written material

Written material has often been used to supplement individual or group meetings. In Finland, the FRC psychologists' preparedness group has adopted the distribution of written material as a separate and independent function.

The first time written material was produced for wide distribution was at the Sally Albatross shipwreck. Six or seven members of the psychologists' preparedness group were at the terminal to meet evacuated passengers and crew. At that point, we had discussions with many shocked passengers, before they continued their journeys home. It became obvious during these discussions that the help we were able to give them at the docks was insufficient. However, all 1300 passengers had travelled to their homes around the country during the night, so that it was impossible to reach them personally. Consequently, we decided to write a letter to the passengers and the ship's company. The next day, the shipping line sent it to everyone who had been on board the ship, and also to staff who had been off duty.

In the letter, we outlined the shocking events they had experienced. In composing these descriptions and assessing anticipated reactions, we drew largely on the conversations we had had the previous night at the terminal. Having described the reactions, we stressed individual differences, but also drew attention to known psychological patterns. In addition, the letter contained advice on how the reactions should be approached, and instructions for the next few days. Instructions were also given on when to seek professional help and where to find it.

We received very positive feedback on the letter. Many people said that until it arrived, they had had a hard time, because they did not understand their own reactions and their intensity. In particular family members, who had not themselves been on the cruise, were surprised at the intensity of the reactions, called the person involved hypersensitive, or suspected that he was going mad. The content of the letter made the reactions comprehensible and gave permission for them. They became normal reactions to an abnormal situation.

After this experience, we have followed the same procedure after all major accidents, adapting it to each situation at hand. To this end, we first had to determine what the people involved in the accident, or their loved ones, had experienced, and then assess what kinds of reactions that particular experience was likely to elicit.

About 8000 copies of material prepared at the MS Estonia disaster were distributed at the terminal to ships' passengers. The material was translated into five languages. It was received surprisingly favourably. During the first days, we did not think to distribute the material to people leaving ferries by car. The mistake was spotted when numerous calls were received on the psychologists' helpline, with motorists saying that other passengers had received such material, but they had not. The material was sent to them by post. One piece of feedback was particularly touching. A Finnish man called the psychologists' helpline and wanted to say thank you for this leaflet. He had been a passenger on one of the ships that participated in the rescue effort. After returning home, he had had a lot of problems. He said that he had read the leaflet at least 60 times and that it helped every time.

Inferences may be drawn about the importance of the letter also from the fact that none of them were discarded on the floors or in trash bins of the terminal. All who had received it had taken it. I have heard that many have kept the letter. I have met people who told me that they re-read it on every anniversary of the sinking of the Estonia.

The leaflet is designed in the form of a signed personal letter. Possibly, this is another reason for the importance of the leaflet. While visiting Sweden or Estonia since the accident, I have occasionally met people who, having learned my name, say that they have received a letter from me. On closer enquiry, it has transpired that they mean the letter that was distributed to the victims of the Estonia disaster.

The importance of written material and its precise targeting was clearly evident also after the 9/11 terrorist strike. In Finland, crisis work was set in motion immediately after the catastrophe, as a Finnair plane was on its way to New York, and it was ordered to turn around after four hours' flying time. There were more than 250 passengers on the plane, a large number of them Russians. At Finnair's request, crisis workers met the passengers, the majority of whom only became aware of the reality at the air terminal or the hotel where they were taken. The captain had explained the reason of their return during the flight, but in its incomprehensibility it had not penetrated the passengers' consciousness.

Most of the passengers were placed in nearby hotels to await clarification of the situation. While receiving the passengers, we crisis workers became convinced of the need for written material in this situation. During the evening and night, the first written material was prepared in the form of a letter, and translated into Russian and English, for distribution to the hotel residents. The perspective was that the recipient himself was not involved in the catastrophe, but he was worried about loved ones in New York and the uncertainty of his own immediate future.

Another version of the bulletin was prepared for those who were in the USA at the time of the catastrophe, and thus experienced it. This material was distributed on the plane to passengers on the first Finnair flight from New York to Helsinki, and for the next week at the air terminal.

When we were meeting the passengers off the first flight after the catastrophe, it dawned on us that the families and friends meeting the passengers also needed information and directions on how they should relate to their loved ones who had experienced moments of terror, and how they might help them. To this end, yet another bulletin was produced, for families and loved ones. This bulletin, too, was distributed by Red Cross volunteers at the airport. All the bulletins were also posted on FRC's website.

The 9/11 terrorist strike reinforced our understanding of the importance of precisely targeted written material. That disaster touched a large number of people whom it was impossible to reach in any other way. When material is well targeted, it addresses and touches people quite differently from that designed for general distribution.

Psychological support of accident victims

Disaster psychologists' special methods, such as psychological defusing and debriefing (to be more thoroughly introduced later) have a crucial role in major accidents, too. The major part of actual professional crisis work consists of leading these sessions for families of those killed in the accident, those injured and their families, those involved in the accident who were uninjured, and other groups closely affected by the accident.

Defusing sessions must be implemented as soon as possible after the accident. Psychological debriefing sessions should be timed preferably on the second or third day after the accident. In major disasters, the first week after the incident is the appropriate time for debriefing sessions.

All recent major accidents in Finland have been so-called centripetal accidents. In such cases, conducting debriefing sessions becomes mainly the task of local crisis groups. However, co-ordinating the activity and informing local crisis groups about victims is a huge task.

Psychological defusing and debriefing for rescue workers

Rescue workers at scenes of major disasters and healthcare personnel receiving the injured at hospitals are subjected to enormous stresses. For this reason, they are usually provided with an opportunity of defusing and processing their experiences in groups immediately after the work is finished. If rescue efforts take several days, a psychological defusing meeting should be arranged for the rescuers at the end of each shift, enabling them to defuse the shocking experiences accumulated during the shift. The actual debriefing session is organized when rescue work is complete.

In major disasters, many other people also work with the victims, apart from those involved purely in rescuing or caring for the injured. It is important that also those who are involved in psychological support work have an opportunity to defuse their experiences. This includes both the volunteers and crisis group members who have attended. The same principles apply to these groups as to other victims. A psychological debriefing session must be proactively arranged for them by an outsider. Frequently, it does not occur to them to request it, in spite of their expertise in crisis work.

At the Estonia disaster, the majority of the work done by the FRC psychologists' preparedness group in Finland focused on the psycho-social support of rescuers, as there were few Finnish passengers on the ship. Some idea of the scale of the work is shown by the fact that the group organised about 250 psychological debriefing sessions altogether, the majority for ships' personnel. Other groups were helicopter pilots and surface rescuers, survivors who had been brought to Helsinki, and volunteers and professionals who had been involved in the psycho-social support.

Instructing organizations and their management

Atle Dyregrov, the Norwegian disaster psychologist, illustrated the need for disaster-psychological knowledge in organizations, using as an example an accident that took place in the 1980s.

> A large shipyard had completed a luxury cruise ship which set out on its maiden voyage. The company wanted to reward its personnel for a job well done, by arranging for half of them to join the maiden voyage. Lots were drawn for who could go.

They were to embark at a Danish port and sail back to Norway on the ship. They flew to Denmark on a chartered plane. They never made it to Denmark: the plane crash-landed and all the passengers were killed. In one blow, the company lost half its workforce and most of its management. Naturally, in such a situation the firm's management needs expert help in dealing with reactions elicited by the catastrophe. (Dyregrov 1994)

We have already seen that crisis and disaster-psychological work is community work in nature. It is carried out within organizations and communities, and it necessitates approval of the activities by the community and its leadership.

At the time of the MS Estonia disaster, we discovered the importance of pre-existing contacts with the organization, and the importance of plans for disaster-psychological services being in place before a disaster happens. It was easy to make contact with organizations we had collaborated with before. Conversely, we had difficulties in initiating our activities in the organizations with which we had no previous contact.

With Silja Line, constructive co-operation was achieved immediately, since the company was familiar with the principles of crisis work from the Sally Albatross disaster, six months before the sinking of the Estonia. But staff at Viking Line had no idea of disaster-psychological work at all. Consequently, it was necessary first to instruct the company management on the principles, aims and benefits of disaster-psychological work, before the doors were opened for crisis counsellors. After the meeting with the management, the company ordered two psychologists for each of its ships that had participated in the rescue, to help and support the personnel. The psychologists sailed with the ships for two weeks. The aim was that the entire personnel should have the opportunity of receiving support.

Activation of disaster-psychological work was not so smooth everywhere. The greatest burden of the rescue work was borne by the helicopter pilots and divers of the Frontier Guard and the Turku rescue centre. In these organizations, disaster-psychological work and thinking were completely alien. When they were offered the opportunity of having a group of FRC preparedness group psychologists provide crisis counselling and help helicopter pilots and divers to recover from the rescue effort that had been mentally very taxing, the leadership delegated the decision to the next officer down in rank. So the decision was passed down the chain four times, and finally an official decided that no psychological support was necessary.

The process of passing the buck was repeated three times with the same result. Then the matter was taken up by the organization's occupational physician, who confirmed that if the men did not receive help in coping with their psychological reactions soon, they would quickly all be unfit for work. The next morning, seven psychologists from the preparedness group started work with the rescue personnel. The work went on for four days, and was later much praised and appreciated.

Today, more and more organizations, in sectors where major accidents are likely, have their own preparedness organization and plan, which now also automatically includes organizing psycho-social support for victims. For example, Silja Line has its own psychological preparedness for the personnel, and trains managers to recognize traumatic events and to outsource appropriate services when required. Airlines, too, have their own preparedness plans, with care of the psychological welfare of staff and passengers and their families a crucial part in accidents and other traumatic events.

In Sweden, the prime minister, leaders of political parties and decision-makers were faced with a difficult question immediately after the Estonia disaster. The media demanded their views on raising the ship and the victims who had gone down with it. Both main party leaders and the then prime minister expressed their views on the first day after the disaster that the ship should be raised without regard for cost.

These views later triggered a heated debate from victims' families, and the question of raising the wreck became a huge political problem. The promises given on that first day are quoted again and again. Since the party leaders have not kept their promises, people do not know whom to trust and what to do.

The crucial mistake was actually made when the politicians formed a view in a situation where they were themselves in a state of psychological shock. The pressure to somehow offer consolation to families who had lost members was huge. In shock, normal capacities for judgement and decision-making disappear; consequently, statements are based purely on emotion and a wish to console the grieving. Disaster-psychological expertise would be useful in such situations. Decision-makers could be warned about the dangers of hasty formulation of policy, however great the pressure to do so.

Another central disaster-psychological principle is that people tend to regress in a catastrophe. Childlike characteristics manifest in them. Thus, in a catastrophe, a strong leader is required in whom others can trust and seek security. This also applies to leadership of a country that has experienced a catastrophe. Repeated reformulation of policy and debating of the issue destroys the basis of trust for people who have lost loved ones: there is no truth that one could accommodate. The country's leaders should have first thoroughly considered their policy in the matter, and later adhered to it. That way, they could have offered their citizens the security and solid foundation they so badly needed.

Psychological support in identifying the dead and saying goodbye

One facet of disaster-psychological work is organizing psychological support for people when they must identify their dead kin and say goodbye to them. In major accidents, identification of the dead and post-mortems are often carried out centrally. Thus, this task falls on members of the crisis group of the location where the deceased are.

At the Estonia disaster, identification of all the deceased was carried out using the Disaster Victim Identification (DVI) procedure. Not in one case was the help of relatives needed in identification. The psychologists' preparedness group had anticipated large-scale support for relatives at identification and viewing of the bodies, but these services were not needed. Conversely, at a more recent train crash, a psychologist from the preparedness group was present at the Department of Forensic Medicine on every occasion when relatives went to say farewell to the deceased.

The task of the support person in this situation demands particular professional skill. The family, especially children, must be well prepared for what they are about to see and experience. I will return to this preparation later in this book.

In smaller accidents and everyday traumatic events, not all types of service provided at major disasters are generally required. In such situations, the work is focused on support in the shock stage and psychological debriefing.

9

The Media and Traumatic Events

At times of major disasters and also some smaller-scale traumatic events, the need for information is great for both those immediately affected and the general public. News broadcasts are watched with great interest. The media, on their part, compete in how quickly they release the news and its impact. They want to bring out something special and unique that other news media have missed.

The role of the media as producers of traumatic experiences

The role of the media in traumatic events is to provide a service, but it can also be traumatizing. For example, TV programmes may evoke new traumas for people involved in the accident and their families. That is why it is important for the media to understand the effects of their actions, and to take them into account.

Rescue and medical personnel often consider the behaviour of reporters and photographers to be too intrusive and crass. Frequently, they actually hinder them in their work. After the Estonia disaster, when staff at a large hospital was asked what the most difficult part of the disaster was, they systematically replied: "The role of the media." The hospital was forced to place police guards at the door to prevent reporters and photographers from entering, to enable medical staff to concentrate on their own work.

> When the hospital doors had been locked and one could only enter past police guards, some reporters posed as patients or victims' relatives in order to get in.
>
> Photographers lurked like vultures in various places, on the lookout for likely targets. When the prime ministers of three countries visited the survivors, and a limited number of reporters and photographers were admitted, the fight over gaining entry was unbelievable.

Similar scenes took place at the location where most of the bodies were taken. Considerable efforts were needed to prevent photographers from taking pictures of the dead when they were brought in by helicopter. Some photographers ripped the black plastic covering the bodies in order to get pictures of them.

Victims of traumatic events, too, see media intrusion as violation of their privacy. For example, in many fires, photographers arrived at the scene before the apartment block was evacuated. People complained that they had no way of avoiding TV cameras when they were evacuated from their homes in their nightwear.

Published detailed descriptions of incidents may also hurt victims. Particularly if the information is false, its publication can produce a new trauma for a person already traumatized. At the Jokela train crash, it was widely reported that the driver of the accident train had a serious brain disease. After a few days it transpired that the information was totally false. However, such reports were deeply hurtful to the driver's family, and clearly added to an already very traumatizing experience.

The media rarely give a thought to the fact that old traumatic experiences often resurface when a new similar incident takes place. It is common practice in such situations to write a historical review of similar incidents. Years after the event, photographs of the victims, their families and the accident may be published again, and quite unwittingly, they are again in the media glare. Often, these victims feel that they are never going to be left in peace; the media will never let them forget or be forgotten.

The role of the media in promoting psychological coping with a traumatic event

On the other hand, the media have a central role in imparting information and promoting psychological coping with traumatic experiences, and in Finland, television in particular has laudably understood this role.

The media have three main tasks in major disasters and other wide-reaching traumatic events:

1. *Reporting the facts.* The primary task of the media is to report the facts about the incident. These facts are crucial in facing and accepting the truth. Although the family often receives factual information from officials, the media have a central role in supplying information to friends, colleagues and relatives outside the immediate family circle. For this reason alone, it is important that the facts reported by the media really are correct.

2. *Imparting information about special services.* At times of major accidents or traumatic events, special services for the accident victims are required. They include, for example, a telephone service to provide information about the victims, crisis centres, and telephone helplines offering psychological support. These special services are set up immediately after the incident, and information on how to contact them must be available quickly to everyone. The media have a central role in this task of imparting information.

3. *Imparting information on human psychological reactions after an accident.* The third essential task of the media, especially after major accidents or other traumatic events that touch large numbers of people, is imparting information on how people react in such situations and afterwards. The Finnish media have performed this function in an exemplary manner. After every large accident, the media have carried interviews with experts about usual reactions and how to cope with them.

   A serious train accident happened on a Friday afternoon. Before five o'clock, a TV breakfast programme contacted the Finnish Red Cross, requesting an expert in the studio for the next morning to explain people's typical psychological reactions after such an incident.

   The interview was broadcast. It covered people's usual reactions after an accident, how they should be approached, where to get extra help, and who should seek such help. The interview was aired three times during the breakfast broadcast, always after the news.

The same procedure had been followed at the Estonia disaster, when the media, particularly TV, were very interested in the impact of such a massive catastrophe on the human psyche, and in how victims may be helped in such situations. About twenty TV and radio broadcasts in all covered these topics during the first fortnight after the accident.

It was significant that TV current affairs programmes in particular attempted to follow the natural human coping process of a traumatic experience, and to promote it. Many reporters contacted us to ask what the most important aspect was at the time. So the reports at first described the effects of a great shock on people, then recovery from the shock, the grieving process and its progression, death and relating to death. This process culminated in a memorial service at sea, also planned and executed with great care.

The process continued on the anniversary of the Estonia disaster, when the programmes touched on the significance of the anniversary, the emotions it elicited, and also recovery that had taken place and the situation a year after the accident.

Reporters' approaches to making these programmes was responsible, careful and sensitive.

> About a week after the Estonia disaster, a very well-known and experienced news reporter contacted me. He said that he had to read the commentary for a documentary entitled 'Mayday Estonia', to be aired the following Sunday. He suggested that we view the documentary together and discuss what he should say in his opening and closing commentaries. He was particularly aware that the programme could also be seen in Estonia, and was likely to attract a large audience.
>
> We viewed the documentary together and considered what was appropriate and important in the commentaries. He later faxed me his commentary text and asked me to check through its content and choice of words, to ensure that he was not using hurtful expressions in his commentary.

The knowledgeable, proactive and positive approach of the media to disaster-psychological work has had wide-reaching consequences. I believe that it has helped our work achieve an accepted status among citizens and decision-makers. This positive attitude is also reflected in the fact that in Finland, these methods were very quickly widely adopted and that in less than a decade, a comprehensive network of crisis groups was established in our country.

Another achievement of the media concerns the general understanding of disaster psychology in Finland. Over the ten years that disaster-psychological work has been carried out, people's knowledge of how we react in shocking situations and their willingness to accept help have increased enormously.

Many people used to think that effects on the human psyche only emerge when there are problems. The general understanding was that only so-called weak people have a psyche. Today, a much greater proportion of people is aware of the existence and importance of the psyche. This knowledge has been significantly increased by internalization of disaster-psychological concepts. Shocking events make people pause and become receptive to new knowledge, and the media have produced it in an effective way, right at the most sensitive time.

People are more accepting and understanding of psychological reactions and psychological processing of an experience. Consequently, in this respect, our country is a better place. However, this knowledge is gradually forgotten; it is important that the media maintain their proactive role as informers in future, too.

Protecting victims from publicity

Those involved in crisis work have an ambivalent relationship with the media. On one hand, the media are necessary to disseminate information on people's reactions, crisis services and how to contact them, on the other, it is our duty to protect victims of traumatic events from the added stress that the media undoubtedly cause them.

The media, on their part, endeavour to give the accident a face, and a prominent part of a news story about an accident is interviewing those involved and their families.

Psychological shock renders victims willing to talk to anybody, including reporters, about their experience. Often, victims who were interviewed and photographed later regret their statements, or agreeing to the interview. Where photographs are concerned, victims' permission is not even sought.

In psychological shock, our judgement is not fully functional. The need to talk about the experience and the accident coincides with the reporter's need to find out. However, our inner psychological state is in total turmoil. This is why people may give statements during interviews that they later regret. Furthermore, one is not fully capable of anticipating the consequences of publicity. That is why protection from publicity should be the policy of crisis work.

A 14-year-old boy became the victim of vicious violence. He died of his injuries on the way to hospital. The hospital staff was prepared for the family's arrival to see their son. The boy died in the early evening. The family did not come that evening or night. They had been taken to another emergency centre for treatment.

In the morning, the hospital telephoned the parents, giving them another opportunity to see the boy. They promised to come and to bring their other children.

The group that arrived later consisted of two adult women, two adult men and two children. The staff assumed that the family had brought people to support them, and did not ask questions as to their identity. They were taken to the hospital chapel. The young mother found it hard to see her dead child, and left the chapel quickly, going into an adjoining waiting room with the children and the other woman. One of the staff members followed them, the other remained in the chapel.

After a few minutes, flash photography was seen in the chapel. One of the men started taking pictures of the dead boy. The men's strange behaviour caused the staff to conclude that something was wrong. It transpired that one of the men was a reporter from a magazine, and he was taking pictures for a story.

It is very difficult to protect victims of traumatic events from publicity. The media usually receive news of the event more quickly than crisis workers, and they are also quicker off the mark than crisis professionals. Often, the damage is already done by the time the crisis worker manages to contact the victim's family.

General education in this area is very important. We should all be aware that no statements should be issued to the media in the first days after a traumatic event, even if we ourselves may find it tempting.

We have gained experience of protecting victims from publicity in major disasters:

Thirty-eight survivors of the MS Estonia arrived in Helsinki on a car ferry. They were met at the terminal by a sizeable group of reporters and photographers. An advance plan had been prepared by the rescue services and the Red Cross for transporting the survivors from the car ferry and their subsequent care. We also agreed to keep the plan strictly secret, in order to protect the victims from publicity.

As the ship arrived at the docks, the reporters and photographers from both terminals were taken on board ship for a press conference. Meanwhile, the survivors were taken via the car deck to two hospitals, where their physical injuries were examined and treated. Afterwards, they were taken by the rescue service to a hotel, where the staff were sworn to secrecy that all the survivors were in their care.

The secrecy was kept completely. It demanded a great deal of work, as at the same time we wanted the survivors' families to be able to contact them. At every call from a family member, we checked the caller's name and relationship with the survivor. Only when the information had been checked with him was he asked to take the call.

In the 24 hours that the survivors were in the care of FRC, not one of the survivors was confronted by reporters or photographers. They were extremely grateful for this freedom from intrusion.

Some hospitals, too, succeeded in protecting victims of the Estonia disaster. An appropriate procedure was applied, for example, in the Mariehamn district hospital.

Eight survivors were brought to Mariehamn hospital. International press also arrived in private planes and helicopters. The interest of foreign reporters was increased by the fact that the only British survivor was taken to

Mariehamn. The reporters and photographers employed the same methods as in Turku.

The hospital doors were locked after the survivors had arrived. The reporters attempted to gain entry by posing as patients, survivors' family members, or by attempting to bribe hospital staff. But unlike in Turku, the Mariehamn crisis group was well prepared to protect the victims and to provide psychological support. The latter was their first priority. Every survivor was allocated a personal supporter to care for his psychological welfare. Not one of the reporters or photographers managed to interview or photograph the victims on the first day after the accident.

On the second day, too, the reporters had to wait. During the morning, the survivors' psychological debriefing session was held, and afterwards, the survivors were allowed to rest. Only after that were they told that reporters and photographers were waiting for an opportunity to interview them, but that they had every right to refuse. If someone wanted to grant an interview, their personal supporter accompanied them. The reporters, too, considered the interviews of the rested English, Swedish and Estonian survivors to have been very successful (Raittila 1996, pp.49–50).

In May 1995, there was a serious hotel fire in Prague. Eight people, two of them Finnish, died in the fire. The Finns were among a group of tourists, 23 of whom lived in the burned-out Hotel Olympia.

The tour operator contacted the FRC psychologists' preparedness group immediately after the fire, for guidance on taking care of the psychological support of the Finnish residents at the hotel. The instruction was that the victims should be returned home to their families as soon as possible. In addition, the necessity of protecting the victims from publicity was emphasized.

Most of the tourists who had stayed in the hotel which suffered the fire were work colleagues. They knew each other well. The fire was very threatening. The rooms were so full of smoke that if one left the window, one was lost, and could not find the way back. The women who had died had been killed by noxious fumes.

The fire was made more threatening by shortcomings in fire and rescue technology. The fire was on the thirteenth floor, and the Finns lived on floors 16–19. The water jets and ladders of the fire appliances reached up to the eleventh floor. Some residents were rescued off the roof by helicopter, but the majority hung out of hotel windows for air. The fire was extinguished and the residents were led away down the stairs.

Most of the Finns took nothing with them from their rooms other than the clothes they were wearing. They had no money, passports, or outer clothing. They were transported to Finland on the first available flight. We agreed with the tour operator that this would not be disclosed. In spite of this, the survivors were met at the airport by a large crowd of reporters and photographers.

However, we had planned for this. The victims were asked to stay on the Finnair plane that had brought them, while the other passengers disembarked. The FRC psychologists had arranged a separate bus to collect the survivors from the plane, and they were taken directly to the terminal, to a boardroom that was completely isolated from outsiders.

There the survivors were given a combined information session and psychological debriefing. Those who had insufficient warm clothing were provided with it by FRC. At the end of the two-hour session the victims were told that there was a large group of reporters and photographers outside, wanting interviews. They were advised that they were under no obligation to grant them. A woman emerged from the group who said that she was a reporter herself. She volunteered to make a statement on behalf of everybody.

She began her statement by saying that they had all agreed that she would give all interviews, and that the others wished to be left alone later, also. After the interviews, the group was taken from the boardroom into a bus, and to their homes. They were told that they would be contacted by phone the next day, and that more thorough aftercare would be organized.

The survivors' wish to be left alone was well respected. No interviews were published. They were very pleased that they had been protected from the publicity mill, having already endured a shocking experience.

The sympathetic approach and authoritative actions of the tour operator and airport officials enabled effective protection of the victims from publicity. However, such efficiency also gave rise to public criticism. For example, the main national newspaper included in its write-up the subheading "Crisis group isolated victims from media". It should be stressed that the idea is not the total isolation of victims from the media. The intention is just that the victims should first be allowed time to process their shocking experience and recover sufficiently to be able to make a considered and independent decision on granting interviews. Are the media really in such a hurry that they want to interview victims at the expense of their psychological welfare and recovery, when they can do so in more restful circumstances a couple of days later?

The majority of the Finnish media approach victims of traumatic events and their needs with respect. Even when it seems that the needs of the media and victims are incompatible, reporters understand very well, when it is thoroughly explained to them, that the victims do not wish to appear in public. However, some of the tabloid press apply principles that allow no protection for the victims.

Reporters' and photographers' needs are exemplified by a photographer's experience from the Estonia disaster.

> The photographer was taking pictures in the Tallinn terminal, when those rescued from the disaster arrived back in Estonia. The terminal was packed with waiting, shocked, weeping families.
>
> The photographer said that he, too, wept and took pictures. He felt that he should not be doing it, but as the photographers of competing papers were taking pictures, he had to do so, too. He said that he wished fervently that some external authority would enter the scene, chase all the photographers away, and forbid all photography.

Some victims of traumatic events use publicity as a means of defusing their distress. In such cases, the media have arrived at the scene ahead of proprietary crisis counsellors, so that processing of the experience has already become public. This might also happen if internal processing of the experience is not possible for some reason, or if the victims feel very frustrated and unfairly treated in the way officials have handled the traumatic incident.

10

Psycho-social Support During the Shock Stage

The form and content of psycho-social support depend on the stage of processing the traumatic experience. During the psychological shock stage, support is different from that during the reaction stage. While a person is in psychological shock, he needs only pure support, not actual help in processing the traumatic experience.

Psychological first aid

The psycho-social support in psychological shock is called psychological first aid. Everyone should know its basic principles. It is a first aid skill much more frequently needed than physical first aid. At various stages in our lives, all of us will face situations where we should be able to support a person who has endured a traumatic experience.

Psychological first aid sounds very simple, but in reality it is extremely demanding and stressful. I will begin the introduction of the principles of psychological first aid by using an example.

> Krister Andersson is the psychologist who brought the disaster-psychological method to Finland. In the summer of 1989, he had attended a conference of Scandinavian psychologists in Iceland, and taken a course there run by Atle Dyregrov, the disaster psychologist. Krister was so excited by the ideas introduced during the course that he decided to set up a crisis group in the town where he was employed as health centre psychologist. He assembled the group, trained it during the autumn, and the group was activated at the start of 1990.

The health centre, hospital emergency room, police and rescue services had all been informed of the new service, and they were asked to contact the group when any traumatic event happened in the area.

In the first week, Krister received a call from the health centre. He was informed that they now had a case for him. They had a mother whose eight-year-old daughter had been run over by a car on her way to school and killed. Krister took the mother into his office, excited to be able to test his skills so soon.

They sat in the office for about an hour and a half. Krister held the mother's hand and frantically searched for something comforting that he could say to her, but could think of nothing. So, they just sat there, and the mother did most of the talking. Sometimes she wept bitterly, sometimes she talked about her daughter, her traits and ways, and sometimes asked: "I wonder where our little girl's school bag got to?" Krister listened, and did not utter many words during the entire conversation.

When the mother left, Krister's first thought was that he was no good at this work after all. He did not know how to help people who were in great pain. His career in disaster psychology was doomed. He felt like this for about a month, until the mother called him. She wanted to thank him for the help he had given her. "I don't know how I would have coped without it," she said.

This experience encompasses what is important and also most difficult in psychological first aid. Comforting or appropriate words do not exist. The crucial point is that the supporter is a tranquil presence and available.

During psychological shock, it is important to create a calming, safe environment, which is also associated with empathy and caring. The crisis centre set up at the previously described train accident achieved this very well, if you recall the experience of one visitor. Many supporters ask: "What if I can't help crying myself?" Becoming moved is generally interpreted as sympathy, and as such it only helps to bring warmth into the situation. However, it must be limited to the extent that the victim is still able to rely on the supporter and his strength.

A 45-year-old man was killed in a road accident, and two other passengers seriously injured. One of them died two weeks later. The elderly mother of the driver, who was killed instantly in the crash, recalled that when she and her husband were told of the accident, he began to suffer symptoms of a heart attack. They set off to the health centre together to see the doctor. He asked the man to come in, and after a short while, the wife was called into the surgery too.

The man had told the doctor about his son's accident, and it turned out that the doctor was acquainted with their son. The mother said that all three discussed their memories of her son and wept. She concluded: "He is such a good doctor."

It is also vital that the victim's reactions are accepted, and an encouraging and positive approach is adopted. Frontline helpers have this skill. Victims of traumatic events talk about the focused and professional actions of ambulance crews, fire brigade or police, and the calming effect it had in making them feel safe. In the section on psychological shock, I have described this phenomenon using case studies.

During the shock stage, the victim of a traumatic event has an enormous need to talk about what happened. He rewinds the event over and over again: the rescue efforts, examinations at the hospital, the treatment. Now and again, he recalls new details of the event. That is why it is beneficial for friends, relatives and acquaintances to call and ask questions about the event. Going over it again and again is helpful at this stage.

It is important to allow the victim to talk about what happened, and not contribute very much. Occasionally, a focusing question may be interjected. We should remember that in the shock stage, the victim needs someone to listen above all else, not to have a conversation or to offer opinions.

There are rare cases of victims who do not want to talk about what happened. This may apply in some cases that engender very strong feelings of shame, such as rapes, and situations where the victim has been subjected to violence. In such cases, one should talk to the victim about the experience, encourage him to open up and share the experience. A calm presence is the most important element.

Providing a calm presence seems like an easy task, but in reality it is anything but easy. Meeting and listening to someone in psychological shock evokes such powerful feelings of helplessness and anxiety in us that they are almost impossible to endure. The worst mistakes in psychological first aid are the results of our inability to tolerate our own emotions, and our efforts to resolve them.

One way of alleviating our own anxiety and helplessness is an attempt to console the victim by saying that others have met with a similar experience, or an even worse one. We tell him all the horror stories we know, and believe that it will help the victim in a state of shock. The contrary is true. The victim thinks that that person has no idea of how he feels. In such a situation, there is no consolation in knowing that others have had the same experience or an even worse one.

The worst thing we can say is that we know how the victim feels. He or she believes that nobody could possibly imagine how they feel, and it is very hurtful to be told otherwise.

Often, we do not consider the victim's needs, but think that what calms us down must work for them, too. We may feel better for being busy and doing something, but the victim may be much better peacefully sitting still and just being there.

We may also attempt to make the victim forget what happened, and divert his attention to something else. This, too, is led by the supporter's need for relief from the situation, and not the victim's needs. The victim may see it as ridiculous and artificial. However, he will understand that the other is only thinking of what is best for him.

When something very shocking happens to a fellow human being, we feel a huge need to console him. We find ourselves in the same situation as Krister Andersson, who desperately searched for comforting words. The situation is perhaps eased by the fact that there are no words of comfort in such a situation. As a matter of fact, it is impossible to console a person in the early stage of a traumatic experience.

You may recall from the description of the processing of a traumatic experience that after a traumatic event, people lose the future perspective. They cannot visualize tomorrow, let alone months or years ahead. Yet, all that is comforting is in the future. Consolation is based on the fact that time will pass and the event will become increasingly distant. It is precisely this that is impossible for a victim to understand after a traumatic event. Providing consolation is, again, a need of the supporter, and it is impossible to fulfil. It is not worth setting oneself tasks that are doomed to failure from the start.

In psychological first aid, it is essential to allow space for the victim's reactions, thoughts and feelings. When a supporter attempts to comfort the victim, he may feel that the supporter cannot bear his anguish and crying. "I must pull myself together, and not express what I really think and feel, or the supporter may be frightened and leave," the victim thinks. Efforts at consolation encroach on the space for the victim's real feelings which he should be allowed to express in a secure atmosphere.

The need to console also involves the need to make excessive promises. 'Tomorrow will be better' is a good example of a false promise. We seek refuge in empty words which the victim may find insulting. Examples of other empty phrases are 'you are young, you have your whole life ahead of you', or for example, in a case of a miscarriage: 'There will be new pregnancies and new babies.'

The use and meaning of frequently used idioms, such as "please accept my condolences", "if there is anything we can do…" have been much discussed. In some languages, such pat expressions do not exist. Many victims feel that they are empty phrases, like greetings for people who have lost someone close. If these idioms are used in such a way, they may be seen as hurtful.

However, the content of such idioms is sharing, participating in the loss, taking on a part of the grief and pain. If they are used in this way and the words really mean what they say, the expression is received positively. Any promises must be kept, and the sadness and loss really shared with the person.

Touch is a much more genuine and effective means of communicating caring and sharing than words. It is totally natural to touch and hold a person in a state of psychological shock, even if he is a stranger. Touching brings security; it calms and expresses sympathy and acceptance. It cannot be misconstrued, it does not set limits.

How does professional support differ from lay support?

The ability and capability of providing support during psychological shock of a so-called lay person, a family member, relative, friend, colleague and also a volunteer helper, and a professional are fundamentally different. It is unreasonable to expect an untrained helper to recognize the emotions the support situation and the victim evoke in him, and to control them so that they do not impinge on the support situation. A crisis work professional must be capable of this.

A professional should be able to allow the victim all the space he needs. He does not respond with his own experiences, give advice or attempt to console in such a way that it would set limits on opportunities to respond. He listens calmly and absorbs the victim's emotions within himself, and does not deflect them back to the victim. Such a method requires thorough training and long experience, and is very difficult after all that.

A crucial question is whether external interventions affect the duration of shock, and whether it is desirable that it should be affected. The function of psychological shock is to protect the self from information and experience that it is unable to endure. Thus, it serves the wholeness and staying together of the self. As long as shock serves this purpose, it should not be interfered with.

If the shock reaction becomes prolonged and starts to serve denial and blocking of the event, its effects no longer serve the wholeness of the self in the long term. In the short term, it is indeed serving this purpose. In a situation of prolonged psychological shock the wholeness of the self would be served if the coping process were helped to move on to the next stages. If the experience remains completely unprocessed, it will develop into a psychological trauma.

It is difficult to identify a positive or negative effect of psychological shock on the wholeness of the self. That is why a volunteer or lay supporter should never attempt to influence the duration of the shock. Their task should be purely to offer victims their support and presence. An attempt to move the coping process forward, for example from psychological shock to the reaction stage, demands the diagnostic ability and professional skill of clinical psychology.

Is it possible, then, to influence the duration of psychological shock, and to move the coping process of a traumatic experience forward by external means, even with good clinical professional skill? Experience shows that it is difficult, but possible in some situations.

One of the characteristics of psychological shock is that the event seems unreal. Consequently, any method that forces the victim to face reality may also further the coping process and aid the transition from shock stage to reaction stage.

> A couple lost both their children in an accident. The parents were unable to face reality, making the shock reaction very powerful and enduring. In this situation an attempt was made to move the coping process forward by taking the parents to the accident location, where the course of the accident was gone over in detail. The photographs taken by the police at the scene were viewed with the parents, and they were accompanied to see the children's bodies. These methods helped to make the experience of the huge loss more real, and the coping process progressed to the next stages.

Psychological shock is often accompanied by dissociation, when the victim feels that the event is not actually happening to him. It is extremely difficult to psychologically process such an experience. However, processing is essential, as an organism has a memory. If the event remains totally unprocessed, the effects of the organism's memory will later manifest as unexplained reactions and feelings.

That is why dissociated experiences must first be made to feel like the person's own experiences. This, in turn, requires strengthening of the self and reducing the inner danger factors associated with the experience. Only through this route is it possible to make the experience the focus of subjective processing. This generally demands a good therapeutic relationship and the ability to process traumatic experiences through psychotherapy.

Psychological defusing

The group method of dealing with the shock stage is psychological defusing. It was developed by the American psychologist, Jeffrey Mitchell, towards the end of the 1980s. Mitchell intended his method for the immediate defusing of traumatic experiences of professionals engaged in work involving a lot of such situations or events. Such professions are, for example, the police, rescue personnel, and hospital casualty or emergency room staff.

The defusing meeting should be held as quickly as possible after a traumatic event or situation. If the event falls early in the shift, work should be interrupted for a while, the defusing meeting held, and working resumed. If the shocking event occurs late in the shift, it should be ended with a defusing session before going home.

The objective of the psychological defusing session is resumption of the ability to work as quickly as possible. It is achieved by systematic and focused defusing of the uppermost feelings elicited by the shocking experience. These feelings will be defused anyway, but generally less effectively and requiring more time off work. Defusing is like defusing a bomb, rendering it harmless; the inner bomb formed by a shocking experience is defused out of people. A psychological defusing session should be attended by all those who were involved in the task where the traumatic experience happened. It is usually best to aim at small, homogeneous groups.

Defusing meetings are led by outsiders. Sometimes, crisis workers act as leaders, but it is also common practice to train so-called peer leaders from within the organization to lead defusing sessions. In other words, people within the police organization or rescue service are selected as peer supporters; they are trained to lead defusing sessions, and also to identify the need for organizing defusing meetings. One-to-one support of traumatized employees is also a part of the support person's duties.

When the leader of the defusing session comes from the same organization as the employees subjected to a traumatic event, it is important that he is sufficiently detached. A line manager or a close colleague cannot act as leader. A psychological defusing meeting takes about 20–45 minutes. If it lasts longer, Mitchell says that it has been unsuccessful.

A defusing session progresses in stages. It starts with an introductory stage, when the participants are told why the meeting has been organized and what has happened. At this stage, they are also briefly told what to expect of the session.

During the discussion stage, the traumatic event itself is reviewed. The central questions are what actually happened, what each participant did, saw, heard and experienced. The aim is to discharge from the mind the uppermost feelings about what happened. If someone goes deeper into analysing their own feelings, Mitchell advises that they must be interrupted by returning the discussion to the event itself, for example by asking: "Who else was there?"

In the information stage, the discussion focuses on how the situation developed, how the victims were doing, etc. At this stage, wider background information for the event may also be provided. For example, in a case of suicide, the number of any earlier attempts is examined, their nature, how common this type of suicide is, etc. In addition, the participants are made aware of common psychological reactions in situations that are similar to the one they have witnessed, and instructed on how to approach these reactions.

Based on the defusing session, decisions are made on the necessity of a psychological debriefing session, or whether the defusing is sufficient to ensure recovery. If the incident is extremely shocking and has given rise to strong reactions and emotions, a psychological debriefing session is desirable. In that case, the timing of the debriefing session is agreed at the defusing meeting.

If there is to be no debriefing session, the follow-up arrangements are agreed after the defusing. The follow-up consists of the defusing leaders checking how the participants are coping during the following days, monitoring their recovery, and if there seem to be problems, directing them to further treatment.

When disaster-psychological methods reached Europe, their applications changed. They were no longer used only in addressing traumatic experiences undergone by professionals in the course of their work, but their use was extended also to other victims of traumatic events. In Finland, families of those killed and rescued in serious accidents form a major target group of disaster-psychological work.

Psychological defusing is a useful method in certain situations where victims of a traumatic event urgently need psychological support. Such situations are, for example, fires where families have lost their homes and have been evacuated, perhaps to a hotel. They need help in coping with their immediate reactions. In such cases, it is expedient to organize the defusing session within a few hours of the evacuation. A psychological debriefing session may be arranged later.

> A fire broke out in a small apartment block in the early hours, and six families were evacuated to a hotel. The mother of one of the families was slightly injured in the fire. The fire was threatening in many ways, and it was only a matter of luck that no one was killed.
>
> The following afternoon, a defusing meeting was organized in the hotel, and all the residents of the burned-out block took part. In the meeting, some practical matters were dealt with first, and then the upper-most feelings evoked by the fire were discussed. At the end of the meeting, a psychological debriefing session was arranged for the following day.

Another situation where psychological defusing is appropriate as a method of emotional first aid is a major accident, where large numbers of slightly injured are taken to hospital for examination and treatment. These accident victims should be assembled in groups and a defusing session run for them before they are released; they are united by their shared, shocking experience.

To my knowledge, such a practice is not yet implemented in any hospitals. It does seem odd that slightly injured or uninjured accident victims are left without any psychological first aid whatsoever. Although they have escaped physical trauma, a psychological trauma will have been formed. Psychological defusing is an excellent method for such situations.

Examinations and possible treatment of physical injuries should be completed before defusing is carried out. The order of administration of care is important. Physical injuries are addressed first, then the psychological.

In the USA, the defusing method is in regular use by police and rescue organizations. Currently, the defusing method is used ever more frequently, and psychological debriefing more rarely.

In Finland, defusing in the above form has not become as popular. Time resources of local crisis groups rarely allow the organization of crisis worker-led defusing sessions. By the same token, few organizations have trained peer support persons for this task.

The Finnish healthcare system is fundamentally different from that of the USA. Finland has a well-functioning national or public healthcare system. The operation of local crisis groups is a part of it. In the USA, organizations must fund all services themselves. This will surely have a bearing on what kinds of services become prominent in addressing traumatic experiences.

In my opinion, psychological defusing gives an erroneous picture of coping with traumatic events and situations. In many cases, the mere superficial defusing of the strongest psychological pressures is not sufficient to ensure coping with the experience. Personally, I would organize a thorough psychological debriefing session for the following day for employees who have endured a traumatic experience in the course of their work, rather than be content with just a defusing session. A defusing meeting is necessary when the traumatic event is so shocking that psychological first aid in group form is required during psychological shock.

Discussing difficult, emotion-evoking tasks immediately after their completion with colleagues and without an independent leader is a natural practice in rescue organizations and the police. Such defusing is no substitute for systematic defusing under the guidance of an external professional, but it serves as first aid in such situations.

The method of psychological defusing offers a model which fundamentally alters the way we tend to act. When something shocking happens in a workplace, those most affected are sent home. Then the incident is discussed for the rest of the day during work, and not much work gets done.

An alternative model would be that instead of sending people home, the whole group sits together for a while and defuses the strongest emotions evoked by the incident, and then gets back to work. This immediate group discussion, even in the absence of an independent leader, is certainly more effective than a disorganized approach to the situation.

11

Coping with Psychological Reactions: Debriefing

History of the psychological debriefing method and its applications

When the coping process of a traumatic experience moves on from emotional shock to the reaction stage, working methods also change. In the reaction stage, we gradually become conscious of what really has happened and what it means to us and our lives. The reaction stage is a period of actively processing the event and the reactions, feelings and thoughts it has engendered. The purpose of intervention methods employed at the reaction stage is to support and promote this active processing. This is why working methods in this stage differ fundamentally from those in the shock stage.

The differences between methods of the shock stage and the subsequent reaction stage may be likened to motoring. In the shock stage, the car engine is running but the gearbox is disengaged. The psychological process is not moving in any direction. Any help is purely support. In the reaction stage, the car is in gear and at full throttle. In this stage, the approach is active, speeding up the coping process and steering it.

The most important method of the reaction stage, and really of all crisis work, is psychological debriefing (PD). This method was also developed by Jeffrey Mitchell. In fact, he developed the PD method first and psychological defusing only later. He spent almost all of the 1980s developing the PD method, because he wanted to be sure that it worked and that it would not be harmful to anyone. Consequently, the development of the method also included a great deal of research on its effects.

PD was also originally developed to aid coping with traumatic situations at work. It was initially used as a part of stress control programmes in organizations where work tasks involved high degrees of risk and danger. Mitchell himself wanted to limit the concept of PD only to this application. From the USA, the debriefing method was brought to Norway, where it was adopted also in addressing psychological reactions of families of accident victims; the scope of application of the method expanded.

Since the method was brought from Norway to Finland, its applications have become ever wider. Earlier, we identified the psychological victims of a traumatic event. In Finland, the debriefing method is employed in addressing the psychological reactions of all victim groups after traumatic events.

Thus, Mitchell defines the concept of psychological debriefing both by the target group of the activity and the content of the method. It would be more expedient to define the concept based purely on the content of the method: in that case, PD would cover all such interventions that correspond in content to the method developed by Mitchell.

However, the PD method is continuously developing and changing. One crucial factor affecting this development is that in Finland as well as in Norway, the debriefing method is only employed by professionals in the field. Elsewhere, it may be applied by, for example, volunteer aid workers. In Finland, use of the debriefing method requires basic training in a human relations profession, training in crisis and disaster work, and in use of the debriefing method.

Aims of psychological debriefing
Psychological debriefing has four fundamental aims. Its effectiveness depends on how successfully each of these aims is achieved.

Facing the reality
THOROUGH REVIEW OF THE EVENT

The starting point of the coping process of a traumatic experience is facing up to the event and accepting it as reality. Psychological shock is characterized by the person shielding himself from the truth. What has happened does not seem real. We have seen that the processing of a traumatic event can become fixated in the shock stage. In such cases, the appropriate defence reaction transforms into denial and blocking of the event. The normal coping process is disabled.

Facing the reality is the starting point of coping with a traumatic event, and at the same time the starting point of recovery. As long as the event is denied or the experience is blocked from one's thoughts, no processing or adaptation is taking place. That is why facing the truth of traumatic events is so important.

Facing the truth is accompanied by accepting what has happened. This means, among other things, understanding that what happened is irreversible.

There is no way of undoing the event. We have no other choice but to accept the outcome of the event. It is an unavoidable fact, beyond our control.

This does not mean that accepting the reality and the truth is easy. Victims sometimes fight stubbornly against acceptance. Accepting the event seems impossible. Yet, it is the only healthy solution.

Another significant outcome of accepting the truth is that the truth liberates. However hard it is to face and hear the truth, when we know the truth we no longer need to trouble our minds with what really happened. Our minds will continue to work and wonder over questions to which the answers are not known, which remain open. For this reason, we should aim at as few gaps as possible.

Our minds will use imagination to fill these gaps. We invent most diverse and fantastic versions of the incident. It will not leave us in peace.

> A young man committed suicide at his home. At the time of his death, his wife was abroad. When she returned home, she insisted that she did not want to know where and how her husband's suicide happened.
>
> In this situation it was already predictable that if the wife's intention of denial was not overcome and details connected with the suicide worked through, questions associated with it would never let her rest.
>
> The prediction came true. During the following year, the wife constantly developed theories of where and how her husband had killed himself. She tested her theories on friends by asking: "Wasn't it like this, as I worked out?" When the friend replied that it was not quite like that, she developed a new theory. It would have been much easier for her and she would have recovered from her husband's suicide much better, if she had been told immediately where and how it took place.

There are two main methods in disaster psychology and debriefing we can use to facilitate facing the truth and accepting it. The first method is reviewing the course of events in as concrete, detailed and thorough a manner as possible.

> Some years ago, a nine-month course in general psychiatry was organized for unemployed Finnish doctors and dentists. The participants wanted the programme to include a large dose of disaster psychology and crisis work. They had diligently practised leading debriefing sessions. At the end of the course, the students requested that I should lead a final practice session for them; they would invent an imaginary traumatic incident themselves which we would then proceed to work on. Normally, I would not agree to such an arrangement, but in this special situation I accepted the suggestion.

The course was to end the following week. They would spend this final week on an island in the Turku archipelago. The incident made up by the course participants was as follows:

During that week on the island, they had spent an evening drinking, dancing and having fun late into the small hours. Then there was a fracas among those who were still awake, resulting in one chap leaving in a temper and saying that he was going to take a sauna. In the morning, he was found dead in the sauna.

To enable the participants to assume their roles and to imagine the details of the situation during the exercise, we agreed in advance who the dead man was. The students chose a chap who had dropped out from the course, and whom everybody knew.

During the exercise, I conducted the factual stage of debriefing thoroughly. Together we went over how the evening had developed. What was the fracas about? Who was there at the time? How did the situation develop? What time did the fellow go off to the sauna? What happened then? Then we got to the morning and how the victim was found in the sauna. Where was he found? Was the sauna warm? What did he look like? Was he still warm? What position was he in? Was he dressed? Who else came to the sauna? Who called the police? Who certified the death? How did the day continue afterwards? Who notified the family of the deceased? Were they intending to celebrate completion of their course regardless of what happened? Who will deliver the course certificate of the deceased man to his family?

I went through the other stages of debriefing at a faster pace. Finally, we concluded the exercise and defused the roles. Then we were supposed to return to our normal routine.

Unexpectedly, the participants of the exercise told me that it was actually almost impossible for them to return the fellow certified dead in the exercise to the land of the living. The thorough reviewing of the events, in spite of the participants only making them up, was so effective that the incident felt real. This exercise showed me how effective a method of facing reality is provided by thoroughly reviewing the facts.

Without the experience gained from this exercise, I might not have such a clear appreciation of the importance of reviewing the course of events and the associated facts in helping people accept the truth. The feedback from debriefing sessions is frequently that the event now feels more real, and one that the individual must, and perhaps will, be able to live with.

Sometimes the problem is that it is not known what happened. An extreme form of such a situation is when a person suddenly disappears without trace.

Then there are no facts on which to attach the imagination, and which would limit the flights of fantasy. People can disappear for years, as if into thin air, and no sign of them is ever found.

These are extremely difficult situations for the families. The adaptation process in such situations invariably takes longer than in those where the facts of what happened are known. When we have speculated sufficiently over various alternatives, some scenario often begins to feel more real than the others. We are forced to create our own reality and adapt to this.

> The father of a family disappeared quite unexpectedly. He went off to view an apartment in the course of his work, and never returned home. The family saw nothing unusual in his behaviour before his departure or his work assignment. The couple had just had a baby after years of trying. The child was only eight weeks old when the father disappeared.
>
> A few weeks after the disappearance, when the family and close relations were reviewing the disappearance at the PD session, I asked them what they thought had happened to the man. Everyone at the meeting had the same opinion. They were certain that the man had been the victim of a crime and died. Consequently, we took this theory as our starting point, and used the session to promote adaptation to it. Naturally, we had previously thoroughly gone over the disappearance event itself, its associated details and thoughts from the preceding days.

Sometimes, it is known what happened, but the body is never found. Occasionally in cases of drowning, the deceased is not recovered in spite of all efforts by the rescue services. One of the worst of such disasters, where all the victims were never found, was naturally the sinking of MS Estonia.

When the loss is not concretized in a way that would enable bidding the deceased farewell by seeing his body, having a funeral and a grave, the grieving process is often hampered. The fact that no body is found places particularly great demands on crisis work, especially in terms of facing and accepting the reality. In such cases, it is necessary to review events even more thoroughly, what happened and how, so that the shocking event and its consequences become so real that the process of adaptation is able to begin.

This work is greatly aided by reviewing the family members' mental images of the body of the deceased, where they imagine it to be, what they think it looks like, etc. This may seem cruel, but is necessary for the recovery process to begin. However, going over mental images does not mean that such images are produced by the process. They already exist, and they are only now discussed and actively processed.

SAYING GOODBYE TO THE DECEASED

When someone has died in a traumatic event, saying goodbye to the deceased is an important way of facing the reality and accepting it. It is really a case of returning to an old tradition.

A few decades ago, the dead were brought home, and saying goodbye to them was quite natural. Today, death has been removed to institutions, and seeing the deceased usually requires special arrangements. The old practice has been abandoned and bidding the deceased farewell has become the exception rather than the rule. In crisis- and disaster-psychological work, we aim to return to the old practice, and emphasize the importance of seeing the dead loved one and saying goodbye.

Families frequently need to be encouraged to go and see the deceased. Encountering death in such a concrete form is alien to people. This method has proved a very successful and important way of facing reality and restraining the imagination. In this way, it aids the grieving process and recovery from the loss.

Some people say that they want to preserve a living image of their loved one, and use this to resist seeing the deceased. However, seeing a dear person dead does not remove, diminish or change memory images of that person alive. It only enables the formation of an image of him or her dead, too. So it diminishes or removes nothing, but adds something new.

The setting of viewing the deceased and bidding him or her farewell must be made as safe as possible. People are often frightened by new, unknown situations, and seeing a dead person is one for many of us. That is why it is important that close family, children in particular, are prepared in advance for encountering this situation.

Most hospitals, health centres and departments of forensic pathology have a small chapel that is used for viewing the deceased and saying goodbye. Often, the viewing takes place at the stage when the deceased is placed in the coffin and handed over to the family.

The family and children should be told in what kind of a room the deceased will be, what colours and furniture there are, etc. Then they are told that the deceased will be in a coffin in the centre of the room, and the way he or she will look is described. Often, the deceased looks both familiar and strange. He or she is the person we know so well, but at the same time quite different, when life has departed from the body. As a rule, people look restful and peaceful in death, which has a particularly calming effect. Often, especially in cases of sudden death, families wonder whether there was pain. Then they are told that the deceased will be cold and stiff, but in spite of it or for that very reason, family members are encouraged also to touch the corpse.

Many people arrive at the farewell occasion bearing flowers, mementoes and objects that were important to the deceased, to put in the coffin. Children often bring a drawing that they have done for the purpose, or a goodbye letter, which is placed in the coffin. At this time, people can talk to the deceased about things that were left unsaid. People can stay with the deceased alone or in various groups; they can linger, talk and touch.

A man aged about 50 died while on a business trip abroad. He left a wife and three children, the eldest 13 and the youngest 8 years old. A viewing of the deceased was arranged for the family and close relatives in the chapel of the institute of forensic pathology. I was present as a support person.

First, I went to see the deceased alone, and then told the family, directing my words particularly at the children, what the chapel looked like. I said that in the middle of the chapel there is the coffin that your daddy lies in. He is dressed in white and resting peacefully in the coffin. It is quite all right to touch your daddy, but remember that he is now cold and stiff.

The mother and children entered the chapel first. The wife stroked her husband's cheek tenderly, and the 13-year-old put his goodbye letter to Dad in the coffin. His younger brother touched Daddy's forehead and drew back his hand quickly, as if it had burned him, and then shook his hand to remove the cold sensation from it.

His eight-year-old little sister had already begun to examine and pat her father. "Here are his toes, here's a knee. Oh dear, the coffin is a bit small, his knee is bent. Here is his tummy; his hands are on his tummy." She went over the whole of Daddy this way, touching. Her 11-year-old brother followed his sister's example, stroking and studying his father in the same way, and the cold sensation disappeared.

I later heard how important this farewell visit was for this family. The mother told me that only when she saw her husband lying in the coffin did his death begin to feel real. The occasion was also important for the children, not only enabling them to face the truth, but also to say goodbye.

Parents are often unwilling to take the children to see the deceased and to bid him farewell. The occasion is at least as important for children as it is for adults. There is no lower age limit. It is vital that children are accompanied by a support person whom they know and trust, because the adults may be unable to take care of them owing to their own emotions. At the same time, the parents are free to concentrate in peace on their own goodbyes. Children should also be told in advance that adults may cry or have other strong emotional reactions. They should not be frightened, as the situation is quite natural and understandable.

Children relate to death much more naturally than adults. It triggers questions which parents or adults should attempt to answer as well as they are able. Most importantly, children must be given honest answers.

Children often process the death of a loved one through play and drawing. This is a way of coping with the experience peculiar to children, and it should be allowed. There is no reason to intervene.

Saying goodbye to a person who has died is also important to a child. If he is excluded, mystification of the event in the child's mind is reinforced. Saying goodbye can also assume great significance in later life. I once overheard a conversation between two young men on the subject. One said that his father had died before he was born. He had, however, been to say goodbye to his father in his mother's womb.

Working through psychological reactions

Another fundamental aim of psychological debriefing is to work through the wide variety of powerful psychological reactions produced by traumatic events. They must be worked through in order to reduce their intensity and to release mental resources for their customary functions. Such psychological reactions include thoughts, feelings and intrusive mental images or flashbacks associated with the traumatic event.

Working through disturbing thoughts and feelings is achieved by actively thinking about them, talking or writing about them, or processing them by other means of expression. The crucial point is that difficult thoughts or feelings are confronted rather than denied or avoided. This is far from easy. On the contrary, these thoughts and feelings evoke fear and anxiety, making denial or avoidance a much easier and more tempting option than facing them.

It is important to attach labels or names to feelings and thoughts, as they will then become things that can be addressed. Verbalizing feelings and thoughts makes them concrete and enables their sharing. It is one step towards confronting them. This is why merely talking about difficult issues will help.

Working through psychological reactions is not just defusing the anxiety and intensity attached to them by talking. Working through also includes moving forward in processing the traumatic experience. Thoughts and feelings form layers, so that access to deeper layers is conditional on first dealing with issues close to the surface. For example, grief may be concealed under a need to apportion blame and to seek guilty parties. It cannot be accessed until the feelings of perceived injustice and the associated anger and aggression are dealt with. If they are not successfully worked through, the grief is never reached.

In a psychological debriefing session, the task of the leader is to help the participants face their feelings and thoughts, defuse them, and advance their coping process. This is an extremely demanding task for both the participants and the leader. The leader must possess great expertise, professionalism, and the ability to receive intense emotions while preserving his empathy, acknowledging his own emotions and keeping them under control.

An important feature of PD is that reactions produced by traumatic experiences are addressed together with others who have experienced the same event. Debriefing is specifically a group method. The major part of its effect results from hearing other group members' descriptions of the event and the reactions brought about by it: it enables an individual to access more of his own feelings and thoughts. The model provided by other group members in coping with their feelings also helps him to find ways of coping with his own. In the course of observing this process, some of his own feelings and thoughts are processed, even if he does not participate in the discussion.

A group also reveals a wider variety of reactions caused by the event than an individual. This facilitates getting in touch with new feelings within ourselves. Working through traumatic experiences and reactions in a group is much more versatile, colourful and effective.

The question of how psychological reactions are processed in practice and how other group members are utilized in the process is described later in more detail.

Deepening and reinforcing social support

An extensive and well-functioning social network is a vital aid for coping with a traumatic experience. We need people around us in order to offload our thoughts and feelings – we need listeners. We also need supporters who will stand by us, however awful or hopeless we may feel. We also need people who are able to share the experience and the reactions it has elicited with us, and understand what we have endured.

Psychological debriefing aims to deepen and reinforce social support. When people review the course of a traumatic event thoroughly together, discuss the thoughts and feelings it produced at different stages, it usually means sharing these feelings. The victim is no longer alone with his experience and pain, and that brings a surprising amount of relief.

An upper-grade pupil at a school assaulted a teacher during a lesson. The teacher was instructing the boy, when he suddenly flew into a rage and attacked her. The teacher was thrown on her back on the floor, and the pupil pinned her down holding a flick-knife to her throat. Somehow, the teacher managed to scramble up and move up towards the front of the class, when the pupil kicked her in the back.

At the headmaster's initiative, a psychological debriefing session was organized at the school a couple of days later, and all the teachers were encouraged to take part. More than 40 teachers attended, including the victim of the assault, although the headmaster had doubted that she would.

At the session, the violent incident was addressed first: how it developed and what happened, what then happened to the teacher, the pupil, and the school in general. Then they discussed whether the assaulted teacher had had previous difficulties with the pupil, and of what kind. The discussion was then extended to the other teachers: had they had problems with that particular pupil?

Next, they discussed the thoughts and feelings elicited by the event both in the teacher who had been the victim of violence and in the other teachers. The whole teaching staff was unanimous in the view that although the target of this act was one individual teacher, it was really aimed at every one of them. The other teachers expressed their concern over the welfare of the victim and her ability to carry on in a very positive, sharing and caring way.

Responsibility for future situations was also seen as shared, and one they had to shoulder together. They agreed common policies regarding treatment of this pupil, but also on treatment of other pupils with a tendency to aggression. Their attitude towards the violent pupil, too, once the feelings of anger, indignation and aggression were defused, was caring and assuming educational responsibility.

After the session, the situation of the teacher who had been the victim of violence had changed completely. Where before she had been withdrawn after the event and avoided contact with other teachers, after the session she was showered with an abundance of support, understanding and warm sharing of the experience. This teacher, the headmaster and also many other teachers agreed that they should share their experiences much more, and that it would make their work much easier.

The mere act of discussing difficult issues together directly and honestly and not skirting around them almost always results in an increased and accentuated sense of closeness. This is always evident in successful debriefing sessions. At the beginning, people are apart from each other, alone and in their own worlds. After the debriefing session the atmosphere is warm, caring and relaxed.

A sudden death of an employee happened in a workplace at three o'clock one afternoon. The victim was a man of around 50, who was employed under a retraining scheme. He was heading an important IT project that was to have a great impact on the work of all the employees.

His death seemed particularly dramatic, as that day was his last at work. His contract was at an end, and although he was a valued employee, the funds for his direct appointment had not been found yet, although a permanent post was in the offing.

In the morning, he had called the telecommunications company and requested two men urgently for a day's work. They were to install a cable between two points, which would complete the system he had designed. He said to the service manager that it was a matter of life or death.

He had just had a meeting with these men when he took the elevator to the floor where his office was. As he left the elevator, he collapsed in the foyer. His colleagues noticed the event immediately, asked the switchboard to call for help and to put out a call for people with first aid skills. The telephone engineers were just about to leave as they heard the announcement downstairs, and because one of them was trained in first aid, they came back to find the man who had just instructed them on the floor suffering from a heart attack.

They started to administer first aid, but soon an ambulance crew arrived, and after them also a flying doctor. They continued resuscitation for half an hour, but it proved to be futile. The man was certified dead.

The next morning, a service of remembrance was organized for the work community. The superior of the employee made a poignant speech, a moment's silence was observed and then the opportunity was taken to hold a psychological debriefing session. We expected to see about ten members of the work community.

About 40 colleagues were present. I assumed that some of them would only attend the service and then leave, but no one left after the memorial service. We did not have enough seats for everyone, and about 15 people had to stand.

At the session, we reviewed the previous day's events before and during the fatal heart attack. The majority of the staff had seen the resuscitation attempt. Some of them had been convinced that the resuscitation would succeed, some had been certain that it would fail. We discussed their feelings during the resuscitation and afterwards. We discussed how they spent time at the office after hours, talking together about the shocking event; we discussed how it felt to go home, and what thoughts had crossed their minds during the evening and night.

They remembered their colleague, cried and grieved over his demise, wondered about the cause of this heart attack, but they also talked about the personal worries that the event elicited. They wondered about the contribution of stress at work to their colleague's death, and how they all had stressful jobs and worked under great pressure. The question was raised as to whether the job was worth sacrificing one's life for. They talked about their fears, shared them and anxieties over the effect of workplace stresses on themselves and each other. They were given permission to feel stressed, and they were told to take care of themselves and each other.

The session lasted a couple of hours. Two-thirds of those present were women, but it was mainly the men who spoke and wept during the session. The deceased was particularly their partner in collaboration. After the session, four men came to speak to me privately. Several of them had had cardiac symptoms the night before; one spoke of the death of his father.

Later, I received feedback on this session. People said that it brought about significant changes in their working community. The death of a colleague was a unifying factor for them. They felt open grief which was no longer disguised as discussion about what happened and how. They talked among themselves a lot about their work, their working situation and stress. Mutual caring and concern increased, and they grew much closer to each other.

The effect of PD in deepening social support is particularly evident in work communities or other groups where it is not customary to discuss sensitive issues. The debriefing session introduces a new model into such a community, and its effect is much more far-reaching than merely addressing the traumatic experience that was the reason for the session.

PD can also have a similar effect in families and among relatives. Many families have secrets that are known to everybody, but never mentioned. PD, at least when successful, ensures that such silent issues are not created. Often, those old secrets also surface and are included in the debriefing process.

A PD session was organized ostensibly because of the death of a common-law husband and father. The family consisted of the mother and three grown-up children. Very soon it emerged that the children's real father had drowned almost 30 years ago, when the youngest was a few months old. The father's drowning and details associated with it were this family's secret.

This unresolved drowning, however, came up repeatedly during the session, interfering with the processing of the new traumatic experience. So, we decided to arrange a dedicated session to address the drowning which happened 27 years before.

At that session, the family's secret was defused. Old records of the police investigation were unearthed, revealing the course of events and the details associated with it. The children were told for the first time what really happened when their father was drowned.

Defusing such old secrets greatly relieves the family's anxiety and aids formation of mutual closeness, since nothing needs to be kept secret any more. Secrets weigh on the mind, prevent the development of trust, and tie up resources.

The PD session also serves as a model showing that it is possible to discuss sensitive matters, too, directly and honestly. Such a change in a family's or community's customary ways of communicating cannot be effected without a detached leader. Sometimes, families claim that they have discussed the event so much that they need no debriefing session. Yet, a detached leader's influence on how subjects are broached and what issues are brought up can be quite crucial. Talking among ourselves cannot replace psychological debriefing. Without a leader, we follow the same rules and practices that have always been followed in the family. Debriefing can open up something new, create new rules and practices more conducive to openness and mutual closeness.

Normalization of reactions and preparation for future reactions

In addition to facing reality, working through psychological reactions and deepening social support, the aim of psychological debriefing is imparting information on how we usually react in traumatic events and afterwards, and how we should relate to such reactions.

Knowledge generally has a calming effect. It enables cognitive control of the situation and also of our inner reactions. That is why in debriefing sessions and in crisis- and disaster-psychological work in general, imparting knowledge, teaching and learning hold a central position. It is very important both before a traumatic situation and after it.

Generally, we are afraid of powerful emotional reactions that we cannot control or influence. Often, medication is used in an attempt to control such reactions. However, knowledge is a much healthier and more effective tool for coping with powerful emotions.

The aim of a debriefing session is to impart information to the participants about human reactions both at the time of the event and afterwards. The purpose of this knowledge is to render one's own reactions, thoughts and feelings normal and tolerable. We are able to endure even extreme reactions and feelings, if we know that they are appropriate, serve a certain purpose, and that they will pass in time.

Pain and intolerable anxiety result when our reactions seem strange, abnormal, and we do not know what will happen next, which way our state of mind will develop. Many people describe their reactions during the first days and particularly the nights after a traumatic event by saying that they feared they were going mad.

> Three students shared a student flat where each had his own room. One Friday afternoon, one of the boys was on his way home when he was killed in a road accident. The news of their friend's death reached his flatmates in the early evening.
>
> One of them went off to stay with a relative and the other stayed in the apartment alone. He described the following night and his vague fears by saying that he really believed that he was going insane.

Those involved in the Sally Albatross shipwreck reported that they thought they were losing their minds. Such feedback came especially from their family members. When they received a letter from the shipping company explaining how people usually react in such situations, they felt better. Knowledge helped to calm them.

In group debriefing, it is also significant that people see and hear how others have perceived the event and reacted to it. They are able to compare their own reactions, feelings and thoughts to those of others. Usually, they find much common ground, and also certain differences. When the material each participant has gathered for himself during the session is combined with the information imparted by the leader on people's typical reactions in such situations, an individual content is formed for the information, which will live and be available during the following months, influencing how one approaches one's own reactions.

Methods employed in processing traumatic experiences have wide-ranging consequences. I will next describe a case study which will demonstrate these consequences. For better understanding, I will first identify the differences between traditional crisis work and disaster-psychological work.

There are three main differences between disaster-psychological work and customary crisis care:

1. Customary crisis care is initiated by the client: he must seek expert help. Disaster-psychological work is proactive, seeking work; the services are offered.

2. Crisis work is typically individual. In disaster psychology, the starting point is processing the experience in a group, a sense of togetherness, and utilization of shared experiences.

3. In disaster-psychological work, the primary aim is normalization of reactions and imparting of knowledge of typical reactions, including future ones. In traditional crisis counselling, on the other hand, the

client is advised to contact the counsellor if new symptoms and problems arise, and they will address them together. Future reactions are, in a way, abnormalized, so that dealing with them requires expert input.

The significance of these two methods and also of imparting information on typical and future reactions is well exemplified by the following experience:

I have already described the disaster-psychological work carried out among ships' employees after the MS Estonia shipwreck. By chance, a situation developed whereby different methods were applied aboard different ships. No crisis counsellors who knew the debriefing method were found for one ship. Instead, the staff had access to two crisis workers who employed traditional individual crisis counselling methods, and who were leading experts in the field in Finland.

These crisis counsellors carried out excellent crisis work on the ship, sailing with it for a week, so that one of them was on board at all times. They carried out customary crisis work among the ship's personnel.

After about three months, employees from this ship began to appear at the occupational health centre, all complaining of the same problem in the same way. They said: "I have developed this neurosis, I can't sleep on the ship during a storm," or "I have developed this psychological problem that prevents me from sleeping on board during a storm." Although a number of them came along at the same time complaining of the same problem, each was convinced that he was the only one with the problem.

Around the same time, three months after the disaster, I went to Stockholm on another ship. There, crisis work was done applying the disaster-psychological model, using the psychological debriefing method, including normalization of reactions and preparation for future reactions.

I saw a large number of the personnel. I asked how they were and, consistently, they replied that they were fine. "Life has almost returned to normal." Then I asked about sleeping on board ship on stormy nights, and the reply was always: "Of course I can't sleep – we all get together in the mess and think of something fun to do."

This example shows the difference produced by different methods regarding the importance attached by people to their own reactions and feelings, and how they control them cognitively. The employees who had no knowledge of typical or future reactions attached psychopathological significance to the phenomenon: "There is something wrong with me." Other employees, who had been prepared for future reactions and given information on them, deemed them to be perfectly natural and appropriate.

The difference between the employees' approaches is very significant. If a person has already developed the identity of a sick, flawed individual, the problem is never resolved by saying that the phenomenon is perfectly normal and you need not worry about it. By this stage, when anxiety has already developed, imparting information no longer has the same impact, but the problem must be treated. Thus, imparting of information has a preventive effect, but it must be correctly timed.

Applications of psychological debriefing

It is vitally important that in each situation, the correct and most effective psychological intervention method is employed. Psychological debriefing is by no means a cover-all method that may be applied to any kind of situation. It is a very specific method, designed for certain specific situations.

Above all, the PD method is suitable for addressing sudden traumatic experiences within a few days of the event. PD is a suitable method in the presence of the following criteria:

- the event was sudden and unpredictable
- the event was traumatic and shocking
- the stress situation is over.

There are also situations where PD, with the inclusion of shock stage support and subsequent follow-up support, does not ensure sufficient psychological support. Such situations are:

- long-lasting, very stressful situations, such as torture, refugee status, sexual abuse of children, etc.
- when the stress situation is ongoing, and includes new traumatic experiences, such as physical injury and disability
- when the traumatic situation is continually repeated, such as domestic violence
- when the victim has suffered previous mental problems
- when the situation has been extremely traumatizing.

In some of these cases, PD may be used as a starting point, but they require subsequent ongoing, regular psychological support.

There are also situations where other psychological methods are more suitable than debriefing. For instance, if the shocking experience has been predicted for a long time and people have been able psychologically to prepare for it, PD is not much use. Such a situation is, for example, the death of a loved one preceded by a long illness.

Timing of psychological debriefing

In the preceding chapters, I have described the stages and progress of the coping process of a traumatic experience. The knowledge we have about the timing of these stages and their distinguishing features forms the basis of the timing of psychological interventions.

The duration of psychological shock depends on how shocking the event was and on its proximity. By the latter, I mean such factors as whether the person was involved in the event itself, whether the event affected his family, or colleague, friend, etc. The more shocking the event and the closer the proximity, the more severe the psychological shock and the longer its duration.

It is crucial that the correct intervention methods are applied at the different stages. PD is a method for the reaction stage. In the shock stage, the approach is different. At that time, not all emotions addressed by debriefing have developed or emerged. That is why it is impossible to address them at this stage, and PD is wasted in a way.

> By chance, two very similar suicides took place in the same week and in the same town. In both cases, the suicides were 35-year-old men, who shot themselves in the bathroom at home using a shotgun. In one of the families, the other members were out shopping at the time of the suicide; in the other family they were out walking the dog.
>
> In one of these cases, the PD session was arranged for the following day, about 24 hours after the suicide. The session was attended by eight people, the victim's family members and close relatives. Five of them sought additional help from various services the following week. Some of them did not even remember that they had taken part in such a session.
>
> In the other case, the debriefing session was arranged for the third day after the suicide. It, too, was attended by eight people, also the victim's family members and close relatives. None of them sought additional help the following week.

In every case, there is one optimal day for the PD session. This optimal day is in the middle of the reaction stage, when all the reactions, thoughts and emotions have already emerged and are at their strongest. If the session is timed too early in the shock stage, not all phenomena requiring processing have yet emerged. If it is delayed, people have had time to develop possibly inappropriate coping strategies to enable them to endure the phenomenon.

The human mind begins to close up after the first three days from the traumatic event. Processing the traumatic experience is most effective while the mind is still open. This psychological work may be compared to cleansing a wound. It must be done while the wound is still open. It hurts at the time, but it greatly aids healing.

> An example of delayed PD is provided by the Sally Albatross accident. The heads of rescue stations had their PD session during the first week after the accident, but the majority of employees attended debriefing sessions about three weeks after the event.
>
> I had the opportunity of meeting some of them about three years later, and I asked them for feedback on the debriefing sessions. Those who took part in sessions during the first week said that it was quite indispensable. "I would not have coped without it," they said. Instead, those who attended after three weeks said: "It was all right, but we rather felt that a wound that was already healing was being re-opened."

Another fitting metaphor is provided by treatment of broken bones. It is important to treat them before the bones begin to knit together. If the bones heal in a wrong position, they must be re-broken, so they can be correctly positioned. In the psychological healing process, too, correct positioning in the right direction is important for the end result.

It is not always possible to organize the debriefing session on the optimal day. Notification of the incident may be delayed, or the crisis group's resources may be stretched to capacity. After the optimal day, there is a reserve period of a few days, when a debriefing session is well justified. In general, the first week after a traumatic event is the appropriate period for processing the experience.

If the debriefing session is delayed, the consequences are evident both in the session itself and its effectiveness. The session leader is forced almost to dig for and pluck out participants' reactions, thoughts and feelings. They do not bubble up and demand attention, as they do when the session is correctly timed. The session is much more demanding for the leader, and the results are also less successful. The bones have already started to knit, in whatever position, and it is difficult to force a change in this development.

Some factors affect the rate of processing of a traumatic experience. If the victim is physically injured, this slows down the psychological processing of the event. All resources are first expended in survival and physical recovery, and none left over for psychological processing. In such a situation, problems are created when the family of the injured person progresses at a different rate from the victim. For the family, the optimal time to address the event is earlier than for the injured victim. If the injured person is at all physically capable, the actual debriefing is best timed according to the family's process. An opportunity should be provided for the injured victim for more thorough processing at a later time.

This is also justified because a badly injured person not only has traumatic experiences associated with the event, but medical examination and treatment may produce additional traumatic experiences. For this reason, PD is often an inadequate method of processing their experiences, which require longer-term trauma therapy.

Another factor influencing the progress of the coping process is the magnitude of the event. At the sinking of MS Estonia, where more than 800 people were killed, crisis reactions clearly progressed more slowly than at smaller-scale traumatic events.

Session planning and organization
Gathering information about the incident

Before the planning for a PD session is embarked upon, the crisis worker has already done a lot of assessment and planning in connection with the traumatic incident. The first task is assessment of whether the event fulfils the criteria of a traumatic event, whether it falls within the crisis group's area of responsibility, or possibly that of some other organization.

If the criteria are fulfilled, the next appraisal concerns identification of the affected people and determining how they are affected. Is it necessary for the crisis group to provide services immediately, during psychological shock, or not until the reaction stage? The object of the appraisal is mapping of the communities that are affected by the event, and selection of appropriate intervention methods for each target group.

This work of appraisal and planning of debriefing sessions demands information on the event and the victims. Crisis- and disaster-psychological work depends on collaboration with officials, and good communication between various officials is a prerequisite of its success.

The main contacts for providing information required by crisis groups are the police, rescue officials and healthcare officials. The more mutually trusting the relations and the more seamless the co-operation between the crisis group and these officials, the better the service provided to victims of traumatic events.

On the basis of information collected from the officials, the crisis worker must make preliminary plans for the necessary action. To do this, information about the incident itself is required: What happened? Where? Are people injured or dead? Were there others involved in the incident? Who (names and contact details)? Were there outside helpers and eye witnesses? Who (names and contact details)? Who are the close family members (names and contact details)? Have the victims been informed about the crisis group, and have they given permission to be contacted?

The following example shows why it is important for the crisis worker to know, for example, the time of the incident:

> The duty officer at the crisis group was alerted by the police about a house fire. They failed to specify the time of the fire, so the crisis worker immediately called the father of the family whose house had caught fire.
>
> The contact number was a mobile phone. The crisis worker called it, introduced the service and asked if it was a good time to talk. The man replied that it was rather difficult, since he was currently watching the fire with the insurance assessor, to see whether the whole house would burn down or if there was anything left.

It is not always possible to extract any information about an incident from the officials, or the information may be very scant. In that case, the only alternative is to contact the victims and glean the necessary information from them.

Contacting the victims

The picture gleaned from officials is supplemented by information received from the victims. Usually, the crisis group duty officer or the crisis worker allocated to the incident first contacts the officials. Sometimes the party raising the alarm is someone other than an official, in which case he is the primary source of information. In any case, the crisis worker must have some idea of what has happened and when, before he contacts the victims.

During the first contact, the victims are usually briefly told about crisis work and the principles applied, and asked how they are, and it is ascertained that the victims are not alone, but have support persons with them. They are also given the crisis worker's contact details and a time is agreed for when the victims will be contacted again for more precise arrangements for debriefing and associated details.

The victims' contact person usually has the task of discussing possible debriefing with other victims, its timing and who should attend. Often, it also falls to him to identify the other interest groups or communities that may need help.

During the next telephone conversation, arrangements for the PD session are usually agreed, its timing and who will attend. There may also be discussion on what other groups require PD and how they may be contacted.

At the planning stage of PD, the following points should be remembered and noted in connection with contacting families:

1. The first contact, when the principles and methods of crisis work are explained, is of paramount importance. The service must be introduced so thoroughly and clearly that people understand what it is about. If they then decline, they know what they are declining.

2. It is important that PD is introduced in the right way. It is good to take as starting point the view that every victim of a traumatic event has the right to receive this service. It is offered to everyone who is involved in a shocking situation, without needs assessment.

3. The crisis worker should always take the initiative in contacting victims of a traumatic incident. The victim does not have the resources to assess his need for help, or the energy to make contact. If the help is declined and the crisis worker assesses the need to be particularly great, it is worth allowing time to pass. The next contact in a couple of days might produce a different result.

4. It is worth remembering that the person who emerges as the victims' contact person is usually the one coping best among the victims. The crisis worker should also bear in mind the so-called trauma and grief hierarchy, so that contact is maintained also with the most traumatized person in this respect.

As a rule, arranging a PD session demands several contacts with the victims. These conversations, too, are very important in coping with a traumatic experience. They provide information on typical human reactions in such situations, caring and social support. Even if they do not always lead to an actual session, many people are helped by these conversations alone.

Declining debriefing

Occasionally, the contact person informs the crisis worker that the group has unanimously decided that such a session is unnecessary. In that case, it is important to ascertain whether he has indeed proposed it to the parties, and in the correct light. Occasionally, the contact person himself may make the decision on behalf of others or someone else, without giving the person concerned any choice. This is justified as 'protecting' a sensitive or vulnerable person.

There are many possible reasons for refusal. Some of them are identified below, and methods suggested for resolving the problem.

1. *Crisis services are associated with mental health services, and people do not want to be labelled as clients.* The crisis worker should stress that access to crisis services after a traumatic incident is every citizen's right and that these services are intended for everyone who has endured a shocking event. Offering the services is not based on an assessment that they particularly need such services, but on the premise that everyone will benefit from them in this situation. Accepting the services will not result in any notes in any healthcare records. In that sense, it is not a mental health service.

2. *Fear of facing and addressing painful emotions and thoughts. Fear of mental breakdown.* This is less frequently cited as the actual reason, and recognizing it is the job of the crisis worker. Fear may be alleviated by increasing the sense of security. This is achieved by describing what happens in a PD session, and assuring the victim that the leaders have the expertise to ensure that nothing alarming will take place. Sometimes, trust is engendered if the victim meets the leader in advance, ostensibly for a preparatory discussion. A personal meeting will create more security than a telephone conversation. Security is also enhanced by holding the session at the victim's home, on safe territory.

3. *Fear of someone else's emotional breakdown.* There may be a desire to protect a family member by fearing on their behalf. In this way, the person is also prevented from receiving the help and support that he needs. In such cases, permission should be sought to speak with the individual in person.

4. *It is desirable and honourable to cope alone.* Discussion of this attitude should begin from closer examination of the concepts contained in it: why is it honourable to cope alone? What is the basis of the idea that people should cope alone? What kinds of experiences does the victim have of coping alone? Does he also expect this from others? This might be followed by descriptions of experiences where social support played a crucial role, and thoughts on courage attached to accepting help, and questioning the original attitude in this way.

5. *We have talked a lot among the family about the event. We don't need outside help.* Talking to family, relatives and friends about a shocking event is no substitute for a PD session. Systematic processing of the event and reactions guided by an outside professional is fundamentally different from a conversation with friends and family. Family

members and friends will avoid talking about the most painful issues. To ensure that the real focal points of pain in a traumatic event are addressed requires an independent expert. This is the feedback invariably received after successful debriefing sessions.

6. *I don't need psychological debriefing. I have no adverse reactions associated with the event.* In this case, the crisis worker must return to the nature of the traumatic event and the victim's role in it, and reassess the severity of the traumatic event, the victim's background (previous experiences and coping with them, education, training) and need for support. On this basis, it is possible to assess whether it is a case of denial and blocking, or whether there really is no need for help. If it is a question of denial and blocking, it is worth referring to one's own experiences and research findings, and trying to motivate the victim to come along, even if only for the sake of others, or out of curiosity.

However thorough and capable the crisis worker, he cannot always succeed in motivating the victims to attend a PD session. Particularly in cases where children are among the victims, or the traumatic experience has been very intense, the crisis worker is often left feeling worried and miserable. He feels that he is not good enough and wonders what else he could have done.

A young couple was expecting their first baby. Everything was fine and they had their lives ahead of them. They had just moved into a new home, the husband had been accepted on a course he wanted to do, and the baby was due in about a week.

The wife had arranged to visit her parents during the morning. When their daughter did not arrive or answer the telephone, the parents became worried and went to see if everything was OK. They found her in the bathroom, dead.

They called the husband and asked him to come home immediately. He was already on his way home when the call came. When he came in, he was told what had happened. He was beside himself, threw furniture around, broke chairs, and the police officers attending had difficulty calming him down.

The police requested crisis counselling for the family. They told me that the husband was staying with the young woman's parents, so I contacted them. The husband would not take the call, so I only talked to the young woman's father. I told him about psychological debriefing, and they were all prepared to attend, the husband too. We agreed on a tentative date, to be finalized depending on the location of the session.

When I called again to arrange the exact timing and location, I was told that the husband did not wish to attend the session. He had more important things to do on that day. He had to attend lectures and study for his exams in the spring. The event took place in September. The husband still refused to come to the telephone. The young woman's parents did not want to attend the session either, since the husband would not be there. He is the one who needs it most, they said.

Overnight, I thought about the situation and what could be done. I ended up with the solution that I would write a letter to both the husband and the young woman's parents, telling them about typical reactions, thoughts and emotions in such a situation. I also suggested how these feelings and thoughts should be approached and how they may be processed. I included my contact details at the end of the letter. The police gave me the addresses. They told me that the husband had been questioned on the same day, and that he was still in a state of shock. The police thought that the husband really needed help.

Four days after I posted the letters, the young woman's father called me. He thanked me for the letter and said that the husband had told him about sitting in his car on a railway crossing, waiting for a train to run over him. But the train had not come and his life was saved. This had happened on the day the letter arrived in the post.

The husband had been incapable of reading through the whole of the letter. He managed to read a few sentences at a time, and then he wept in anguish. After a while, he would read the next few sentences. The letter had succeeded in bringing out the tears and the pain, defusing it. The psychological coping process of his shocking experience had begun.

However, everybody has the right of self-determination. It must be possible to refuse psychological debriefing, too. The important thing is that the person understands what he is refusing and what the possible consequences are.

Imparting information on the PD session and motivating people to attend is an event based on interaction. Its course and outcome are affected by both the receiver of the message and its transmitter. If the crisis worker himself is not convinced of the need for a debriefing session, he may well get a negative answer. If the crisis worker's own motivation for crisis work in general or the task at hand in particular is weak, it is immediately reflected in his reception. The old proverb 'As you sow, so shall you reap' holds true in this situation, too.

It is up to the crisis worker to motivate the contact person to ensure that the debriefing session is as comprehensive as possible, or that everyone involved attends. Here, too, the way the matter is marketed is the crucial factor. Is it presented as a unique, once-only opportunity to address issues associated with the event in depth, systematically and with the guidance of an expert, or is it a chore generally undertaken with reluctance? The contact person should present the event so that everyone is expected to attend and express that it would be a pity if anyone cannot come.

> A group of young people was celebrating Midsummer Eve on an island. They had spent the evening on the mainland and were returning to the island. There were twelve of them and the small motor boat was registered for five. The boat's skipper wanted to make two trips, but the passengers would not agree. They said that the boat had carried that number of people before. The skipper was forced to choose between steering the boat or allowing someone else, who had been drinking, to do it.
>
> When the boat was nearing the island and slowed down, it took in water and overturned. All aboard were thrown into the water. The water was cold, below 10 degrees Celsius.
>
> One of the girls drowned; the others managed to get ashore. The drowned girl was the best swimmer in the group. She was also one of the three wearing life jackets. Some heavy object from the boat had got caught on her foot, dragging her down, and she did not succeed in shaking it off.
>
> Two debriefing sessions were arranged, one for the girl's family and another for her friends, including those who had been in the boat. The teenagers themselves took charge of getting everyone together for the session. They had 24 hours to get the message to their friends.
>
> Twenty-three teenagers attended the session, people who had been in the boat or on the island or friends who had celebrated Midsummer elsewhere. Two of them were doing their national service. They had requested leave to attend the session. The girl's brothers and their girlfriends also attended the session. In fact, they took part in two sessions on the same day. The other session, held before the teenagers' session, was one for the family.
>
> Only a couple of the girl's good friends were absent from the session. This is an example of how a debriefing session was marketed in a motivating way, so that everyone felt the need to attend.

Structure of debriefing groups

Above all, psychological debriefing is a group method. Particular care is required when assembling the groups. Often, there are several alternatives in group structure. By selecting one alternative, something is achieved, but simultaneously something may be lost.

Family groups are often assembled by agreeing the principles with the contact person, and the actual structure of the group being left up to him. The guiding principle is that everyone affected should be encouraged to attend.

Often, the session leaders do not know exactly who is present, in spite of having agreed in principle. Surprising absences may occur, and sometimes people turn up unexpectedly.

> A successful man of about 50 committed suicide by piping his car's exhaust fumes into the vehicle in an isolated spot. He had thoroughly prepared his suicide, by, for example, putting his financial affairs in order and making arrangements with his grown-up sons.
>
> He and his wife were getting divorced, but the divorce had not yet come through. However, he lived in his own home. He had three adult sons from a previous marriage and an 18-year-old daughter from the current marriage.
>
> His eldest son made the arrangements for a debriefing session for the family and relatives. All the above family members were to attend.
>
> The son went to his father's home and played back the messages on the answering machine while he was there. There were numerous messages from a woman. While the son was there, the phone rang, and the caller was the woman who had left the messages. It transpired that she and the man who had committed suicide had had a very close relationship for the past two years. When she heard of the man's death, she was severely shocked, and the son invited her to the debriefing session. It turned out that the woman had a 16-year-old daughter who also knew the dead man very well. She, too, was invited to the session.
>
> All the above-mentioned people arrived at the session. The leaders had no knowledge of the two additional people, and their attendance came as a total surprise. In addition, the wife of the dead man had no idea even of the existence of the other woman, let alone of her presence at the session. The leaders complained that the session was extremely difficult, which is quite understandable.

In general, the aim is the formation of homogeneous groups. This means that people in the same position are assembled as a group. For example, those assisting at the scene of an accident form their own group, the victim's family another.

This has not always been the case. In the early stages of acute crisis work, it was customary to gather everyone connected with a traumatic event to a communal session. Thus, for example, in the case of a road accident, the same group would contain the survivors, families of those injured and killed, and the rescue personnel and police officers who attended the scene of the accident. The idea was that everyone together could discuss their reactions, thoughts and emotions associated with the incident.

However, this proved to be impossible. For example, rescue personnel are unable to express their insecurities, doubts about taking the correct action, or their feelings of guilt, in the presence of bereaved families. In such a heterogeneous group, in effect nobody is able to express his emotions quite freely, because the presence of others inhibits them. That is why the recommended course is to organize separate groups for the family, rescue personnel, police, etc., if all these groups are necessary.

However, frontline helpers (rescue personnel and police) may be utilized in a PD session as experts to present the facts about the incident. Families are generally extremely interested in the details of the event, and they feel that the most reliable sources of information are people who were at the scene. If a frontline helper is present, families can also directly ask them questions that arise during the session. When frontline helpers act as experts in a session, their role must be clearly defined in advance, and it must be clear that they will leave the session when the facts have been reviewed.

Often, the victims themselves are the best experts in structuring groups.

A student committed suicide in an educational institution. His friends knew that he was planning suicide, and they had devised a 'duty roster' among themselves, taking turns to stay nights with him. On one occasion, the person 'on duty' fell asleep, and when he awoke, he could not find his friend anywhere. He was afraid to go out to search alone, so he alerted a couple of friends to go with him.

They found their friend, dead, in the attic of their apartment block. The suicide was reported to the institution, where the decision was made to organize a separate PD session for students on the victim's course and for the teachers. The course tutor requested permission to attend the students' session, but after a moment's consideration I decided that it would be best if she attended the teachers' session.

The students' session was attended by 16 people out of the group of 20. Gradually, during the session, it emerged that the absentees were the closest friends of the deceased, those who watched over him and who found him. I took their contact details and called them after the session.

They told me that their absence was deliberate and considered. There were two reasons. First, they knew certain things about the deceased that they did not want to tell everyone else. They would have felt awkward at the session, unable to speak directly and honestly about their thoughts and feelings. Second, they felt that if they had attended, everyone else would have wanted to focus on their emotions and thoughts and to allow them space. Then, the more distant friends would have been unable to address their own thoughts and feelings.

Both grounds for absence were correct. These close friends had their own session, and both sessions were a great success. The wise action of these students created excellent conditions for both sessions, because homogeneous groups were formed.

I asked the students at the end of the session how they would have felt about their course tutor being present. The students' unanimous opinion was that in that case they would not have said anything.

One factor determining homogeneity, then, should be closeness to the deceased. In the above example, the students' action ensured two very homogeneous groups in this respect. If a student in an educational institution dies, the homogeneity of groups on the closeness–distance continuum should be considered. Then, at least two debriefing sessions should be arranged: one for the deceased student's class and another for his friends. Thus, some people may attend two sessions.

A similar situation may arise in a work community, if a member dies. The whole community needs debriefing, but the employee's closest friends should also have their own session.

The objective in structuring debriefing groups is to ensure facility and openness of expression. For this reason, the group should contain nobody who might prevent someone from speaking out, or whom he cannot trust. Such people are particularly superiors at work, and teachers at schools.

A superior's participation in the debriefing session may adversely affect the subordinates' courage in discussing their reactions, thoughts and feelings. But sometimes the presence of the superior is quite crucial. Let us take for example a situation where the community has experienced a medical error or a near-miss situation. In such a case, the superior has a pivotal role in the debriefing session. As a general rule, if the superior is an important and seamless part of the working community, 'one of us', he should attend, but if he is a distant administrative superior, then he would not naturally participate in the community's session. However, the superior's participation should always be assessed: what would be gained and what lost by it.

In schools, participation of the teacher in debriefing depends partly on the age of the pupils, and partly on the teacher's personality. In lower grades, it is quite natural that the teacher participates in the class session. In upper grades, the general rule is that the teacher does not take part in the class session, unless his relationship with the students is particularly confidential and close.

One guiding principle in forming debriefing groups is respecting natural groups. If people have experienced some traumatic event together, they are also offered the opportunity of processing this experience together.

A natural group is also formed for example by those who work together.

> After an incident that deeply traumatized the whole community, it was decided that debriefing sessions should be organized for the whole work community of more than 80 people. The sessions were structured in groups of 12. These 12 people formed a working unit, who were on the same shifts and whose members worked together.

In natural groups, the degree of traumatization should also be taken into consideration. If a part of a work community has had a particularly shocking experience, for example being taken hostage in a very threatening situation, and the other community members have watched the incident from the sidelines at the scene or been off duty at home, it is important to consider whether the experience should be addressed communally by the work community, or whether the victims of a particularly traumatizing situation should form their own group. The homogeneity of the work community and maximization of social support favour a communal session, but confidentiality and depth of processing favour separate sessions.

There are experiences of extremely threatening hostage situations that were addressed with the whole work community. Those who were taken hostage felt that the others attended out of sheer curiosity, to hear the details of the incident. In that case, the degree of traumatization was so different for the actual hostages and other members of the work community that separate debriefing sessions for these two groups would have been preferable.

Another central factor in structuring debriefing groups is the question of guilt. As a general principle, those culpable in the incident and their families have their own session. Occasionally, however, good results have been achieved by allowing the victims and the guilty parties to meet.

In the above example, where a young girl was drowned, the person in charge of the boat was legally culpable for the accident. He attended the teenagers' session as one of the members, and this greatly relieved his anxiety. At the session, his emotions were allowed a lot of space, and the other young people also gave him enormous social support.

A shared session for the victims and perpetrators may enable effective processing of guilt feelings and aggressions, anger and need to apportion blame, but this kind of communal meeting also entails many risks. That is why it is better first to run separate sessions for the victim and his family and the perpetrator and his family. If the meeting of these two groups looks as if it could be fruitful, it can be arranged after the separate sessions. Such a communal meeting, however, requires particularly strong professional skills of the leader.

> A little boy was knocked down by a car and killed. The driver of the car had a pressing need to meet the dead boy's parents. He expressed this need also to the investigating police officer, who arranged a meeting with the boy's father.
>
> The meeting took place at the police station. The officer left the men alone, and the boy's father pulled a photo album out of his case. He had reacted to the boy's death through photography. He took pictures of the boy's room as it was around the time of the accident, the headline posters at the newspaper stand, etc. He also assembled photographs of his son at different ages in his album.
>
> He wanted to look through the album with the driver. He justified it by saying that the driver had such a mangled image of his son. He thought that the driver would feel better if he had an image of the boy before the accident.
>
> The last picture in the album showed the boy waving, saying goodbye. The motorist said that he leafed through the album out of courtesy, but was far from able to look at the pictures. He saw them as if through fog.
>
> The boy's father spoke to the motorist about how this event united them, saying that he had nobody else with whom he had experienced anything so important. He invited the driver to the funeral and expressed his wish that they should keep in touch in the future.
>
> The motorist wept continually for three days after the meeting. His family were anxious and worried about him, and at the same time incredibly angry with the boy's father. The motorist sent a wreath to the funeral, but did not attend himself.

This example demonstrates how unpredictable the effects of meetings between victims and perpetrators can be. Indeed it is best if, for example, those killed in an accident remain unknown and distant for the person who caused the accident. In spite of this, many mental images are associated with them. Before meeting the dead boy's father, the motorist in the above example had already endured thoughts of how the boy could never grow up, how he would never graduate from high school, get married, etc. These thoughts become even more painful, if the victim becomes familiar.

Large debriefing groups

The size of a psychological debriefing group is not regulated by the laws of group dynamics as powerfully as the size of groups in general. Usually, the optimal group size from the group dynamics point of view is 5–8. In PD, both smaller and larger groups are functional, if they fulfil the criteria of homogeneity and open and honest expression as described above.

Often, a natural group is relatively large, such as for example a school class or work community. In that case, an assessment must be made on whether the group should be divided into smaller groups, or the debriefing carried out with all the community members together.

We have gained experience of large (20 or more members) groups by chance, by virtue of being unprepared for large numbers of participants, when we have had no alternative but to manage with the resources at our disposal. Had we had prior knowledge of the numbers on these occasions, we would no doubt have recruited more leaders and divided the community into small groups. However, then we would not have discovered how a large group functions in a debriefing session.

There are certain advantages in conducting PD with all the community members in one communal session. When the course of events and related facts are presented and worked through with the whole community, a shared truth is formed. All the members know the same amount and the same facts. There is no further need to compare information and ideas, or to speculate. A shared truth has a calming effect and frees the atmosphere.

When the whole community participates in the processing of a shocking event, it also affords maximization of the sense of social cohesion and support. The experience becomes an issue common to all, from which they will also recover together. Responsibility for possible follow-up actions will be shared, too.

Let us return to the case where a high school student attacked a teacher, brandishing a knife. The teacher escaped the threatening situation with minor injuries.

One of the most beneficial results of the debriefing session was that many teachers voiced their own fear of the violent pupil, and said that they dared not discipline him properly. During the session, a common policy was agreed on how to deal with this pupil and other potentially difficult students, too, in the future. All the teachers undertook to follow the same principles.

When it is possible to agree common policies for the future, and everyone undertakes to share responsibility for the issue, the community's unity and efficiency are improved.

When the debriefing session is held for the whole community, the session, too, becomes a shared experience for everyone. At the same time, formation of subgroups and cliques is avoided. It is also crucial for the community's cohesion that everybody hears everybody else's experiences.

In some situations, the whole community processing the experience together, in spite of having different experiences and perspectives of the traumatic incident, is more important than the homogeneity of the groups and the corresponding depth of the processing.

> At the sinking of MS Estonia, the personnel of the attending car ferries fell into three distinct groups that differed in respect of their experiences. Some of the employees took part in the rescue effort in a concrete way by plucking victims from the sea and attending to their first aid. Some were working on board ship, but engaged in their customary duties, and some were ashore, off duty.
>
> In the procedure that evolved, these groups were mixed up in debriefing sessions. Most sessions were attended by people from every group. At these sessions, they had the opportunity of hearing the experiences of others, and sharing their feelings with each other. The result was that no subgroupings were formed that would otherwise have been unavoidable. This was one of the most important and valuable outcomes of the psychological work carried out on the ships.

In the same way, in communities where the aim is unity and sense of belonging, the fact that community members who were in different positions in relation to the traumatic event share and hear each other's various experiences will increase understanding of others and community cohesion.

Large debriefing groups also raise problems. One of the most prominent is that not everyone gets the chance to talk about his or her personal experiences and emotions. Otherwise the length of the sessions would become intolerable. This is usually resolved by selecting representatives to describe their experiences and reactions. All aspects do generally emerge even in large groups. Participation and commitment may be increased by saying that this is a common reaction: who else felt this way in connection with this event? Then you may ask if anyone else wants to describe his or her own feelings. After this, the topic may be extended to different experiences of the same phenomenon.

In a large group, the level of intimacy is impaired. Many people find it difficult to discuss very personal issues in a large group. That is why in a large group special attention must be paid to developing a sense of trust in the debriefing situation. This is increased by belief in absolute confidentiality. In a large group, it is worth drawing particular attention to this by actively committing the participants to confidentiality, by saying at the start of the session: "This meeting is bound by confidentiality. Nobody must discuss outside this session anything that anyone else says here. Naturally, you may talk about what you have said or experienced yourself. Does everyone agree?" Then the leader looks at everyone present, after which he can say: "So, we are all agreed."

Because it is difficult to discuss personal matters in a group, it is important that the leaders stay behind at the venue, so the participants have the opportunity for one-to-one conversation. In my experience, this opportunity is taken up in large numbers particularly after large group sessions. These conversations often reveal an earlier trauma that has surfaced along with the new one, and the victim now wants to talk about it. Some personal issue connected to the traumatic event, for example a personal issue connected to the deceased person, may also emerge that is so personal that the victim does not want the whole community to hear it.

Usually, large groups are also heterogeneous. That is why in large groups emotions are not processed in as great depth as in smaller homogeneous groups.

When the whole community is present, it also affords the possibility that some attend out of sheer curiosity, and not to process their own traumatic experience. In a smaller group, the leader is able to extract that personal experience from all participants. This is not possible in a large group.

One way of resolving the problems caused by a large group is by periodically splitting up into small groups, each with its own leader. This is useful at least in groups of children. They have difficulty in maintaining concentration in a large group, but effective work can intermittently continue in small groups.

The coach of an ice-hockey team of juniors aged between 10 and 12 died in the middle of a training match. He was 38. He just suddenly collapsed on the ice. The ambulance was called, and an attempt made by the crew to revive him, but the efforts were futile. The boys saw the ambulance rock for a while, then the rocking stopped and the ambulance drove slowly away. Then they guessed that their coach had died.

The assistant coach telephoned all the children on the same evening and told them that the coach had died. A PD session was arranged for the children for the next training session. At the same time, a letter was distributed to the parents, informing them that instead of training, the death of the coach and emotions elicited by it would be processed. The letter also contained the information that a debriefing session for the parents would take place the next evening.

The boys were taken to a nearby school, where the course of events and the associated facts were run through together. Then the boys were split up into groups of four. The discussion within the groups was led by a trained adult leader. In the small groups, they went over the thoughts, emotions and other reactions caused by the event. Afterwards, all were gathered together again and they discussed how to move on from here.

The boys' debriefing session was very successful. In the small groups, the children were able to deal with emotions and thoughts elicited by the sudden death of their coach in surprising depth and very personally. On the other hand, the session was shared by the whole team, and it reinforced the team's unity and sense of belonging, and helped the boys cope with this difficult event.

The same method may be applied in work communities, school classes and other communities, where the emphasis in PD is on togetherness and unity of the community and maximization of the community's social support.

Leading a PD session always demands excellent ability to read the situation, flexibility and a wealth of ideas. In large groups, these requirements are even more necessary. In each situation and each group, a method appropriate and suitable for its specific needs must be found.

In large groups, the role of the leader is often magnified. His task is to keep the group together and to ensure that the processing progresses even more distinctly than in small groups. A method that is generally emphasized in large groups is lecturing and teaching. In large groups, normalization of reactions and preparation for future reactions takes the form of a small-scale lecture.

In my view, the advantages of large groups mostly outweigh their disadvantages. Today, I like to keep the whole community together when debriefing work communities, because this enables fulfilment of objectives that benefit the community even after it has recovered from the traumatic event.

What, then, is a large group? I would define a large group as having more than 15 participants. The largest group I have led was an entire school staff of 48 people. Everyone was present, the discussion lively, very confidential and profound. As a matter of fact, I feel that organizing a debriefing session that the whole community attends together is an expression of respect and also of confidence in the community.

Practical arrangements of a debriefing session

Psychological debriefing should be organized within an external framework that supports the objectives of debriefing. The circumstances must facilitate talking through the shocking experience, so that participants can freely express and discuss their emotions and thoughts without outside interference or fear of it. The external framework must contribute towards feelings of trust and security.

PD demands peaceful, pleasant surroundings. The session venue must be neutral, so the activity is not branded as, for example, a church event or mental health service.

In the case of frontline helpers, it is important that the debriefing session, even if it is 'work', should not take place within the workplace, and that the participants are not in uniform. PD addresses experiences caused by a work situation for the employee as a human being, not in his professional role. Removing the session from the workplace and conducting it in civilian clothes supports this aim.

PD is very intensive and demands great powers of concentration from everyone, both participants and leaders. Consequently, it is of primary importance that a framework is created where there are no extraneous distractions. External noise, ringing of phones, doors opening or other disturbances will seriously disrupt the intensive work.

It is said that the best is an enemy of the good. It is not always possible to find the optimal venue for the session, or leaving the workplace may seem so complicated that people may want to forget debriefing altogether. In such cases, we must be satisfied with the facilities that are available, but the session venue should always fulfil certain minimum requirements. These are that the venue is an enclosed space with no outsiders wandering in, and that intrusions and interruptions are minimized by prior arrangement.

The victims' home is not always the optimal venue for the debriefing session, but there are often many factors in its favour. It is a safe and familiar place for the family and relatives. When the thought of PD seems very frightening, an offer to hold the session at home may alleviate the fear sufficiently for people to agree to the session.

Sessions conducted in homes give leaders access to significant additional information, which may be of primary importance in correctly assessing the situation. Conversely, working in people's homes, in a way on their territory, may hinder the adoption of a sufficiently strong leadership role. Leaders are responsible for the session, even if they are working in someone's home. During the session, they determine the course of events, not the residents of the house.

When the session is held in a home, it is important to agree certain ground rules in advance and at the start of the session. If coffee is to be served, it must be done right at the start before the session, or at the end, after the session is over. Telephones are turned off for the duration, and if the doorbell rings, one of the leaders answers it and informs the caller that the residents must not be disturbed right now.

Preparations for the session include, as well as finding a suitable venue, also making sure that the facilities are comfortable and appropriately equipped for the occasion. A table with a white cloth, candles and flowers, a jug of water and glasses, and tissues are necessary provisions for a PD session. If it is attended by children, paper, crayons, and maybe some toys and books are needed for them. Some crisis groups have assembled a 'debriefing case', which contains all the necessary equipment.

Debriefing session leaders

It is customary to have at least two leaders in a PD session. Sometimes, if there are very few (one or two) participants, one leader is adequate. If the number of participants is known to be large or if children will take part, a third leader is required.

The necessity for two leaders is due to a number of factors.

1. In a debriefing session, many significant things happen simultaneously. Four eyes perceive more than two, and even then, some crucial matters may go unnoticed.

2. When there are two leaders, they support and complement each other. Acting as session leader feels safer and easier. At the same time, the quality of the work improves, too.

    > During their preparedness training, the FRC psychologists' preparedness group carried out a major disaster exercise which included a PD simulation for firemen, a first aid group and their supervisors. The session was a kind of demonstration of PD, with the emphasis on educational material.
    >
    > In analysing the exercise, all seven pairs stressed the importance of their working partners. Although many had not worked together before, the same theoretical background and shared wide practical experience created a feeling of security and good co-operation for the leaders.

3. Debriefing sessions often contain material that is very shocking and anxiety-provoking. While leading the session, the leaders are also subjected to this material. They must face very difficult experiences, powerful emotions and heart-rending thoughts. Defusing these experiences after the session is essential in order to avoid traumatization of themselves. When there are two or three leaders, this defusing is possible immediately after the session.

4.   The session itself always evokes emotions and thoughts in the leaders, too. Discussing the course of the session and the thoughts and emotions evoked by the different stages is important not only for the sake of the leaders' learning and development, but also for their endurance.

The leaders must be outsiders. Ideally, they should not be previously acquainted with session participants, have prior therapeutic relationships with them, or belong to the same organization as the participants.

> The mother of a family, a teacher by profession, committed suicide. She had been on sick leave for several weeks owing to abdominal problems. During her sickness absence, her condition continued to deteriorate. She used a lot of painkillers and sleeping tablets and was often 'woozy' and absent-minded during the day, too. Her husband was concerned and encouraged her to visit her doctor to request proper hospital tests.
>
> When he came home in the evening, he found his wife in bed, unconscious. He called an ambulance and a doctor arrived with it. The doctor certified the wife dead, slumped into an armchair and said: "This was not supposed to happen." He had noticed an empty tablet bottle on the edge of the bed. The wife had visited his surgery during the day and asked for stronger painkillers. The doctor had prescribed the medication. The woman had taken them all at once.
>
> The doctor invited the whole family, the husband and three children, to a PD session at the health centre the following morning. After a sleepless night, the family arrived at the health centre to be met by the same doctor who had been to the house the night before, and who had prescribed the tablets the wife had used to commit suicide. The school psychologist and school nurse from the woman's school were also present. When the children realized who was leading the session, they clammed up and would not say a word. The husband tried to be polite and spoke a little, but he saw no opportunity for opening up in the situation either.
>
> Since the session was unsuccessful, the leaders decided to end it after half an hour. As they were leaving, the nurse took one of the children by the arm and said: "We will meet again." The next session was agreed for the following morning. This time, it was attended only by the husband, who in this context had the opportunity of discussing the matter more closely with the doctor.
>
> The timing of the PD had been quite wrong, but an even greater problem was the identity of the session leaders. The doctor was himself a victim, and the other two leaders came from the same organization as

the deceased. The children attended the same school where the school psychologist and the nurse worked, and the children were quite unable to trust them.

If the leader knows the victim or someone attending the debriefing session well, he, too, becomes a victim, and cannot keep his own emotions separate from participants' emotions, or at least it requires a superhuman effort.

Sometimes it becomes apparent only at the session that the leader knows the deceased or one of the victims. If this is found immediately, it should be declared right at the start of the session. If it is revealed during the course of the session, it should be disclosed at the end. The main thing is that the matter is acknowledged. It is important in maintaining trust and an honest and open atmosphere.

> A middle-aged man suffered a heart attack and died. He was just about to leave on a journey. There was no advance warning, so the man's death was a great shock to his family.
>
> In the course of the debriefing session, the principal leader realized that he knew the man well from a leisure activity. He recalled how the man had talked to him about his stress levels and physical symptoms.
>
> The leader completed the session, utilizing all his resources in order not to allow his own emotions and thoughts to impinge on the session. At the end, he revealed to the family that he knew the deceased and the activity they shared. He did not disclose their conversations.
>
> After the session, the leader suffered a total breakdown. He was overcome by his own feelings of guilt in not taking the man's symptoms seriously enough and encouraging him to see a doctor.

If the leader realizes during a session that he knows the deceased or one of the participants, or that one of them has a therapeutic relationship with the leader, there is no alternative but to conduct the session and try to keep his own emotions under control. Alternatively, the second leader may assume main responsibility. If a leader finds during the session that one of those present is a former patient, it is wise to acknowledge that they have already met, but patient confidentiality must naturally be maintained. He must not disclose how he knows the participant.

In small towns, everyone knows everyone. It is not always possible to find leaders who are not known to the victims. An effort should be made to find leaders who are as detached as possible. The leader should also always reflect on his ability to conduct the session. If the town's own crisis group cannot provide sufficiently neutral leaders, they might be borrowed from other crisis groups.

Sometimes, victims request that the session leader should be a person they know and trust. They are looking at the issue from a completely different perspective, and cannot foresee the difficulties caused by such a choice. They should be given a thorough explanation of why an external leader is preferable. If their request puts the whole session at risk, a compromise of at least one of the leaders being an outsider could be suggested.

Occasionally, victims set an ultimatum: we will agree to a session only if you will lead it. If explaining why the session is better led by an outsider does not produce a result, the leader should assess whether he is up to the task. If he thinks so, then the session should go ahead. Otherwise it must be abandoned.

The importance of the independence of PD leaders came home to me in a completely new way in connection with the 9/11 terrorist strike. I was offered the opportunity of leading debriefing sessions for Finnair staff in New York about ten days after the strike. I was hesitant at first, as I thought that cultural differences and language difficulties would significantly impair the sessions, but my experience was quite different.

The sessions were mainly attended by local people and they were conducted in English. All the participants had been personally touched by the event. Many had family members, relatives or friends, who had been in the World Trade Center at the time of the disaster. However, nobody had lost people who were very close to them. Many people had friends who were missing. Many had seen the catastrophe with their own eyes; one was in the area at the time. Everyone had difficulty getting home. In the worst case, the journey home had taken eight hours.

The sessions revealed how profoundly everyone's sense of security had been shaken. The majority had extremely strong fears. They were unable to enter tunnels, the metro, bridges, or go near high buildings. We who had come from Finland noticed an enormous difference between our experience and theirs. We were able to visit all the places they feared without any feelings of fear or threat.

This neutrality proved to be incredibly important in leading the sessions. We were able to state with conviction that the fear was in their minds, not in their environment. In fact, I became aware of the fact that if we, the leaders, had experienced what the participants had endured, we would have been wholly incapable of leading these sessions and helping the participants overcome their problems. The importance of the leaders being outsiders also in the sense that they do not have the same traumatic experiences as the participants was shown to be a particularly significant prerequisite for leadership of debriefing sessions.

It is crucial that the session leaders know each other well and are familiar with each other's working methods. Then the leaders benefit most from the colleague's support. Indeed, crisis groups should organize their work in such a way that formation of such working partnerships is possible. Practical situations are the best settings for learning a partner's way of working. The important thing is a thorough analysis of the session afterwards. The less familiar the leaders are with each other, the better they should prepare themselves for the session, by agreeing precisely the division of work and their mutual roles.

The leaders' mutual division of work could be based on the solution that one is the principal leader and the other the assistant. This solution is worth adopting if the leaders do not know each other at all, or not very well. The task of the principal leader is to keep the session under his control and to keep it moving from each stage to the next. The assistant leader observes what happens in the group, intervenes in matters that the principal leader has not noticed, and assists the principal in problem situations.

The role of assistant leader is actually incredibly difficult, because he must follow events in the group, what the principal leader is doing, and in addition, he must be capable of anticipating the principal's solutions. He must be able to intervene in the discussion without undermining the principal's authority or hindering the group process. Thus, the timing of interventions is important. On the other hand, even more important is that the main issues are processed at the session. The assistant should return to an issue if its processing has been interrupted or forgotten, even if the process has already moved on to something else.

All participants should be allowed sufficient attention and space. If the principal fails to notice that one of the participants is sidelined and does not take part in the discussion for a long time, the assistant should draw him into the discussion. He could, for instance, put a question to the withdrawn person, or say: "You have been silent for a while; I am interested in your view on this matter."

If the leaders know each other well and have led numerous sessions together, they can erase the difference between principal and assistant leader and act as equal leaders. In that case, the leaders need only agree on who will start the session.

In session leadership, the essence is building and preserving trust among the participants. Sometimes the leaders need to communicate something to each other during the session. This should be done directly and openly so that all participants hear it. Sometimes one sees instructions that leaders should agree in advance signs they can use to communicate during the session. Most participants will notice such messages, and they create suspicion and mistrust rather than trust. Conversely, mutual open communication during the session creates trust and increases the leaders' authority.

The leader of a debriefing session is an authority in the eyes of the participants. He must assume this position. His authority and participants' trust are weakened by the leaders referring to instructions and papers. Participants will suspect that the leaders do not know their stuff. The leaders should memorize participants' names and get them right. Participants are particularly hurt if they are called by wrong names.

Seating arrangements at the session have a great bearing on its course. When the leaders are inexperienced and insecure, they seek safety by sitting close together. Physical proximity creates security. The problem is that the leaders cannot see each other's expressions. More experienced leaders usually try to sit among the participants. This way, they are better able to follow each other's work. There is another advantage in this seating arrangement. The leaders reflect security also on participants nearby, and if the leaders sit in their midst, more of them are party to this proximity. Furthermore, the leaders have better eye contact with those sitting on the opposite side; thus, the leaders' eye contacts cover everyone.

12

The Debriefing Session

The psychological debriefing session proceeds in stages. They are the result of careful experimentation and research by Jeffrey Mitchell, the creator of the debriefing method. He tested its structure extensively before finalizing the present format. Mitchell wanted to be certain that the method was not harmful if used according to his instructions and principles.

The starting point of the PD process is the uppermost, superficial issues. Through the Factual Stage, the event itself is entered. At the same time, penetration towards deeper psychological layers takes place. The Thoughts Stage directs the work towards cognitive processes. The process is at its deepest during the Feelings Stage. This is also the most important stage of debriefing. After that, an ascent through the mind's layers begins. The Reaction Stage is next, where somatic reactions are addressed and the process is directed towards the future. People's reactions, facing other people, arranging the funeral, returning to work are discussed. Then follows the Normalization or Teaching Stage, and by the Summary and Closure Stage, return to the surface has been completed.

The structure of PD has proved to be relevant and very effective. It also clearly fulfils the needs of people who have suffered traumatic experiences, and they perceive it as very appropriate. However, PD has developed, along with increased professional skill and experience of the leaders, in a more process-like direction. Mitchell himself holds the view that a principal PD session leader must be a professional crisis worker, but as assistant leaders he uses lay people trained for this task, such as policemen in a police organization and rescue workers in a rescue organization. In Mitchell's model, each stage begins with the leader presenting a fundamental question descriptive of the stage, for example: "Now, I'd like you to tell everyone what you know about the event and its course." Each participant in turn then answers the question. The leader asks the next question, and so the session progresses. The leader does not comment on participants' answers other than by thanking them and then moving on to the next participant. They may ask each other questions, comment on each other's experiences, but their mutual interaction is relatively slight.

The effectiveness of such a PD session is based largely on the fact that it is helpful to express sensitive issues and emotions and to hear the reactions of others, and on the knowledge gained from the leader about typical reactions in traumatic situations.

However, PD offers an opportunity for much more effective and productive processing of experiences, when it is developed in a more process-like direction. In that case, however, it demands that the leaders are thoroughly conversant with the group process, and possess the ability to move it on to addressing the emotions and thoughts that the participants are unable to manage on their own. It also requires that the leaders have thorough expertise in the psychology of disasters and traumas.

In Finland, the majority of the members of local crisis groups are human relations specialists who have received special training in acute crisis work. The level of basic training of these leaders is higher in Finland than that of debriefing session leaders in general. For this reason, the majority of psychological debriefing sessions are process-like in nature.

The stages of psychological debriefing

The stages of psychological debriefing are: Introduction, Factual, Thoughts, Feelings, Symptoms and Normalization, and Closure. The progress and depth of the debriefing process are shown in the Figure 12.1.

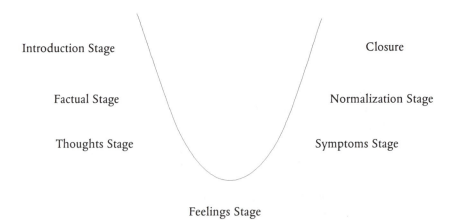

Figure 12.1 Stages and depth of psychological debriefing

The Introduction Stage

The aims of the Introduction Stage are to create a positive atmosphere, reduce participants' anxiety, and build up trust. The Introduction Stage creates the foundation and framework for the process. In this sense, it is very important, and leaders should understand this and focus on it sufficiently.

At the Introduction Stage:

- The session leader explains why the session has been organized. The first sentence of the session should explain directly and honestly the reason for the session, for example: "We have met here today because John Smith committed suicide on Friday." Thus the leader immediately gives an example that at this session things are called by their real names and discussed directly.

- The leader explains what will happen at the session, what actions will be taken and why.

- The leader sets himself up as an authority by outlining his background and emphasizing his experience in debriefing.

- The assistant leaders introduce themselves and outline their background.

- The leader explains why such sessions are organized, what their aims are, and what kinds of experiences have been gained from them, for example: "Some of you may feel that you can cope with this situation alone. That is possible, but in our experience, people working through the event alone will need more time than those who take part in psychological debriefing. People who participate in sessions generally get over the situation and start living again sooner, which is shown in better sleeping, appetite and ability to work."

- The leader motivates the participants to work. Some may resist debriefing. They can be told: "Some of you perhaps don't want to be here. You are thinking that this kind of discussion is unnecessary. However, your presence may be important to others. They want to hear what you know about the course of events, and how you perceived the situation. That is why your presence is important."

- The leader stresses the differences in reactions, and the importance of an accepting and respectful attitude to the reactions of others.

- The leader runs through the session rules and justifies their importance, for example: "For the session to be successful, it is important that certain rules are followed."

The rules are:

1. PD is not technical debriefing, where strategy and tactics applied during the work are gone through, but processing personal impressions and reactions during and after the event.

2. The session is confidential. The leaders are bound by a duty of confidentiality and the participants must undertake not to divulge outside the session what others have said about their own impressions, reactions, thoughts and feelings. They are free to discuss their own impressions and feelings after the session, as well as the facts associated with the event.

3. No notes are taken at the session. If the leaders make notes, they explain the reason for and content of the notes, and destroy them within sight of the participants.

4. The participants are encouraged to talk freely about their reactions and feelings. It is essential that they talk about their own reactions, and not those of others. So, everyone speaks for himself, including any children present at the session.

5. The participants do not have to say anything other than their names and how they are connected with the event. However, they are encouraged to talk about their own reactions.

6. There are no breaks. If someone needs to leave the room, they are asked to leave quietly and return as quickly as possible. Everyone should also stay to the end, as "there are important issues at the end, too, that we would like everyone to hear".

7. There is no hierarchy at the session. Everybody's views are equally important.

8. Anything expressed at a session must not affect an employee's work, position or promotion prospects. It is important to stress this at work communities.

9. No outsiders must be permitted at the session. Everybody present must be in some way connected to the event under discussion except the leaders, who must be outsiders.

Finally, the leader asks whether anyone has any questions, before moving on to the next stage.

The Introduction Stage can involve particular problems:

- Confrontation at the beginning of the session is hard. Verbalizing the reason for the session in the first sentence may cause the leader insurmountable difficulties if he does not rehearse it and concentrate on his words 100 per cent.

- Too little attention may be paid to the Introduction Stage, with the result that important things are left unsaid. The leader may be nervous at the start of the session, and therefore tend to rush through it rather quickly.

The Factual Stage

The aims of the Factual Stage are:

- *To facilitate facing the truth.* I have already discussed, in connection with the aims of debriefing, the great importance of the Factual Stage in facing and accepting the truth.

- *To reduce the scope of the imagination.* Our imaginations are much more inventive than the truth. We are capable of imagining the most horrific scenes, which is why going over the truth is usually a relief. The truth liberates. If we do not know the truth, too much scope is left for the imagination.

- *To create an overview of the event.* Although our perceptions of a traumatic event are very detailed, we do not perceive everything that happens. A typical feature of the shock stage is so-called tunnel vision. It is essential for recovery that the victims of traumatic events gain an overview of the course of events. This is possible only by combining the perceptions of all parties.

- *A shared and general understanding of the event.* The social situation is considerably calmed if it is possible to create a shared and general idea of what happened and how. This will increase social support and liberate people from agonizing over the course of events. The processing of the traumatic event can progress to the next stages.

The Factual Stage usually starts with introduction of the people present and how each is connected with the event. Sometimes the participants of the session have already been introduced, in which case this stage begins with a discussion of the role each person had in the event: whether he was there at the time and what happened, how and when he heard about the event, etc.

At this stage, the focus of the session shifts from the leaders to the participants. That is why it is important that all participants answer the first question, and that the discussion is not allowed to stall with one person for long.

Everyone should have the opportunity of saying something within a reasonable time. If someone starts to describe the event in great detail, he should be gently interrupted: "We'll return to this presently, but let's finish this round first."

After everyone has had the chance of recounting how he was connected with the event, the group begins to reconstruct the detailed course of the event. It is best to start off from the period preceding the event. If the traumatic event happened during the day, you could start from the morning. What was the morning like? Was there anything unusual about it? Those preceding shared moments usually assume a huge significance later on. The objective is thus to ascertain when the person last saw the loved one alive, and what that contact and parting were like.

> A middle-aged man died on a business trip. An important part of the Factual Stage of the debriefing session was recalling how each family member had heard about the event. What were they doing when the message came? When had each of them seen the deceased last, and what was that meeting like?
>
> The wife's impression of the final meeting was particularly poignant. She recalled: "Although we have been married almost 20 years, our relationship still contained strong love and tenderness. I felt my husband's love in a particularly concrete way when we said goodbye as I was leaving for work. His eyes and his voice were filled with love. That moment was to be the last we shared. Two days later I received the message that he was dead."

We should then move on to the actual event, and the preceding moments: what did those involved in the event manage to perceive and think before it happened? A typical description by a person involved in a road accident follows:

> We had just left Gran's house, where we had collected the Christmas tree. The weather was awful. It was snowing and dark. Dad was driving too fast. I told him off about it, but he wouldn't slow down. He started to overtake a lorry and I shouted from the back seat: "Don't, there's a car coming." Dad managed to avoid the first car, but then the car skidded into the opposite side of the road and there was a car coming that crashed straight into the side of our car. After that I can't remember anything.

It is important that a clear picture of the course of events is formed. The experiences of those involved, eyewitness reports and reports of the police and rescue services are crucial. Family members often obtain information about the events before the debriefing session, but to be doubly sure, the leaders should familiarize themselves with available factual information. Sometimes it is fitting for a police officer, fireman or doctor to be present at the session as an expert, to describe the course of the events. The expert must be instructed beforehand that he must leave after the Factual Stage, to enable family members to discuss their deepest feelings without the presence of an outsider. If necessary, emergency personnel should have their own debriefing session. The family's session is not appropriate for them.

> A shooting incident took place in a private apartment, resulting in the death of one young person. The others present were so drunk that they could remember nothing about the event.
>
> At the debriefing session for the young man's family, a police officer was present as Factual Stage expert. He had been the first to enter the apartment and to see the whole horror of the situation. His task was to describe what he saw and to answer the family's questions, of which there were many. Then he left, and the family members continued the session among themselves.

Sometimes the best expert is the other party in the accident.

> Two people in the same car were killed in a crash. They were good friends and knew each other well. Separate debriefing sessions were held for the two families. At the time, it was not known how the accident happened. Firm information started from the call for the ambulance.
>
> Both families were troubled by not knowing how the accident happened. There was another party to the accident, the car that hit the friends' car. For the families to gain a complete overview of the event, a shared session was organized for the families of the deceased and the driver of the other car. During this session the driver described in detail how the accident happened.

During discussion about the course of events, those who were involved take centre stage. In the Factual Stage, a careful and detailed analysis of each person's memories of the incident is important, including their sensory perceptions (sight, sound, smell, taste, touch and motion) during the event. These will be crucial later, when intrusive memory images or flashbacks are dealt with. Next, the discussion will move on to what people have heard about the incident afterwards: what the police, rescue personnel and eye witnesses have said.

Essential facts are also the rescue operations and how they were perceived. Often, discussing the events takes relatively little time. Conversely, the rescue operation and the positive or negative perceptions of it take a lot more time.

> We will return to the accident where a boy was run over by a truck on his first day at school. First at the scene was a group of military police officers. The truck driver said that they stopped, quickly took charge of directing traffic at

the accident spot, moved him aside and took care of him, as well as immediately calling the emergency services. The driver perceived the military policemen's action as incredibly important and supportive of him. At the debriefing session he requested that these officers, who happened to be at the scene, be sent particular thanks.

When the ambulance arrived at the scene, the driver was removed into the ambulance, and was at all times attended by a staff member. He was very well looked after. The officer in charge of the military police patrol also came into the ambulance to talk to him. He, too, was very kind and friendly. Another of the officers also came into the ambulance. He did not actually say anything accusatory, but the driver thought that he recognized an accusing tone in his voice anyway.

Often, initial medical examination and treatment is very painful and conducive to further traumatic experiences, which should be addressed during the Factual Stage. In cases of serious injury, painful examinations and treatments continue for days, even weeks after the accident. In such cases, accumulation of traumatic experiences continues after the debriefing session, and further psychological support for the patients must be organized. PD alone is not a sufficient form of psychological support.

An interesting observation is that victims endure painful procedures relatively well, but clumsy, uncaring or unkind treatment by personnel is perceived as particularly traumatic. It may become the most traumatic experience of the entire event.

Three six-year-old girls were crossing a busy road. They were in a hurry to buy sweets, and nipped across the road between cars. Two of the girls were hit by an articulated truck, which drove completely over them. The girls were momentarily knocked unconscious when their heads hit the tarmac, but neither was otherwise injured.

A nurse working at the nearby hospital saw the incident through the window. The girls were taken to the hospital unconscious, and when one of them came round, the nurse was standing by her bed. The girl did not know what had happened and where she was. The first words she heard in hospital were from the nurse: "You girls were incredibly lucky. If the truck wheels had gone over you, you'd have been just a wet blob."

These words and the nurse's attitude became the most traumatic experience of the incident for the waking child. Luckily, the girl's parents helped a great deal because of their supportive approach and total lack of blame.

Frontline personnel and hospital staff largely determine whether victims amass more traumatic experiences, or whether these experiences are positive and conducive to recovery. The experiences following the incident are particularly important, because the victims are in a state of particular emotional sensitivity and vulnerability. Their significance is great compared to experiences acquired in a normal emotional state. A caring, considerate and encouraging attitude goes a long way to alleviate even severe pain and suffering.

During the Factual Stage, experiences of participants who were not at the scene of the incident itself are also discussed in detail. How did the policeman deliver the tragic news? What happened then? Did you go to the hospital to see the deceased? What happened there? What did the deceased look like? What did you do then? What time did you get home? How did the evening at home go? How was the night?

Sometimes, the participants do not want to hear the truth. They may decide right at the start of the Factual Stage that they do not want to hear about such things. Then the leader can motivate the participant by saying that experience shows that we continue to be troubled precisely by the things we do not know. The truth allows peace, however terrible it may be. Next, the facts should be discussed one by one, and when the point is arrived at that the participant did not want to hear about, the leader might turn to him and ask: "How about it? You said that you didn't want to hear about this. Do you still feel the same?"

Usually, they will have changed their minds. As the Factual Stage has progressed, the person has already discovered that discussing the facts brings relief, and at the same time, the need to know overcomes fear. The task of the session leader is to bring such a sense of security to the session that with his leadership and help it enables the victim to face facts that would be impossible alone.

A PD session was organized for the circle of friends of a young man who had been killed in a motorcycle accident. It was attended by almost 20 friends and acquaintances of the dead youth.

The accident happened in the small hours. The youth drove a light motorbike into a bus stop and died. First on the scene were two of his best friends. One went off to get help. The other stayed with him. I asked the latter what his friend had looked like, as he was lying there on the ground. He looked into my eyes for a long time and asked: "Do I have to tell you?" I said, "Yes."

I began to ask him things that I thought were shocking. Was he bleeding? No. Was his face badly disfigured? No. Was his skull smashed? No. Then he said that the thing that had shocked him most was that one of his friend's arms was half a metre longer than the other.

It was incredibly important that he was able to express the sight that had most shocked him. I am convinced that he would have otherwise told no one, and he would have been forced to live with this secret. It was also important that the dead boy's other friends learned what he looked like, as it is one of the things that usually trouble us after an accident.

Generally, people have a need to know what has happened and how. On one hand, we are frightened to hear detailed descriptions of the event, but on the other, we want to and should know those shocking details for the incident to leave us in peace. However, we should also avoid subjecting people to unnecessary shocking material. Thus, the leader should be able to decide whether discussing the details is necessary for all session participants. If the leader considers it to be important, then he must encourage discussion of the issue and assist it by asking probing questions. If the incident is, for example, a private experience of a rescuer or policeman that is in no way connected with the other rescue workers, the leader might suggest discussing the experience privately after the session.

> Atle Dyregrov gives an example of a private experience. There was an accident in Norway involving a Swedish school bus. The brakes failed and it crashed into a mountainside at great speed. Almost 20 children and some adults were killed.
>
> The rescue effort was begun at the back of the bus. It was already well under way. A long row of children's bodies was laid on the grass. All that was left was the well at the front of the bus, the entrance with the steps and the door. The well was almost intact, but there was a hole through which the rescue worker was able to push his arm. The worker in question said that he hoped to find nothing when he pushed his arm through the hole. Consequently, the shock was enormous, when he felt a small hand in his own.

This is an example of a powerful sensory perception that is private in nature. There is no need for other rescue workers to know about it, and the knowledge would not bring them any relief. Therefore, it was pointless to subject them to this experience and the best solution was to address it alone with the rescue worker.

Facing and sharing the truth is vitally important. We have become used to secrets. There has not been sufficient courage to tell or hear the truth. Yet, these secrets persistently trouble the minds of both its keeper and of those who know of its existence, but not its content. One of the objectives of PD is to prevent further formation of such secrets.

The Factual Stage is a very important and significant stage in PD. If the facts are not discussed in sufficient detail, the participants will return to them later and the session will stagnate. On the other hand, the stages become more difficult as the session progresses. In the Factual Stage, the participants in a way enter the event and reconstruct the event for all to examine. This facilitates subsequent addressing of thoughts, emotions and reactions.

At the end of the Factual Stage, it is a good idea to ask the participants if there is anything else they would like to know. Sometimes, this question produces issues that have been missed. Mostly, it produces questions that remain unanswered, to which nobody knows the answer. It is useful to bring out these troubling unanswered questions, too, and discuss them.

Sometimes the facts are unknown. If someone mysteriously disappears, facts are scarce. In such cases, mental images of what the participants think happened to the disappeared person must be addressed. If the ideas are common to all, they may form the starting point of the discussion. Then, the mental images become like facts to which people can adapt. If the participants have different ideas of what may have happened, they are discussed, and each is allowed to keep their own idea.

> At the start of the semester in August at a social science college, one of the fourth year students did not report to school. On the third day, her friends decided that it was not like this student to stay away without notification. They began to suspect that something had happened to their friend.
>
> A rumour arose in school that one of its students had been murdered during the summer. The form tutor called the police and asked if they had any information on the student, and was told that she had been murdered. On the third day after they learned this, a debriefing session was held for the class.
>
> As I was preparing for the session, I called the police for more details on the incident. I was told that the investigation of the case was secret, but that it would be heard in court the following week. It was an open court and he invited me to attend. After the hearing, the officer would be able to supply details of the event.
>
> I considered delaying the debriefing session, but decided to go ahead as arranged. At the session, we had no information other than the date of the incident and that the murder had been committed by the student's partner at their home.
>
> Consequently, the Factual Stage largely focused on the participants' mental images of what had happened at the girl's home. Many classmates had visited her home and some had babysat her little boy. Thus, many had a concrete picture of their home and family, resulting in very eloquent and diverse ideas and theories of the events of that evening and night.
>
> At the close of the Factual Stage, I suggested that the students attend the hearing the following week to learn the details of the incident. They took

my advice. They listened to the hearing all day, heard the course of events in detail, met members of the girl's family, and to close the day, we held an hour's session, where we discussed the shocking things that had emerged during the day. At the end of the session, at the students' request, we agreed on a follow-up session in a week's time.

The day before the follow-up, the class representative called me and said that they had coped so well that the session was unnecessary. He thanked me profusely for helping them come to terms with the experience, and said: "Those who addressed the experience actively at the debriefing have overcome the shock much better and faster than the other students, although the experience was much more shocking for them."

This example shows the importance of thorough discussion of the facts in overcoming the experience. It also shows how important it is to address the participants' mental images of the parts of the event where no factual information is available.

Such gaps often exist in, for example, suicides. In such cases, I always try to include addressing the mental images of session participants about the suicide's final moments. What went through his mind? How did he act? These are the questions turning over in everyone's mind, and they should therefore be openly discussed.

Every stage in PD has its own difficulties. The greatest potential problems in the Factual Stage are the following:

- The stage is not being completed or sufficiently held together. The conversation of the group often goes off at tangents in the middle of the Factual Stage to thoughts and feelings. The leader should then intervene: "This issue is important, but let us return to it in a moment. Let's first go over the facts of the event properly." A good criterion for the leader to use is whether he has himself learned from this session how the event progressed, who was involved, what happened to them, how others learned about it, and what they did then. When his own picture is complete, the facts have been sufficiently established.

- The leader does not have the courage to support and encourage, or help the participants describe their most shocking experiences. It has become clear even in debriefing practice sessions, how difficult it is for a leader to move the debriefing process towards the most shocking and harrowing experiences. The participants cannot face these details alone, and need the leader's help and support. By asking questions, the participant is helped to describe his experience and thereby to share it with the others. The systematic recounting produces an experience of catharsis, relief and a psychological state of well-being.

- The right questions are not asked of the right people. Going over the facts demands enormous powers of concentration and memory from the leader. The same questions must not be asked twice. The leader must remember what each participant has experienced and direct questions to each that precisely fit their experience. For instance, strong sensory impressions are formed primarily by those who were at the scene. It is rather hurtful if such questions are repeatedly directed at those who had only heard of the incident.

- It may be hard to assess when discussing details would be helpful to the participants, and when it would constitute unnecessarily subjecting them to shocking experiences. Generally, family and close friends want to know in detail how their loved one died, if he was in pain, what he looked like and what he experienced. For more distant persons or rescue workers' colleagues, such information only adds to the stressfulness of the event.

The Thoughts Stage

The stages of PD partially overlap and the line between them is fluid. This is also true of the Factual and the Thoughts Stages. If the facts are addressed as thoroughly as described above, some of the content of the Factual Stage is directed at cognitive control of the incident.

In the Thoughts Stage, the focus gradually moves wholly to cognitive control of the traumatic event. In processing a traumatic event, cognitive control precedes emotional reaction. We are capable of coping with a traumatic event cognitively sooner than emotionally. For example, during psychological shock, we cognitively know that a shocking event has taken place, although it does not feel real.

Everyday language does not distinguish between thoughts and feelings very clearly. For example feelings of guilt are 'what if' thoughts, where through thought, we endeavour to keep hold of control and management of our life. Apportioning guilt or accusing others is also associated with an attempt at cognitive control of the event. This is partly the reason why it is so difficult to keep thoughts and feelings separate in processing a traumatic event.

However, it is crucial to stress the importance of the cognitive processing of a traumatic experience. Addressing the thoughts associated with a shocking event is quite as important as addressing the feelings.

Usually, the Thoughts Stage begins by mapping the participants' first thoughts after they heard about the event or were involved in it. At this stage, experiences of psychological shock usually emerge. People describe their thoughts that they seem to have been sucked into an American action movie, their thoughts that they cannot believe that what they heard or experienced was real.

It is also important to run through the participants' experiences of time: how they estimated the passage of time and the duration of specific events. This may have already emerged during the Factual Stage, when the chronological progression of events was discussed.

Description of reactions associated with psychological shock is often very uniform, and it forms its own self-contained unit within the process of coping with a traumatic experience. Often, it contains astonishment over one's reactions and those of others, and questions about the normality of one's behaviour, etc. For this reason, I often normalize experiences contained in the psychological shock reaction at this stage. When the participants have described their immediate reactions, I explain to them how people generally react and think in such shocking situations, and how they are often devoid of feelings. In this way, they are helped to understand reactions that seemed strange.

The Factual Stage usually reveals the powerful sensory perceptions that the participants were subjected to. At the Thoughts Stage, we must address their intrusive memory images. They are often at their most powerful during the first few days after the event, and then begin to fade. It is important that the participants gain an understanding of what these mental images are, their origin, and the fact that they usually decline in time. If someone has a very intense and disturbing mental image that troubles him constantly, he should be directed to seek additional therapy. Mostly, however, thorough discussion of intrusive mental images at the debriefing session is adequate.

Some of us react to shocking events by seeking someone to blame. All our energy and attention is directed at identifying the guilty parties and bringing them to answer for their actions. In a way, this is a defence reaction against more difficult emotions, such as feelings of loss and grief. As described above, some people may become fixated on this apportioning of blame, and the process is prevented from moving forward.

Debriefing instructions usually state that if anyone is seeking to apportion blame or to accuse, the leader must inform the participants that this is not the place for dealing with such issues. A debriefing session is not a court hearing. The police investigations and judicial proceedings are conducted elsewhere. For some people, however, seeking and accusing the culpable are the only thoughts they have about the event. Denial of its discussion results in such persons angrily leaving the session, without receiving any help.

For this reason, the debriefing session should also offer the chance to discuss thoughts and feelings associated with seeking and accusing the culpable. Usually, these thoughts weigh heavy on people's minds, and emerge almost immediately. The leaders should accept the thought: "It is quite understandable that you feel the need to seek the guilty party and to bring them to justice, but we will address this issue later. First, let us go over the facts of the event."

In order that other phenomena may be addressed at the debriefing session, thoughts of finding the guilty party should be addressed right at the start of the Thoughts Stage, often even before the shock stage reactions. It is essential that these thoughts are confronted. If the need to find the party responsible for the event has already become apparent during the Factual Stage, it should be referred to at the transition to the Thoughts Stage, and the discussion focused on it. The person is asked to describe his thoughts in more detail, he is asked relevant questions, and other participants may be asked if they have similar thoughts and how they feel about searching for the guilty party.

After sufficient discussion of the issue, the leader may bring it to a close, saying again: "It is very understandable that you feel the need to find the person responsible and to bring him to answer for his actions, because what happened seems so unjust." This summary is usually true and it diverts the focus from outsiders back to their own experience.

It is very important that seeking the guilty party and accusations are addressed at the debriefing session. This is actually the only stage where it may be influenced. Ideally, the processing should be so thorough that the issue is closed, and the person moves on to the next stages in coping with the traumatic experience. If addressing the accusatory behaviour is neglected or it is unsuccessful, it is very likely that the coping process will become fixated and channelled into police investigations and court hearings.

Guilt feelings are other important issues that require attention. Basically, they are thoughts, too. They are very common after traumatic experiences. Almost everybody feels guilty about something done or said, or something not done or said. Because guilt feelings are so common and such significant thoughts, addressing them at the debriefing session is important.

Guilt feelings usually emerge spontaneously very early in the session. Then, the procedure is the same as with accusations. The leader should accept the thought by saying, for instance, "You said that you have strong feelings of guilt. Let's come back to them later, but first we'll go over the facts."

The Thoughts Stage should begin with addressing shock stage reactions and accusations, if they exist in the group, and after that guilt feelings could be approached together: "We already heard that some people have strong feelings of guilt. Let's spend a moment together being wise after the event, or thinking: if only… What kinds of 'if only' thoughts have you had about the event?"

If a person is not taking part in the discussion, the leader may ask him whether he does not have feelings of guilt about the event. Often, hearing other people's guilt feelings will open a participant's eyes to the fact that it is a way of thinking and perceiving events that is typical of us all. The leader may reinforce this discovery: "Do you see how common guilt feelings are, and how we have them about many different things? They arise because we want to preserve the idea that we can control our lives. Most guilt feelings are about how we might have been able to prevent the event."

Some people try to apply their ultra-rational approach to traumatic events, too. They usually say that this kind of 'what-if-ing' should not be indulged in. It is a quagmire with no return, they warn. They are actually denying a characteristic feature of human nature. These 'if only' thoughts cannot be wiped out by denying them. Rather, they can be alleviated by going through them and processing them.

If an individual has such powerful guilt feelings that the above approach does nothing to alleviate them, the leader can utilize the group to help by asking the other members what they would like to say to him. In this situation, people are generally very understanding.

Sometimes culpability is clear. Then it is important to discuss whether the perpetrator intentionally harmed the other, or whether it was accidental. Legal culpability and psychological culpability are often two different things. If a person is really responsible for, for example, the death of another, he must be helped in this situation to live with his guilt.

A young woman committed suicide on a Wednesday evening. The night before, she and her boyfriend had had a fight and agreed to break up. However, they arranged to meet the following evening. They were to agree the precise time by phone around six o'clock.

The boyfriend was not yet home at six o'clock. He arrived a few minutes later, listened to his messages, and as there was none from the girl, tried to call her. The girl did not answer. The boy pottered around at home and tried again. There was no reply. The boyfriend became concerned and went over to her apartment.

He rang the doorbell. Nobody answered. Then he used his own key to get in and found that his girlfriend had hanged herself. When he took her down, he felt that she was still warm. But she could not be saved.

The boyfriend suffered terrible guilt feelings about the girl's suicide. He was certain that if he had not ended their relationship, the girl would be alive. Nobody else held him responsible, not even the girl's family.

In this case, the boyfriend learned to live with his guilt. It was hard, but gradually he was able to adapt to the situation. Although many years have passed since the girl's suicide, the boy still holds himself responsible for her death. However, he has been able to cope with his work well and to establish new relationships. Within these criteria, his recovery has been good. A PD session alone is not sufficient psychological support for a person battling this way with guilt; he needs more intensive and long-term psychological help.

At the end of the Thoughts Stage it is worth asking the participants if any thoughts are still troubling them, or which thoughts trouble them most. These questions may bring totally new material into the process.

A debriefing session was originally organized because the 45-year-old father of a family had died in a road accident. Two other men in the same van were seriously injured.

The session was delayed, so that it took place the evening before the funeral. A week after the death, the man's son's wife gave birth to a stillborn baby. So the family had to endure two deaths in the space of a week.

The debriefing session had progressed to the end of the Thoughts Stage, and I asked the participants about the thoughts that troubled them most. The son became agitated, stood up and said: "I'm most furious about a relative, an old woman, going around saying that I beat up my wife and that's why the baby was dead. If that old bat comes to the funeral, I'll push her into the grave." A totally new issue emerged, not addressed at all during the session.

The greatest difficulties in the Thoughts Stage are the following:

- Blurring of concepts. It is difficult to distinguish thought from feelings. Many everyday words rather describe thoughts, even though they are called feelings. In other ways, too, we have trouble telling thoughts and feelings apart. Personally, I think it more important that certain thoughts are addressed. The order they are addressed in is also important for the session to progress.

- Difficulties in processing accusations. The need to apportion guilt and to bring the culpable to justice tends to be very strong. It takes real courage and great professional skill to address it in such a way that victims can leave it to official bodies, to enable them to focus on the inner feelings that the traumatic event has evoked. It is difficult also because accusation is used as a defence for precisely this inner processing that seems frightening.

- Processing guilt. The leader must have the patience to stay with guilt feelings long enough for them to be thoroughly processed. For the processing to work, people must first be allowed to wallow in their guilt feelings. They will be alleviated only after sufficient discussion.

- Learning to live with guilt. In some situations, it is impossible to defuse or alleviate feelings of guilt. This is particularly true of traumatic events that are results of negligence, and where legal culpability is clear. In such cases, the objective is for the person to learn to live with his guilt.

The Feelings Stage

The objective in the Feelings Stage is to work through the feelings brought about by the traumatic event so thoroughly that the outcome is:

- reduction of anxiety
- prevention of avoidance behaviour
- promotion of coping strategies
- sharing of feelings and reinforcement of social support.

Seeking to apportion guilt and accusatory behaviour contain feelings of anger and hatred. They should be addressed along with accusatory behaviour. The anger should be confronted with the aim of getting 'inside', rather than avoiding it or hushing it up. It is also important that feelings of anger are accepted and that they are considered understandable. In this way, such feelings gradually lessen and space is made for other feelings.

Loss always contains grief, longing, emptiness, even despair. Often, these feelings of loss are strongly present throughout the debriefing session. They should also be addressed together, by confronting them and lingering with them. The participants are asked to describe their feelings. When are they at their strongest? How do they feel then? What are their thoughts? The leader's task is to assist the participants in confronting difficult emotions. For example, he can encourage people to describe the feeling in more detail, to elaborate.

Occasionally, feelings of loss do not surface at all. Then, the leader should direct the process in such a way that feelings of loss are also faced and discussed. The process may be directed, for example, to confront grief by asking participants to describe the deceased person. What kind of a person was he? This usually feels very natural and may also bring a lighter stage into an otherwise difficult process.

An even more direct question to lead into feelings of grief and loss is: "What do you miss most about this person?" This question is more personal and channels even more deeply into the grief. The leader does not need to interpret feelings of loss away. The point is that he accepts them and allows people to stay with them. At this stage of the session, silence plays an important part. It should not be feared, and the leader should not be anxious about it. Rather, the leader should allow silence and utilize it to reinforce effectiveness of the process.

Feelings of loss make people cry. Often, people are afraid or ashamed to cry in public. On the other hand, we are unable to respond to crying, but become uncomfortable and helpless. People often cry a great deal at debriefing sessions.

Space for crying should be allowed. It ceases in time, if we wait patiently. The leader should show an example in tolerating crying: "Don't worry about crying. Take your time." If the person is able to talk, he is encouraged to talk, even interspersed with crying. If his weeping prevents him from speaking, a moment is spent lingering with it, giving space for the weeping. Then, another person is addressed, and the first person is returned to when he is more composed. The cause of the weeping should never be left unaddressed, but should be worked through.

Leaders are also frightened by facing and processing despair. Family members may express their despair by saying that they do not know how they are going to carry on. Despair, too, should be boldly faced, for example by asking: "What kinds of thoughts do you have about not being able to carry on? What exactly do you mean?" It is precisely this confrontation, a more detailed analysis of a vague feeling, that will help. At the same time, it becomes subdivided in the person's mind into smaller concrete entities which no longer feel like despair.

A frequent problem at debriefing sessions is that one of the leaders or participants is unable to endure another's grief or despair, and embarks on consolation too soon. Then the person who was describing his feeling perceives that there is no space for his feelings, and consequently they are overlooked. Thus, the leader should refrain from consoling; the objective of PD is working through difficult emotions, and this does not happen through consolation. If one of the participants consoles too soon, the leader should interject and allow space to the person overcome by grief or despair: "Let's get back to what you were saying. Can you describe your feeling in more detail?"

Two cars collided in the small hours, and one person was killed. One of the cars contained a Finnish woman and two immigrant men. These men came from a very different culture.

A debriefing session was organized for everyone involved in the accident. Every time the woman spoke about her feelings of guilt or her grief and pain brought about by her involvement in a fatal accident, the immigrant men firmly opposed such talk. They said that they would under no circumstances allow any such thing. The woman was not culpable for the death, and she should not think or talk that way. They were prepared to testify to the family of the deceased to this effect.

The men's attitude was so domineering and unequivocal that the woman's own feelings and thoughts remained entirely unaddressed.

The nature of many traumatic events is such that they involve shame. Becoming a victim of violence or rape, or a family member's suicide are events that bring about powerful feelings of shame. Surprisingly, many accidents or deaths also often induce shame.

Feelings of shame are rarely voluntarily expressed at a debriefing session. The feeling is so powerful that it resembles the need for apportioning guilt. It must be addressed, to free up space for working through other feelings. In processing feelings of shame, the salient issues are first acknowledging and confronting them, and second, sharing them socially. People are often unaware of their shame. Thus, the leader must recognize it from participants' expressions. If this is unsuccessful, the leader himself can sometimes bring it out: "In my experience, such situations often evoke feelings of shame. Nobody has yet said that they feel ashamed about what happened. Does this mean that you don't have such feelings, or is it just that you haven't mentioned them?"

Shame is a social feeling based on social norms and breaching them. That is why it is most effectively addressed in group discussion. Often, people in the group express views that alleviate shame. Shame, too, is easier to bear when it is shared with others, when it does not have to be borne alone.

In a debriefing session, it is important to encourage people to face others, and at the same time their shame. Mostly, people's attitudes differ from the expected, and the shame lessens. However, the shame will not lessen if other people are not faced and the event not openly discussed with them. Relief is preceded by a steep hill that must be climbed first.

Feelings of shame engender withdrawal and avoidance behaviour. Feelings of fear, too, that are associated with almost all traumatic events, produce avoidance of difficult situations. The group should be told that it is perfectly natural to be fearful after a difficult experience. Fear need not be denied or blocked. Often, the traumatic event increases the fear that the person himself or a loved one will meet the same fate. These feelings of fear should be addressed at the session. Their mere acknowledgement, talking about and sharing them suffice to process the feelings.

Some traumatic events produce such powerful feelings of fear that such processing is inadequate. Becoming a victim of violence, armed robbery, rape or attempted rape engender powerful fears. If the fear is not addressed, it takes on a life of its own and starts to control the person. It expands and gathers strength, rather than weakening with time.

Processing fear at a debriefing session progresses from acknowledgement of the fear to describing how the fear now impinges on the person's life. What, where and how the person fears is identified. Processing the fear extends outside the debriefing session. It is possible to accept fear in itself. However, it should be confronted and not allowed to take control.

At the session, the following scenarios may be talked through: what would it feel like to go to the workplace where you were a victim of violence? How would you feel walking past the park or the doorway where someone tried to rape you? What are the circumstances where you would be able to do so? In daylight, with a male friend, with your best friend? In this way, the victim is prepared for the task to be accomplished after debriefing.

Victims of traumatic events are encouraged to confront their fears in a concrete way, to return to the frightening place and to study it. However, these visits should be contrived so that victims feel as safe as possible; they should be accompanied by a person or persons who provide feelings of security.

The old rule we learned as children still applies to fear: if we came off a bicycle or a horse, we should immediately get back on to prevent formation of a fear. Confronting the fear-inducing issue is the most effective method of overcoming it.

Fear is often accompanied by suspicion. Fear-inducing traumatic experiences cause victims to observe their surroundings much more closely than usual. They appraise people; they wonder whether that man could be a robber or if that bag could hide a weapon. Such suspicion brought about by fear should also be addressed at the debriefing session. When it is talked through in a safe environment, its irrationality is revealed to the victim and he may be able to discard it.

The objective of the Feelings Stage is to reduce anxiety and avoidance behaviour. Above, I have given a detailed account of how this is achieved through confrontation of feelings of shame and fear.

I began the description of the emotions processed in the Feelings Stage with anger. This is a feeling that emerges with great force right at the start of the session, or else it is concealed, regardless of its power. We believe that we should not speak ill of the dead or hate them. The death of a loved one also engenders feelings of anger, especially in cases of suicide. A widow said about her husband's suicide: "On top of everything else, he did this to me."

An accident victim may also evoke feelings of anger: "Went and died and left me to suffer and take care of everything." But these feelings of anger are forbidden, and they are rarely brought out into the open by participants themselves. Before they can be processed, they must first be permitted.

If no feelings of anger emerge at the session, and the leader clearly feels that participants have such feelings, he might initiate the discussion: "In my experience, this kind of situation often brings about feelings of anger. I haven't heard anyone express them. Is it that you don't have such feelings, or do you find it hard to talk about them?" After this opening, participants usually willingly describe the feelings of anger and frustration that the death of a loved one has evoked.

At the Feelings Stage in particular, traumatic situations previously experienced by participants may emerge. They may have remained unprocessed, and now flood back with all the feelings and thoughts associated with them. Sometimes, old traumas are shared by all or the majority of the participants. In such cases, part of the session should be used for processing the feelings and thoughts brought about by the old trauma.

Mostly, old traumas are individual and only concern one participant. Then, the leader should comment that after a traumatic experience, old traumas often flood back, but since this only affects one person, he suggests addressing the issue privately after the session.

At the close of the Feelings Stage, the leader may summarize by asking the question: "What was the worst feeling?" The question also helps to check whether all the most important feelings attached to the traumatic event have been brought out and addressed.

The problems in the Feelings Stage are:

- The leaders are frightened or unable to help participants confront difficult feelings. Difficult feelings scare leaders, too. However, it is their job to help participants confront and talk through the feelings they are unable to face themselves.

- Leaders console or present soothing interpretations too early, thus preventing processing of the feeling. Offering consolation and presenting a summary or interpretation usually puts a stop to processing a feeling. If it occurs too soon, participants feel that there is no space for their feelings, and they are left unaddressed.

- Some crucial feelings remain unaddressed. It is important that all the main feelings elicited by a traumatic event are addressed.

The Symptoms Stage

Sometimes the Feelings and Symptoms Stages are combined as one, the Reactions Stage. I like to use Mitchell's original way of separating them, because I want to emphasize the importance of addressing both feelings and somatic symptoms in psychological debriefing. These stages are also different in that psychological processing is at its deepest during the Feelings Stage, and at the Symptoms Stage, the ascent back to the surface is already beginning.

The objectives of the Symptoms Stage are to provide:

- understanding of somatic reactions and symptoms
- preparedness to meet people and to discuss the traumatic event with them
- preparedness to face media representatives and published articles
- preparedness to plan and take part in rituals.

In the Symptoms Stage, the group is informed that the human organism reacts to traumatic events in a holistic way, resulting in both psychological and somatic reactions. The somatic reactions associated with psychological shock are usually processed while discussing the shock reaction. The Symptoms Stage should focus on somatic reactions that emerge later.

The discussion may be opened by asking whether the participants have suffered from somatic symptoms after the traumatic event. The most common problems are a sensation of pressure in the chest, feeling the heart is about to burst, rapid pulse, gastric problems, nausea and lack of appetite, muscle pains and fatigue. Such symptoms are adequately processed by acknowledging them and assuring that everyone has some problems, as we all react physically, too.

The leader should stress the importance of taking care of oneself also after a traumatic event, even if the mind is filled with other things. The participants are reminded to eat regularly in spite of not feeling hungry or having no appetite. Exercise reduces stress, and it is important to take some. Overall, the importance of preserving everyday routines is emphasized, as they keep one connected with living.

> Pets often attend debriefing sessions held at home. On one occasion, the cat played an important role in the Symptoms Stage. He sat patiently in his place in the circle for over an hour, while the family talked through the shocking experience that had befallen the father.

We were about to close, when the cat departed for his meal. Then it occurred to the leaders that the instructions about preserving normal life routines had been completely forgotten. So we all returned to our seats and addressed the importance of eating, exercise and performance of other everyday tasks after a traumatic experience.

Sleeping should be discussed, too. Have the participants been able to sleep? Insomnia is probably the most common symptom after traumatic experiences. Doctors frequently prescribe sleeping pills at the shock stage, before there is any certainty that the patient will suffer from sleep problems. A psychological dependence on sleeping pills develops easily. Initially they are taken 'just in case'. Then people are scared to try managing without, and the vicious circle is complete.

Problems in sleeping should be addressed at the debriefing session and directions provided on how to overcome them. Use of medication should be discussed, too. The recommendation is that it should be avoided.

Gradually, the focus is steered towards the next few days and weeks. Funeral arrangements may be waiting, then return to work and children's return to school. These topics may be approached by talking about outsiders' attitudes to the participants and the shocking event.

People's curiosity and thirst for information is annoying, and meeting people who are slightly more distant may be frightening. Often, this fear is undefined; people are not sure quite what they are afraid of. That is why it is helpful to address it at the debriefing session.

People are often afraid of their own reactions when meeting people for the first time after a traumatic event. They are afraid that they will cry. This is indeed likely, but it also makes the meeting and talking about the experience more natural. The reaction brings the event to the fore, so it cannot be bypassed.

We may also be afraid that others do not know how to approach the issue and find the meeting difficult. This, too, is true. Many of us find it difficult to meet a person who has recently experienced something shocking. This difficulty must be faced. At the first meeting, the traumatic experience may be broached by saying that we have heard about it, and then ask the victim how he is and offer our support.

The most difficult problem for a family that had experienced a cot death was that they always had to bring the matter up themselves. Few outsiders would mention it, although they knew about the tragedy.

The debriefing session should be used to prepare for future events and the anticipated problems. When the session takes place because of the death of a loved one, one of the central questions is saying goodbye to the deceased. In the modern world, death has been removed from the family. Consequently, the family members usually need to be encouraged to go and see the deceased to say goodbye to him.

I have touched on the importance of goodbyes and viewing the deceased in more detail earlier in this book. I want to stress that motivating the family to see the deceased and preparing for it is one of the most crucial functions of PD. If necessary, one of the leaders might volunteer to act as support person for the occasion.

If the family has already seen the deceased, the visit and the associated experiences should be discussed. What did the deceased look like? What were the emotions elicited by seeing him? What thoughts have arisen since?

If the family has visited the deceased to say goodbye before the funeral, this occasion will become more like a memorial service. Funerals, too, often engender fear in family members. People are afraid of losing their self-control, violent weeping, etc. It is helpful to address these funeral fears in advance at the debriefing, analyse them and discuss their meaning. Then they can often be faced without tranquillizing medication.

Many traumatic events arouse the interest of the media. Protection of victims from the media is discussed elsewhere in this book. The debriefing session should also cover experiences and reactions caused by the media. They may cause the victims new traumatic experiences that demand attention. The victims should also be prepared for future approaches by the media.

The main problems of the Symptoms Stage are:

- Both leaders and participants become tired and the intensity of the processing is impaired. Consequently, some important issues may remain unaddressed.

- There may de difficulties confronting set attitudes of participants in relation to viewing the deceased, processing such attitudes and motivating them to organize an opportunity to say goodbye.

- Debriefing may be too late for some issues. Errors may already have been made (e.g. use of sleeping pills, agreeing to interviews).

The Normalization or Instruction Stage

The aims of the Normalization or Instruction Stage are:

- victims acquiring terms of reference for their reactions
- victims accepting their reactions, thoughts and feelings
- avoidance of processes that increase fear
- reinforcement of coping strategies.

Many of the issues addressed towards the end of the Symptoms Stage serve to build the foundations of the Normalization Stage. In discussing reactions, the focus has now shifted to the future, and the process has progressed from the most profound phase to more superficial topics.

At the Normalization or Instruction Stage, the session participants are informed on how the process of coping with a traumatic event will proceed, and what kinds of reactions, thoughts and feelings are characteristic in each stage. The aim is to give the participants a frame of reference, against which they can superimpose their own experiences. This knowledge and frame of reference of typical reactions is extremely important. When we know that our thoughts and feelings are quite normal, space is allowed for such feelings, and we are not alarmed or nervous even with severe reactions. Furthermore, the knowledge that the worst stages will pass with time brings relief and increases tolerance of reactions. We are able to endure these difficult days better, if we need not worry about how we feel.

In order to recover from a traumatic experience, it is not enough that we understand our reactions and feelings. It is not until we are also able to accept them that we find relief and our recovery is speeded up. Therefore, in normalizing reactions, the aim should be acceptance of the reactions, not simply their understanding.

In most successful sessions, a large part of normalization has already taken place before moving into the Normalization Stage. Here, the importance of the group format is evident. The fact that participants see and hear other people talk about their reactions, thoughts and feelings enables their recognition within themselves and the realization that the event has engendered powerful emotions in everybody. Normalization is more effective when we hear and see the reactions of others, rather than the leader describing them or reading out passages. Often, the Normalization Stage is a summary of issues that have emerged during the session, and the role of the leaders is vital. At the outset, the leader draws together typical thoughts, feelings and symptoms that have emerged during debriefing by referring to participants' words. He stresses the similarity of the reactions, but also how they differ from one another. Then he adds that all these reactions are perfectly normal in their situation.

Once the main reactions, thoughts and feelings have been dealt with, the session moves on to impart information and describe future reactions. The participants are told what to expect in the following days, weeks and months, and how they should approach these reactions. The leader continues to stress that they are common and normal on one hand, on the other that there are individual differences. An example of the importance of the Normalization

Stage and particularly preparation for future reactions is included in the chapter on the aims of psychological debriefing.

The Normalization Stage is also called the Instruction Stage. This means that all educational methods may be utilized. Particularly in large groups, I have used transparencies showing the stages of the coping process as a teaching aid. The participants should be given information on normal reactions, including those to come, in written form, so they can refer to them later.

When instructing victims on the stages of a traumatic crisis and their characteristic features, people often comment that they can identify with them all. When the same things are presented on a transparency prepared in advance, normalization of the reactions is guaranteed.

An important part of the Normalization Stage is also identification of control methods or coping strategies and their reinforcement. Discussion should be initiated among participants on what they usually do when they are feeling particularly bad. What kinds of methods do they employ to afford some relief? Some people take exercise, some take a sauna, listen to music, read poetry, paint, talk to themselves, some call a friend. There is any number of ways.

> After the Estonia shipwreck, a group of crew members at a debriefing session was discussing ways of controlling fear. They were talking about how they all set out their clothes carefully on a chair, so they could find them quickly in an emergency.
>
> The group also discussed things that increased their feelings of security in general. Someone had a good luck charm which made her feel safer; some said that a phone call home was the best possible security blanket.
>
> A young woman said that she felt safest when she felt her husband's chest hair against her cheek, and his special smell. The group came up with the idea that she should cut some of her husband's chest hair, put it in a little sachet and keep it on her pillow.

Another description of control methods comes from a person who was involved in a serious train crash. She describes the days following the accident:

> "I wanted to go cross-country skiing. Into the sparkling ski tracks and onward. I remembered that I needed new ski boots. There was a sports shop next door to the pharmacist's.
>
> I made a list in my mind of things that were good about my life at the moment that gave me strength and enjoyment. The list was surprisingly long.
>
> I walked to the lakeside and onto the long wooden pier, where last summer I had sunbathed on the hottest days of the century. The lake,

covered by ice and snow, glistened empty and vast; I visualized it with water skiers and sailing boats. The birch trunks gleamed white.

From the pier, I watched people taking a dip in an ice-hole nearby. Steaming, red-skinned figures popped into the black hole and everyone was laughing. There was something animal and alluring about the activity. I decided to try it one day.

I bought the ski boots and cold weather ski wax and visited the pharmacy. I laughed at myself when I stuffed Diazepam and Rex Blue ski wax in the same pocket. I swung the carrier bag containing my new yellow ski boots. I imagined the pharmacist wondering whether I would take my Diazepam before skiing or immediately after.

In the morning I had been full of anxiety and despair, but by the afternoon I was looking at the slippery line of ski tracks. I was as proud of my ski boots as a small boy.

The next few days were spent skiing on the snow-covered lake. It was as if Nature had helped the mind of the woman on sick leave; the sun shone every day. The cloudy sky and snowfall of the day of the crash became a more distant memory with every day." (Jokinen 1999, p.45)

The above is also an example of a very effective control method, namely writing. The problems in the Normalization Stage are:

- Normalization is begun too early, immediately after the Feelings Stage. Normalization is unsuccessful if the processing of the traumatic experience has not turned towards more superficial topics. If the transition to normalization comes too soon after discussing very profound topics, normalization seems artificial and the message does not get through.

- The leaders do not appreciate the importance of normalization and spend too little time on it. This is a problem especially with experienced leaders. They have been through normal reactions countless times and forget that this is a unique experience for those present, and the knowledge is quite new to them.

- Advance preparation is poor. A good teaching period needs to be properly prepared in advance. Literature handouts and transparencies or other materials must be ready.

- Important issues are omitted in normalization or in preparing for future reactions. We should remember that people take everything that is not named as normal in normalization to be pathological, unless the issue is mentioned separately.

The Closure Stage

The aims of the Closure Stage are:

- ensuring future coping
- direction to further therapy, if necessary.

Finally, the course of the session is briefly summarized and conclusions drawn on lessons learned from the session and the whole traumatic experience. At the Closure Stage, possible follow-up sessions are also agreed.

If the reactions of the participants are severe, or if it is likely that new material will emerge in the following weeks that may affect people's reactions, a follow-up session is arranged. This usually takes place, with the same participants, in about four weeks' time. If the debriefing session was held too early, during the shock stage, the follow-up should take place sooner, in a week or two.

The leaders should initiate the arrangements for a follow-up session. They can justify it by saying that it is only a few days since the shocking event, and that it would be useful to meet again in a few weeks to reassess the situation. They may emphasize that the purpose of the meeting is to ensure that everyone is coping.

A follow-up session is useful for the leaders, too. It is important to get an idea of how the coping process has progressed, especially with participants whose coping concerned the leaders. At the same time, the leaders have an opportunity of receiving feedback on their work.

Occasionally, reconvening the same group seems pointless or inappropriate. The group may have been too heterogeneous or contained awkward sub-groupings. In such cases the follow-up session could be held only for some of the participants, or perhaps the group could be split into two separate sessions.

The venue and date of the follow-up session should be fixed at the end of the debriefing session. It should not be left in the air. In that way, a sense of security is ensured for the participants, as well as continuity.

Sometimes, a full follow-up session seems unnecessary. Then the leaders may arrange to call certain group members in a couple of weeks.

Often, the call is made to the contact person who also helped arrange the session. This person is usually the most able to cope in the group. If the follow-up call is made only to him, a completely distorted picture of how the participants are coping may be the result. The leaders should call all the group members whose coping gave cause for concern.

After debriefing, an experienced leader can pretty reliably identify the participants who may require further therapy. The leader might ask them to stay behind after the session, in order to discuss the options alone and in confidence. Sometimes it falls on the leader to take charge of organizing further therapy.

The leaders should also instruct all group members on when to seek further therapy. A common rule of thumb is that if the symptoms continue to be as severe or more so for about a month, they should seek further help.

The timing of the follow-up session, too, is determined on this same basis. After a month, it is usually possible to assess whether the participants will cope with the help of debriefing, or whether they need further therapy.

Finally, the leaders should say that they will stay for a while, in case anyone wishes to talk to them in private. They give the participants their contact details and say that they may be called any time. After this, the session is closed by thanking the participants.

Role and duties of the leader in psychological debriefing

The leaders' role is central to psychological debriefing. In the model developed by Mitchell, the leaders keep the session together and control the transition from one stage to the next, in the correct order. In process-centred debriefing, the leaders' tasks and demands on them are increased and more diverse.

In customary debriefing, the leader does not usually comment on participants' words. He just thanks them and moves on to the next speaker. The participant tells him about some important, difficult feeling or thought, and then the focus moves on to someone else, who talks about some new issue that is important to him. Thus, the participants are left alone with their feelings and thoughts and they are not processed with the help of the leader and the group.

In my opinion, the leaders should take a more active part in the discussion in order to increase interaction. For example, when a participant describes something very important to him, the leader should acknowledge and accept the message: "This issue you mentioned is very important." He might also repeat the message content: "You have severe feelings of guilt." Once the leader has acknowledged and accepted the message in this way, the speaker is no longer alone with his feeling or thought.

PD is a group method. The significance of the group may be reinforced by analysing the discussion, not only based on the stages but also within them, so that a feeling or thought mentioned by an individual is discussed together. The leader's task is to direct the discussion. Once he has accepted a participant's feeling or thought, he could say: "Let's talk about this thought together. Do any others have feelings of guilt?" If a message emerges in the middle of another discussion, the situation may be organized by saying: "This issue you mentioned is important, but let's talk about this current issue first. We'll return to the new matter later." It is vital that the leader indeed remembers to return to the issue.

So, the leader's job is to organize, direct and move forward the coping process of the group and its members. The process may be moved on in three ways: deepened, expanded and moved forward.

Deepening takes place by asking the participant to describe his thought or feeling in greater detail. This helps the person himself gain a more organized and profound idea of his feeling.

In expanding the process, the group is utilized. The phenomenon – thought or feeling – is shared with other group members. The leader can facilitate sharing by asking whether others have similar thoughts or feelings. In this way, both similarities of reactions and individual differences are emphasized.

When the leader moves the process forward, he may present an interpretation of the phenomenon as a kind of summary. For example, he could say: "As we've seen, accusation is very common in such situations and the reason is that the event seems so unjust." Through the summary, the leader moves the discussion on to the next issue.

If the leader is able to organize the debriefing session in this way also within the stages, the session becomes much more profound and structured, which helps participants process their reactions more effectively.

In addition to directing the processing of a traumatic experience, the leaders should ensure that the participants are given equal space to discuss their feelings. One cannot be sure that a participant is silent during the session of his own free will. A traumatic experience can cause regression. Childlike needs arise within us, among them the need to rely on authority and to receive attention.

At a debriefing session, the participants test the leader, to see whether their presence is important to him. If the leader pays no attention to a person, although he has been silent for half an hour, he begins to feel hurt: "Am I not an important member of this group?" For this reason, the leaders should constantly monitor the members' participation in the discussion. If someone withdraws and is silent for a long time, he should be given space by having a question directed at him. Generally, people are very willing to talk about their feelings at the debriefing session.

A further task of the leaders is to help participants address feelings and thoughts that they are unable or afraid to process alone. This is achieved by the leader asking specific questions that move the process forward. This is what I mean by facing or confronting an issue. With difficult thoughts and feelings, it helps to confront and analyse them, so that the person is helped in a way to travel through the feeling. Avoidance, which is natural to us, only leads us astray.

Participants also often test whether an issue might be discussed by hinting at it in passing, as an aside. The leaders must be sensitive enough to recognize such hints. They should bring the issue into the discussion and process it.

> The debriefing session was drawing to a close, and the participants stood up to leave, when one person suddenly said: "One has all sorts of thoughts, but they can't be discussed because they might make others feel guilty."
>
> At this, the leaders said: "One moment, please sit down again. What do you mean by that?" She then disclosed thoughts that she had about the reasons for her daughter's suicide, and her boyfriend's role in them. We continued the session, and the thoughts and reactions they engendered in others were thoroughly discussed.

No relevant issue that surfaces at a debriefing session should be left unaddressed or put off till the follow-up session. It is the leaders' job to notice and address all important issues that emerge. The only exception is the case of individual earlier traumas which can be addressed after the session, but they should still be acknowledged at the session.

After a traumatic experience, people need authority. This also applies to leaders of debriefing sessions. They must take on the role of authority that is offered to them, and thus respond to the participants' needs. Anything that reduces this authority will simultaneously reduce the participants' sense of security. The leaders must prepare for the session diligently, to enable them to take on the necessary authority.

> After a debriefing session, the leaders learned second-hand about criticism by the participants that the leaders were insecure and needed papers to back them up. They had to look up instructions as to what to do next. Another criticism was that the leaders could not remember the participants' names.
>
> The leaders were concerned and dismayed by the criticism. They had felt that the session was very successful. The critics did not imply that the session had not been useful or that it had been unsuccessful. The crux of the criticism was that the leaders were unable to fulfil the participants' need for authority.

This is why the leader must never disclose that he is taking this role for the first time. The leaders must be able to present a more assured image than they feel inside. In order to maintain authority, the leader should not use notes, but must learn his lines well and rely on the assistants' help.

Leading a debriefing session is an extremely demanding task, as it involves working with people whose state of mind is particularly sensitive and vulnerable. Consequently, the professional skills of debriefing leaders should be a matter for special attention. To lead a session in such a way that all the above-mentioned objectives are fulfilled and opportunities fully utilized, the leader should possess at least the following:

- thorough knowledge of crisis and trauma psychology
- knowledge of group dynamics and group leadership skills
- thorough knowledge of the psychological debriefing method and practical skills in session leadership
- teaching skills.

So many diverse phenomena and issues arise at a PD session that all the objectives are never reached. Something is always missed. All the issues that arise are never successfully addressed. The leaders must accept this. In spite of it, they must strive for perfection every time.

The follow-up session

At the Closure Stage of a PD session, the time and place of the follow-up session should be fixed. These arrangements should be left open only in exceptional cases, because fixing them affects the coping process by adding continuity and security.

At the follow-up session, the same issues are no longer discussed as at the actual debriefing session. If something particularly concerned the leaders at the actual session, they may bring it up, but otherwise they should only refer to the actual session for feedback. The follow-up session may well be started by discussing how the participants perceived the actual session, and how they have been since.

The focus of the follow-up session is what has happened since the actual session. If a loved one has died, the possible occasion of viewing the deceased and saying goodbye may be talked through, as well as the feelings it evoked. Similarly, the funeral and the thoughts and feelings that arose from it are discussed. If the participants were given, for example, tasks connected with controlling fear, execution of the tasks and the experiences gained are discussed.

Overall, the function of the follow-up session is to ascertain how the processing of the traumatic experience has progressed, and whether the aims set for debriefing have been reached. In addition, an assessment is made of how far the participants have come in facing the truth and accepting the event, and how far they are in working through the thoughts and feelings evoked by the experience. Do they still suffer from intrusive memory images, somatic symptoms, are they able to sleep, do they have nightmares, and how do they view their reactions? Have they returned to work, how are they coping with work, and have their lives otherwise returned to normal?

At the follow-up session, opportunities for actual interventions are rather slight, as the mind is already closed up. Thus, the follow-up session no longer involves objectives that affect the actual process.

An important function of the follow-up session is to assess whether the participants are able to continue processing their traumatic experience, so that the process is not disrupted and a trauma formed. If the experience is denied or blocked, and the person cannot begin to accept what has happened, or if the process has become fixated in another stage, the person should be referred for further psychotherapy.

Quick and comprehensive referral to further therapy is vitally important. Psychological traumas tend to ruin people's lives by stealthily affecting their decisions and choices, without the person being aware of it. If they are directed into therapy sufficiently quickly, this is avoided.

A general practitioner referred to my clinic a man who two years previously had been subjected to a serious armed robbery and held hostage for several hours. The seriousness of the situation is well illustrated by the fact that he was forced to load the weapon with which he was to be shot.

Now, two years later, he had problems in meeting people. He avoided them by crossing the road, he avoided eye contact with them, and he even found it hard to leave his home.

In my assessment, it was obvious that a traumatic experience had given rise to a severe psychological trauma, which had led to serious mental breakdown. I made him an appointment for the following week.

He did not turn up at the clinic. Instead, I received a letter from his mother at my home the day before. In the letter, the mother elucidated the events between the traumatic event and seeking help from his family doctor.

The traumatic event took place at his workplace. Subsequently, he visited a psychiatrist a couple of times, but did not feel that this was helping him. A couple of days after the event he took a holiday and spent it drinking heavily.

He applied for a place to study a subject that interested him, and was accepted. But he was unable to study. His heavy drinking continued, and gradually led to total alcoholism and uncontrollable spending. The mother doubted that the son would turn up at the clinic, and predicted that he would cover up his alcohol misuse, as he had with the doctor.

She was right. The son never turned up at the clinic, and never contacted me. However, this case is a good example of how quickly a person's life can be ruined, if he fails to receive expert help with his traumatic experience quickly enough.

Early referral to therapy is such an important issue that the achievement of this goal alone justifies psychological debriefing as worthwhile and economically viable.

13

Children as Victims of Traumatic Events

Children are underestimated

Where traumatic events are concerned, adults tend to underestimate children in practically every respect. Adults are particularly dismissive of children's ability to notice and perceive events:

- 'Children notice nothing.' Parents often think that children do not notice that anything special has happened in the family. For example, research has shown parents to believe that children do not hear their nocturnal fights, and that consequently they need not be discussed with the children. Children usually notice everything, but keep their knowledge from the parents.

- 'It is not necessary to tell children the whole truth.' A facet of the same belief is the idea that difficult traumatic events can be kept hidden from children, or that partial truth is sufficient for them. In this respect, too, children are much more observant than adults think.

- 'A child is only superficially aware of traumatic events and will forget them quickly.' Children are also underestimated in respect of their ability to understand traumatic events. The fact that the child does not talk about them does not mean that they do not prey on his mind. Adults often think that because the child does not talk about a subject, he does not remember the incident.

- Children are also underestimated in respect of their ability to process shocking events. Crisis workers are constantly surprised by children's incredible ability to work through difficult and shocking experiences.

- Children's ability to recover from traumatic experiences is underestimated. If children are provided with optimal opportunities for processing the traumatic experience, they will recover from it more quickly and fully than adults.

The greatest problem in children's processing of traumatic events is posed by the fact that their ability to do so is dependent on the ability of adults to process children's experiences with them. Since adults almost invariably underestimate the child in every respect in relation to traumatic events, it follows that they are incapable of offering such an optimal opportunity.

Special features of children's traumatic experiences

Children as victims of traumatic events

Children may become victims of traumatic events in many ways. A child may be involved in the incident, or his loved ones may die, be injured or become disabled. The child may be forced to call for help or to give first aid, if he is the first on the scene. A child may also be an eyewitness or hear about the incident from friends at school.

Naturally, the nature of the incident and the child's role in it has a bearing on what the child experiences and how he reacts. A child's experience is largely determined by what kind of significance attaches to the event in the child's world. Younger children may be frightened only by the loud noise, rapid movement, or the parents' shocked reactions, for example in a road accident. Through the parents' reaction, the incident may evoke insecurity as well as fear. If the child does not immediately see his parents, or the parents do not respond to the child as usual, his insecurity is increased.

As children's semiotic worlds expand, the impact of traumatic events on them resembles adult experiences more and more. The fear that something bad will happen to a loved one, that the parents or siblings will die, is typical even in relatively young children, especially if they have experienced long separations or losses.

The Finnish actress, Satu Silvo, recalled in public the first moments after her accident [Ms Silvo was crushed by a snow compacting machine on a ski slope. She was seriously injured, but later made a good recovery.] Her young son saw the accident. The boy came up to his badly injured mother and said: "Are you going to die, Mum?"

Children may take the role of eyewitness, or give first aid and call for help.

> A family lived in two adjoining apartments in an apartment block. The mother lived with their three children and the father alone in the flat next-door. The mother was out and the children were at their father's.
>
> Suddenly, an unknown man and woman forced their way in, and the man began to threaten the father, pointing a gun at him. The father stood up, and the man began to shoot. The woman yelled: "Kill him!"
>
> The eldest of the children surreptitiously took the smaller children to their mother's home and hid them in a closet. Then he ran to the nearest phone booth and called for help.
>
> He returned to the vicinity of the building to wait and to warn his mother, in case she was returning home. The boy was aged 11.
>
> The police and ambulance arrived before the mother. The strangers had already left. The father was taken to hospital by ambulance. He was hit in the leg, but survived. When the father had been taken to hospital, the boy remembered that the younger siblings were still in the closet. They had been in the closet, terrified, for over an hour.

The youngest child was aged six, but she fully understood that both the father's and the children's lives had been in danger. Parents usually have difficulty in telling children about a shocking event. They often think that the children may be told later, when they have overcome their own shock a little. At the beginning of this book, there is a good example of what happens if parents delay telling children shocking news.

> The father of two children died on his way to work. The children, aged 10 and 12, were staying with their grandparents hundreds of kilometres away. The mother was unsure how to tell the children, whether to wait until they returned home, or tell them as soon as she could contact them.
>
> I suggested that she tell them immediately, but first she should tell the grandparents the shocking news, with instructions to take care of the children. Then she should tell each child personally that their father had died. This she did. The mother first gave the tragic news to the grandfather and talked to him. Then she told the grandmother that her son had died, and that she would tell the children. She told first the elder child, and finally the younger child about their father's death. During the phone call, they agreed that the grandparents would bring the children home the following day.

Children's thinking reflects on traumatic experiences

The child's developmental stage has a bearing on how he experiences a traumatic incident. Typical characteristics of children are:

- *Short attention span.* A child is unable to concentrate on one thing for very long. This is why children's reactions to a traumatic event are intermittent. For example, if a child's loved one has died, he may grieve desperately for a moment, and then become immersed in playing with friends as if nothing had happened. This does not mean that his grieving is over. It will return at some point, only to pass again relatively quickly. A psychologist who works a great deal with children described children's grieving as 'brief grief'.

- *Concrete thinking.* Children think of traumatic events in a concrete way. They are interested in concrete things. Parents may be surprised by the questions children ask. For instance, if the children's father has died, they may be interested in whereabouts he was hurt, what he looks like now, and where he is.

  > An 11-year-old girl was knocked down by a car on a pedestrian crossing, where she had the green light. The girl was on her way to school. She was thrown 18 metres by the force of the collision.
  >
  > The girl recovered from her injuries quickly and was sent home from hospital after 12 days. During the first days, she was angry with her parents who kept saying that she had been run over by a car. "I was not run over by any car!" she raged.
  >
  > The parents thought that the child was so shocked about her accident that she was completely denying it. When the girl was asked to describe the event in more detail, she said that the car ran into her and she flew many metres through the air, but she was not run over.

  This example shows how concrete a child's thinking is, which in fact in this case also helped the accuracy of her perceptions.

- *Egocentric thinking and perception of the world.* To a child, he is the centre of the world. Often, a child finds an explanation for life events in what he has done or thought. That is why children often suffer from guilt feelings in connection with traumatic events. To adults, the feelings may seem senseless, and they do not listen to the child but belittle his words. This may cause the child unbearable pain. Children may imagine that their thoughts come true. This is sometimes interpreted as superstition. However, the important point is that we recognize children's ideas that their bad thoughts have come true, and that consequently they must be responsible for what happened. Children's thoughts should be taken seriously.

A young family had two children, a four-year-old girl and a baby boy a few weeks old. One morning, the mother found her son in bed blue and limp. It was a case of cot death.

I visited the family to offer support on the same day. I told the parents that siblings are often very jealous of the baby and wish that it did not exist or for it to die. Now that the baby had died, his sister might believe that it was her fault, as she may have had such thoughts about her brother.

The actual debriefing session was arranged in two days' time. At the session, the father said that his daughter had asked him the day before if she had been the cause of her brother's death. The father had asked her what made her think that, and the girl had replied, "Because I sometimes wished that my baby brother was dead".

The father was very glad that he had been warned about this. He said that he had thought the idea strange when I mentioned it. However, it helped him respond correctly to the girl's words. He was able to take them seriously and discuss the idea thoroughly with her, thus alleviating her guilt feelings.

Children's special needs reflected in their reactions

Children are dependent on their parents in many ways. For this reason, the parents' reliability is vital from the child's point of view. After a traumatic event, children's need to trust their parents and families is particularly great. On the other hand, shocking experiences often sorely test this trust.

Parents sometimes try to conceal the whole event from the children, or delay telling them about it, so they sense something is wrong and their imagination is fired. They may develop various theories about the event, and because children are egocentric, they often think that they themselves have done something to cause it.

Delaying telling the truth, or telling only a partial truth, is always perceived as a breach of trust. If the child hears about the event from outsiders, it is often impossible to rebuild the child's trust in his parents.

I described a case earlier, where a bomb was thrown into the yard of a drug squad officer at his home. The family had two young children. The parents sent the children to their grandparents out of town immediately after the incident. They thought it best to allow the situation to settle. When the children returned home, there was no need to tell them about the incident.

I advised them that their plan was doomed to failure. The children were in daycare. Their friends would rush to tell them on the first day that someone threw a bomb into their yard, and then the children's trust in their parents would be destroyed. I encouraged them to tell the children, to answer their questions honestly, and to talk to them about all the issues that the incident elicited in their minds.

They followed my advice. The elder of the children asked: "Was the bomb like the one in the Donald Duck cartoon?" The children viewed the whole incident in a concrete way, and it did not concern them for long. No particular reactions were evident.

Thus, the fundamental issue in all shocking events is that children are able to maintain their trust in their parents. The parents should also try to alleviate children's fears associated with the parents' reactions. Children may be frightened by the parents crying, being sad, not managing to do things, being unable to concentrate. The parents must tell the child that crying is not dangerous, and include the child in their grieving. The parents should be able to accept their own reactions and be open about them. This is then transmitted to the children.

If parents are embarrassed about their own reactions, the children will pick this up. They try to protect their parents and avoid mentioning things that they know will affect them. In this way, children are left alone with their thoughts and feelings, and they cannot find solace in their parents' support.

Protecting the parents may go to such lengths that if they have not told the children about a shocking event and the children find out about it elsewhere, they do not tell their parents that they know, fearing their reaction. In this way, the children are bound in an atmosphere of secrecy that leads to suffering for everyone. The consequences will manifest in all future situations where the children's trust in their parents is required.

Children also need security. A traumatic event always causes feelings of insecurity. Consequently, children's need for security after a shocking event is generally exaggerated and shows in their behaviour. They want to be near the parents more than usual. They particularly crave physical contact; the parents should hold and cuddle their children much more than usual.

Conversely, an exaggerated need for security may manifest as fears. If a family member has died, children are afraid that something may happen to others, too. This is why it is important for the parents to pay particular attention to keeping promises. If they have promised to be home at a certain time, they should stick to it. For example, a father had died in a road accident. The mother took the children to daycare and said that she would pick them up later. "Will you come for sure?" the children asked. The mother replied: "I will, if I'm alive."

Making children feel more secure takes priority even over honesty. In the above example, the mother gave an honest answer, but she also increased her children's sense of insecurity. In children's eyes, adults are omnipotent. When something very shocking happens in the family, the adults' omnipotence must be reappraised. The parents were unable to prevent the accident, fire or death.

Adults sometimes try to maintain the children's idea of their omnipotence by concealing their emotions. Difficult experiences are not discussed in the children's presence and emotions must not be expressed, in case the child is upset. Thus, adults give children a distorted idea of how they perceive the event. This also restricts the children's opportunity of expressing their own feelings and thoughts. At the risk of delivering a serious knock to adults' omnipotence, it is important that emotional reactions are allowed in the family for all its members. By showing an example and by explaining and talking about their feelings and about expressing them, the adult becomes human, and the child, too, is able to express his feelings more openly.

In the traumatic, threatening situation itself, children may seek safety by hiding. For example, in fires children are frequently found under beds, in closets or other hiding places.

Rescue personnel should be aware of this tendency of children, as it helps find them in critical situations. It is worth looking for children in so-called good hiding places. This is true of both fires and other dangerous situations.

> Atle Dyregrov reports a shocking experience from the Rwandan war. A 12-year-old boy was forced to witness a horrific bloodbath, when his entire family of 13 was murdered. The parents, grandparents and all his siblings were slaughtered in their home and left in a heap. Finally, a soldier came back to check that nobody had survived. The boy hid under his family's bodies and survived.

Sometimes children lose both parents, or the parents are so shocked that they are unable to provide security for the children. In such situations, the importance of substitute adults is great. Grandparents, aunts, uncles, and parents' friends can assume the role of substitute adult. They can support the children and concentrate on them differently from the parents, who may themselves be broken by grief and absolutely drained.

Long-term effects of children's traumatic experiences

Children's ability to cope with traumatic experiences is thus largely dependent on the ability of their closest adults to help with processing the experience. Children do not always receive sufficient support or manage to recover from a shocking experience without long-term effects. A typical long-term effect is regression to earlier developmental stages. The child may lose skills already mastered in any area. He might wet the bed again, his speech might regress or his motor skills weaken.

Children who have experienced a shocking event are often restless and have difficulty in concentration. Consequently, their education may suffer. Another typical response is a short future perspective. For example, the child may think that he will die young. He cannot envisage himself as an adult, has no career ambitions, dreams of his own family, or generally any dreams for the future. Compulsive repetitive games are also associated with deep anxiety.

Children may also present with somatic problems. Headaches, abdominal pains and muscle pains are typical long-term problems after traumatic experiences. Their appetite may also fluctuate and their physical development slow down.

I have touched, above, on reactions to traumatic events that are especially typical of children. Some clear differences from adults are apparent. They result from levels of thinking characteristic of children and from their special needs. However, it is surprising how mature and adult-like children are in their reactions to traumatic events.

Children's ways of coping with traumatic experiences

I have repeatedly stressed the importance of adults in facilitating children's processing of traumatic experiences. However, children also have their own means of coping with them. One of them is play. Through play, they defuse pressures built up by the traumatic event, re-enact the event itself, examine it from a different angle, from different roles, with different outcomes.

> After the Estonia disaster, children were often seen at swimming pools playing 'Estonia'. This was a game where each drew his lungs full of air and then sank to the bottom of the pool. The children competed at who could stay underwater the longest.
>
> Adults were horrified. But through this game, the children familiarized themselves with the disaster and experimented how long it was possible to stay underwater without breathing. It is quite likely that they were also defusing the anxiety evoked by the disaster.

After a close person has died, children often play at dying, hospitals or funerals. Through their play, they personally get to know the phenomena that preoccupy them, but in a secure atmosphere.

Adults may be horrified and forbid such play. But they do the children a disservice: they are denying them the processing of the traumatic event they have experienced and that preoccupies them, in their own way. Adults can rarely offer them an alternative method.

The crucial dimension in play is pretending. This means that children incorporate and fulfil their creativity in play. Play is based on children's imagination, and imagination must have its place also in playing at traumatic experiences. Then the games are healing and promote adaptation.

I have already mentioned repetitive play, from which creativity and use of imagination has been lost. The play is compulsive repetition of a certain experience, and does not bring the child relief or promote processing of the traumatic experience. In this case, adults should help the child modify the play, to help him control its traumatic content better. This is achieved by changing the outcome, changing roles, or through other ways of bringing new perspectives to the play.

For children, too, communication of the facts is vitally important in creating a sense of security. However, the information must be concrete and appropriate for the child's thinking.

Some years ago, I saw an interesting video at a psychology conference. The subject was therapy of children traumatized by the Armenian earthquake. Local psychologists had no idea about modern disaster psychology, but they had developed many original solutions that fully corresponded with current knowledge.

One of these solutions was taking children to see houses being built, and particularly how they were built to be strong enough to withstand earthquakes. In this way, the children's fear of being inside houses was alleviated. In their experience, houses collapsed.

Mental imagery exercises can also help produce a sense of security in children and enable them to control their fear.

Another interesting method described on the video was one named 'aromatherapy' by the film makers. Apparently, one of the traumatizing factors in an earthquake is the strong foul smell following the quake. In children, these bad smells were associated with a feeling of threat and caused them fears.

The children were lying down on mattresses and they were relaxed both physically and mentally. They were told to imagine the smell of baking bread. By learning to control their fear on an imaginary level by imagining the smell of fresh bread, the children's sense of security was enhanced.

Drawing is another way of processing traumatic experiences that is characteristic of children. By drawing, they express features and details of the incident that are important to them. Adults should discuss children's drawings with them, ask them what they have drawn, what their story is. This is an entry point into processing important issues from the child's perspective.

At the start of this chapter, I described an incident where the father of three children was the victim of violence, and where the eldest brother first hid the younger children and then went to raise the alarm. The younger children stayed hiding in the closet, terrified, for over an hour, before their big brother came to save them. The youngest children refused to speak after the incident. However much the mother and brother tried to encourage them, they would not say a word.

At the psychological debriefing session, the silent children became enthusiastic about drawing the incident. The leaders had equipped themselves with considerable quantities of paper and crayons, but the paper ran out in the middle of the session. The youngest child's first words after the incident were "more paper". By drawing, the six- and eight-year-old children were able to describe and process what they had experienced during that shocking hour.

After the session, the children began to speak. Drawing had unblocked their channels of self-expression, and now they were able to process their traumatic experiences by talking, too.

Even babies, who cannot yet talk, find a channel to enable them to process a traumatic experience. Parents report that babies' traumatic experiences may result in restlessness, irritability, sleeping problems and clinging, so that the child cannot bear to let the parent out of his sight.

With older children, writing may be the easiest channel of processing a traumatic experience. A method often employed, for example, in cases of sudden loss is to ask the children to write the deceased person a goodbye letter, to say everything that remained unsaid because of the sudden death. Writing the letter makes the event more real and easier to accept.

Some adolescents write poetry, some work through their traumatic experiences using music, either making it themselves or listening to it. The crucial thing is that children and adolescents should find some method of processing their traumatic experiences, so that their adverse impact does not emerge later in life.

Children and psychological debriefing

Children should always be included in PD. Provision of debriefing is often justified particularly by the children's need for support. The same phenomenon is also evident in the approach by crisis workers. A debriefing session is recommended particularly if there are children in the family.

There is no age limit for participating children. If it is known in advance that children will be present, a special leader is usually provided who is experienced in working with children. Drawing equipment, books and perhaps toys, too, are provided.

Sometimes an incident may touch a large number of children. For example, the target group may be the children of a playground, residential community, daycare centre, a school class or a sports team. In such cases, two parallel sessions might be organized, one for the children and one for their parents, so the children can together process the incident with a specialized children's leader, and the adults can do so among themselves.

Young children are usually incapable of paying attention throughout the session. For this reason, it is best to go through the Factual Stage together with the whole family or group of relatives. Afterwards, the children can withdraw to their own corner or another room to draw and play with their own leader. Finally, the children return to the main session, and everyone discusses what they have drawn and talked about.

If a separate session is held for the children and there are a number of them, the facts should again be addressed together, and then the children may be divided into small groups, each with its own leader. The children's thoughts and feelings are discussed in the groups, and the session is closed with everyone together. In this way, the exhaustion of children's short attention span is prevented, and the processing is intensive and deep.

Children are surprisingly capable of processing traumatic events. Seven–eight-year-olds are perfectly able to work in an adults' group, provided that there are not many of them. The important thing is that they are allowed space to address their reactions, and that their reactions and feelings are respected as equal to those of adults. The leader must ensure that parents do not speak for their children, but that the children themselves are permitted to describe their feelings and thoughts.

Seven- or eight-year-olds astonish by their ability to describe both the course of events and their own thoughts, feelings and reactions at various stages of the incident. Children's approach is uniquely fresh and genuine, qualities that may be lacking with adults; children often bring a completely new dimension to working through the event and the reactions elicited by it.

We will return to the family where the 11-year-old daughter was knocked down on a pedestrian crossing, while crossing the road on a green light. The debriefing session was held the day after the girl had been released from hospital. The session had been prepared with care. The leaders had discussed it with the parents. Both were very worried about how the girl would cope with reviewing the facts, because they felt that she was denying the incident. They wanted to make sure that the leaders observed the child's reactions and kept the discussion on a level appropriate for her.

The session was held at the girl's home. She arrived a little late, on crutches, so we had to wait for a while. She had three books with her and pretended to read. She had a book in front of her at all times.

We began in the customary way, explaining the purpose of the session, what would happen, the rules, etc. Then we moved on to the facts. The girl pretended to read, but followed the discussion closely, as she always gave an immediate answer when she was asked something.

We began to go over the incident from the morning of the day of the accident. What kind of a morning was it for each family member? We got to setting off to school, and the parents to work. We talked through the journey to school with the girl, and what she remembered of the accident. Then we moved on to how the other family members learned about the accident, what they were doing at the time, and what they did on hearing the news. We also went over the parents' arrival at the hospital and the events there.

I had prepared for the session by contacting the investigating police officers, and learned from them the course of events at the scene. The father had talked to an eyewitness, who was also the key police witness.

We returned to the moment of the accident, after which the girl remembered nothing. She regained consciousness in hospital, and her next memory images were from there.

I asked the father to tell everyone what he knew about the course of the accident. He became extremely anxious, his pulse raced, his breathing quickened, and he asked what he should disclose and whether everyone present would be able to cope with the information. We encouraged him to describe the accident in as great detail as possible, exactly as the eyewitness had told him. We assured him that everyone would be able to cope.

The father described the course of the accident, how the car struck the girl, how she was thrown through the air a distance of 18 metres onto the grass verge, how the ambulance arrived quickly and the paramedics administered first aid and got her swiftly to hospital. Then we asked the girl what the description sounded like. She said that it was exciting, and asked a couple of specific questions. The father described the incident very accurately. I confirmed this by saying that I had spoken to the police but had no new information to add.

After the Factual Stage the girl relaxed. She put down her books and participated actively in the discussion. This is a good example of how parental anxiety is transferred to children and causes inhibitions that they may not otherwise have.

The following example demonstrates children's ability to address very sensitive and traumatic experiences:

A family had broken up some years ago and the 11-year-old son lived with his mother. The parents had got along better recently, and the boy entertained hopes that they might get back together.

The father committed suicide in rather suspicious circumstances after spending the evening out of town with a group of friends. Regardless of the circumstances, it was clearly a case of suicide.

The mother learned the tragic news during the night. The boy was asleep and did not wake up, nor was he woken. The mother told him in the morning that his father was dead, but not that it was suicide. Encouraged by the crisis counsellor, however, she told the boy the truth later that day.

The debriefing session was held at their home. When the leader arrived, she saw the boy slip into the bathroom. He emerged with his hair slicked down with water and announced that he was ready to start: "You did come here because of me."

The session proceeded in the usual way. They went over what was known about the events, where and how the father had killed himself, how they were told, who else was present, etc. They talked about when the boy last saw his father, what the meeting was like, and how they parted. The discussion went on to when they had arranged to meet again and what their plans for the future had been.

The participants', including the son's, thoughts about the death and particularly the suicide were addressed. The boy recalled memories of his father and what they had done together. He got a photo of his father to show the leader what he looked like. He talked about the trips abroad they had made, and suddenly he said to the leader: "Wait a minute." He went to get a pine cone they had brought back from a shared trip. He extracted a seed from the cone, gave it to the leader and said: "This is a lucky seed. I'm giving it to you."

In their honesty and directness, children may also bring out very important new perspectives on the incident:

We will return to the incident when a truck ran over a seven-year-old boy resulting in his death. At the debriefing session, the truck driver's fifteen-year-old daughter expressed her anger towards the dead boy: "Barging into the road so carelessly and causing my dad such pain."

This was a point of view nobody had expressed before, as it was thought that the deceased could not be accused or criticized. However, the daughter's view helped substantially to relieve her father's guilt feelings.

Children also provide feedback about the importance of the debriefing session:

The thirty-year-old father of a family was killed in an accident. The family had three children, the eldest eight years and the youngest four weeks old.

It was the family custom always to ask the children at bedtime what had been best about that day. The question was asked also on the day the family had their debriefing session after the father's death. The eight-year-old replied: "The session." "Why?" asked the mother. "Because we did some straight talking about important things."

When the participants of a PD session include parents, children's typical reactions to traumatic incidents are always discussed, as well as how the event should be addressed with them. This must be done regardless of whether the children are present at the session or not. Parents always need coaching in how they can alleviate their children's anxiety, how to go about helping the child to process his own experiences. Children have a phenomenal ability to process shocking experiences, but they always need an adult's help and support.

Parents have a hard time coping with traumatic experiences. In order to be able to help their children, they must themselves courageously confront difficult thoughts and feelings. If they are unable to do so, they are also unable to help their children.

A child's anxiety and pain is heartrending. Parents may protect themselves from witnessing such pain, and attempt to 'protect' the child from shocking information and feelings. However, this is an impossible task. Parents cannot protect the child. They may succeed in protecting themselves from facing the child's pain, but at the same time they are not helping the child at all in processing his suffering.

As well as their parents, children also have other adults in their lives, such as daycare staff, teachers, coaches and club leaders. With children under seven, it is advantageous if traumatic experiences are processed with them by an adult who is familiar and safe. Sometimes it is appropriate for crisis counsellors to help daycare staff work through the event and the associated thoughts and feelings. In this way, the staff is coached in crisis work with the children in this special situation.

For example, in cases where a pupil has died, it is usually expedient for the school to utilize expert help. The teacher should be present in debriefing sessions for lower grade pupils. With older students it is usually best that there are no teachers present at the class session.

In connection with children's debriefing sessions at daycare centres, schools and leisure activity circles, it is important to inform the parents of the session in such a way that they understand their children's reactions and questions and are aware of the issues that were discussed with the children. In some situations, it is useful to organize a special session for the parents. It gives them the opportunity of airing their own thoughts and feelings about the event. They can also be informed about children's typical reactions and ways of processing traumatic experiences, and how parents can help and support them.

Addressing children's traumatic experiences is at least as important as addressing those of adults. Many psychological traumas that impinge on our personalities and lives stem from childhood. Children's and adults' reactions to and processing of traumatic incidents are surprisingly similar. In this chapter, I have touched on the specific features of children's reactions. The majority of previous descriptions of adults' reactions and processing of traumatic experiences also applies to children.

It would seem that children's ability to process traumatic experiences develops very early. In many respects, children cope better than adults, but they do need adults' support and help.

14

When Work Traumatizes

Traumatic experiences and stress

Psychologists working with professional people approach traumatic incidents from the perspective of stress. Traumatic incidents cause considerable stress to employees. It may be compounded by other factors, such as excessive workload, continuous rush, duties that are too demanding, monotonous work, interpersonal relations in the workplace and management problems.

In this chapter, I will focus specifically on stress caused by traumatic incidents and its impact. In addition, I will look at the concepts of cumulative stress and burnout, and their relationship with traumatic stress.

Distinguishing features of stress

Stress is a concept of relativity. It describes the relationship of extraneous circumstantial factors or so-called stress factors to personality factors, such as abilities, skills and goals. If these factors are badly out of balance, we experience stress.

Few extraneous circumstantial factors in themselves cause stress. Its development is always related to internal personality factors. For example, if an employee has so much work that he cannot complete it, this will cause particularly severe stress for an employee whose goal is to finish all his work. It will cause a negligible amount of stress for an employee whose attitude to his work is *laissez-faire*, with the principle that he will do as much as he can and leave the rest.

Excessively undemanding and boring work is not a stress factor for an employee who has no confidence in himself and his abilities. On the contrary, he is very happy with easy work, and feels that he is competent. But an employee who feels that he has the resources for much more demanding work would be stressed by the work being too easy.

Development of stress usually sets into motion so-called coping mechanisms directed at reducing the stress and coping with the situation. There are many kinds. Some aim to reduce stress by denying or blocking it, or by distancing oneself from it. Others contain emotional reaction to stress, or attempts at resolving the situation and permanently reducing stress. Some coping strategies are more effective than others.

Some examples of denial, blocking or distancing of stress are refusing to recognize stress, denying its existence, or using alcohol, drugs, medication or, particularly with women, excessive cleaning, washing up or other activities in order to have something else to think about.

An emotional coping pattern includes, for example, accusing or directing aggression towards others, or else self-accusations, crying and depression. The coping patterns directed at permanent stress reduction contain actions aiming to resolve the problem: discussing it with people, thinking about it, considering what has led to the situation and how it could be solved, or active stress-reducing tactics.

Pöyhönen (1987) identified two principal strategies in stress processing. 'The pain avoidance strategy' is characterized by negative assessment of work stress and an avoiding, evasive and emotional approach. 'The growth strategy' includes flexible, optimistic and problem-solving activity in stress situations at work.

Stress is not intrinsically bad. Moderate stress is actually a prerequisite of effective working. Even severe, reasonably sustained stress may lead to a positive outcome, feelings of success and increased self-esteem. Good examples of such stress are preparing for a difficult examination or completing a demanding work assignment.

However, at least once in every 24 hours, we should attain a stress-free state. Mostly, this is achieved at night in peaceful sleep. We can endure continuous stress over several days if we can detach ourselves from it, for example, at weekends or days off. A person can endure sustained stress over several weeks if he knows that the endpoint is in sight, when he will be able to rest and defuse the stress.

The most problematic is cumulative stress. No end for the stress is in sight, but various factors cause and add to the stress continuously. Such cumulative stress will lead to burnout if it is not possible to defuse it.

The individual will burn out and be no longer able to control the stress, as it takes on a life of its own. By now, the usual relaxation and stress reduction strategies no longer help, but what is required is detachment of months or even years from the work environment, psychotherapy to treat self-esteem and other problems, and structural reorganization of the work. Burnout, particularly in its scientifically defined form, is a very serious condition.

Traumatic incidents cause very severe stress. External stress factors are so powerful that personality does not have an effect on the phenomenon to the same degree as in cases of less severe stress factors. Traumatic events put everyone's endurance under extreme pressure. Figure 14.1 represents traumatic stress and cumulative stress.

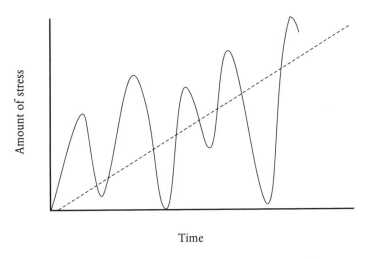

Figure 14.1   *Traumatic (——) stress and cumulative stress (----)*

If traumatic stress can be effectively processed, it will reduce from its maximum point relatively quickly. If, on the other hand, it is compounded with other work-related stress or several successive traumatic incidents, there is a danger of accumulation of stress with all the associated risk factors.

Traumatic experiences at work

Some occupations create continuous traumatic experiences for employees. Such occupations include, for example, rescue work, police work, many healthcare professions, some assignments of journalists and photographers, and acute crisis work.

These occupations or assignments bring about two kinds of occupational stress. On one hand, the employee must deal daily with people who have experienced traumatic incidents. Meeting these people and witnessing their pain and suffering in itself causes stress and traumatic experiences also for the workers, the helpers.

In addition, these people are sometimes subjected to threatening situations in the course of their work. The situations are not always resolved in a positive way. Thus, the workers themselves may experience traumatic events in the course of their work, causing them personal shock.

There are certain factors that contribute to the fact that similar traumatic events do not cause experienced helpers such severe traumatic experiences as they do so-called laymen. Such factors are:

1. *Self-selection.* Such occupations are usually sought by people who possess high levels of stress tolerance and who cope with difficult situations better than is usual. The selection process, too, attaches importance to factors demonstrating high stress thresholds.

2. *Training.* Training usually includes preparation of employees for their future duties and their traumatic effects.

3. *Experience.* Accumulated experience naturally affects our perceptions of various situations. When experience is gained in a great variety of incidents, it brings a calm approach and ability to cope with these situations. However, the prerequisite of coping is that the person is able to process the traumatic experiences 'out' so that they do not become encapsulated.

4. *Practice.* Practice exercises, when difficult tasks are rehearsed, create preparedness for dealing with them. Situations that are new, with no prior experience of them, are usually the most stressful.

5. *Preparation.* Emergency personnel are usually given some information on the nature of the incident when the alarm is raised. In the few minutes that it takes to reach the scene, they are able psychologically to prepare for what they are likely to encounter and experience. This prior preparation has a significant effect on how traumatic the experience becomes. Sometimes the information is inaccurate or the incident involves an element of surprise, such as the helper knowing the victim. Then the experience is more traumatic than usual.

6. *Professional role.* The role of the professional protects a person from his own personal emotions. While concentrating on the task at hand, there is no time to see and perceive everything. Often, the reactions come when the professional role is discharged, making space for personal reactions.

The above factors raise a professional's perceptual threshold of traumatic experiences, so that they do not perceive as traumatic incidents what the rest of us would consider shocking. In private life, this difference does not exist. When a doctor, fireman or policeman loses his wife or child in an accident, his experience of the incident is just as shocking as anybody else's.

However, certain work situations may be classified as traumatic incidents, even taking into account the above factors that increase tolerance to stress.

Such situations are:

- when the victim is a child
- when the worker's life is in danger while performing his duties
- when a colleague is injured or killed in the course of his duties
- when the task is prolonged, particularly taxing, or unsuccessful
- when one is forced to shoot at, injure or kill a person in the course of one's duties (police)
- when the number of victims is large (major disasters).

These situations are usually perceived as traumatic, however experienced and well trained the worker may be. In addition, the work may contain individual incidents that engender a great deal of traumatic stress, either owing to personal reasons or the special features of the incident. An example of such a situation is cruel sexual abuse of children that an official is forced to investigate in the course of his work.

When work continually causes traumatic stress and traumatic experiences, the employee must somehow cope with the situation. If no opportunities are provided for appropriate defusing of traumatic stress and traumatic experiences, employees will adopt undesirable coping strategies.

A frequently used protection mechanism is distancing of the experiences, a cynical approach to work. This phenomenon is easily discernible in employees who have experienced a great deal of traumatic stress. The person's unemotional, cold and cynical approach is not only applied to his work, but also to family, friends and life in general. The result is problems both in interpersonal relationships and at work. The person is no longer able to discharge his duties properly, for example to support victims in traumatic situations and relate to them with empathy. Such workers add to victims' traumatic experiences instead of helping them.

Lack of adequate professional help for employees' traumatic stress may manifest in their excessive alcohol consumption, a poor atmosphere at work, difficulties in home life, frequent absences from work, early retirement due to incapacity for work and even suicide.

Psycho-social support and services for professional helpers

Particular attention should be paid to psycho-social support for employees who encounter traumatic stress and experiences in the course of their work. Originally, the entire operational model of psycho-social support was developed to fulfil this need. The greatest problem, however, is the general atmosphere of such organizations, which is disparaging of human characteristics, and prevents employees from recognizing their own natural needs and feelings and from expressing them.

Psycho-social support during ongoing assignments

Sometimes traumatic assignments or situations may continue for a long period. Such situations are major disasters, where rescue work can take several days, siege situations and other similar incidents. In such cases, it is important that the employees' psychological support and adequate rest are provided while the assignment is ongoing.

Stressful work should not be done as overtime, but the employees should have the opportunity to rest after an eight-hour day. After a particularly demanding assignment and before the employees disperse and go home, both the physical and psychological well-being of the personnel should be ensured. The employees must be given the opportunity to talk among themselves and with crisis counsellors about experiences that may prey on their minds.

The aim of demobilization and defusing meetings is the alleviation of traumatic reactions, normalization of experiences, reinforcement of the social network and prevention of isolation and withdrawal. The fundamental premise is that return to everyday routines should take place as soon as possible, and that not all the day's experiences need to be held on to or taken home to be shared with the family, but that the majority of them should be shared with colleagues and left behind at the workplace.

Aftercare of reactions caused by traumatic situations

If a question is put to, for example, the Finnish police force on how the aftercare of traumatic experiences is organized, the usual response is that the services are good. The aim is always to arrange help for an employee, if he requests it. Let us look at the issue from the perspective of an employee who has been involved in a traumatic incident. When the general atmosphere in the organization is that a healthy and competent police officer who is well suited to the job does not have emotional reactions to shocking incidents, the employee finds it very difficult to ask the organization for help, as he is then labelled weak, incompetent and unsuitable for the job. The usual solution is to seek help from the occupational healthcare services, sick leave and tranquillizing medication.

Many frontline emergency organizations are very hierarchical and authoritarian in nature. Such organizations are, for example, the emergency services, the police and hospitals. It is vitally important that the management and supervisory staff of such organizations understand the needs of the employees and the importance of defusing traumatic experiences. Only then is it possible to implement psycho-social support and services and produce results.

The optimal preconditions for productive work exist when supervisory staff appreciate the importance of addressing employees' traumatic experiences, recognize the situations when professional help is necessary, and through their own decisions give support, for example conducting a PD session. The usual response to supervisors' question to employees about the need for debriefing is negative, even if the need is dire. This response is again influenced by the general organizational atmosphere. Nobody wants to admit to being 'weak' or 'soft', for fear of the attitudes of colleagues and supervisors.

> Earlier, I described an incident when a bomb was thrown at the home of a drug squad officer. The incident took place on the eve of Independence Day. The next day, the officer concerned came to work, along with his colleagues. Their superior officer asked them if they required debriefing. The reply was unequivocal: "We don't need anything." However, the superior did not leave it at that, but listened in to the men's conversation, and then decided that the whole unit (80 men) should undergo debriefing, and another session should be arranged for their spouses.
>
> About ten debriefing sessions were conducted in connection with the incident. Later, the general opinion was that the sessions were very necessary, and that they helped the organization to recover quickly from a critical incident, and the officers' capacity for work and their mutual trust were preserved. This was all thanks to the exemplary action of the unit superior.

Psycho-social support and services should become an accepted, everyday part of an organization's work. Whenever an employee or a group of employees is involved in a traumatic incident, a debriefing session should automatically be held the next day. The organization should also take care of employees' families and provide them with support when necessary.

PD leaders from outside the organization

The position of debriefing session leaders is crucial. It is often thought that the threshold of making use of the service is lower if the leaders come from within the organization. It is also argued that external leaders are not sufficiently familiar with the organizational procedures and employees' duties, which would adversely affect leading the session and engendering trust in the leader.

My opinion is precisely the opposite. Leaders from within the organization, particularly when they are hierarchical and authoritarian, often have a dual role when required to lead debriefing sessions within their own organization. They may have positions of authority that negate the primary rule that anything revealed during debriefing should not impact on the employee's promotion prospects, his position or subsequent assignments. It is impossible for both the leader and the employees to control this effect. This is why an external leader has a better chance of success. Furthermore, an external leader is not as likely to be drawn into the organization's dubious procedures or reinforce them, as would a leader from within.

Before the session, the external leader should familiarize himself with the organization and the characteristics of the employees' duties. This knowledge is relatively easily available, and the extra work is preferable to the harmful factors associated with using people from within the organization.

Emergency personnel, the police, doctors and other healthcare professionals, social workers and even journalists should be given sufficient information about traumatic stress and the impact of critical incidents during their basic training. This would enable them to deal with victims of traumatic incidents in the course of their work in such a way that they alleviate their suffering, rather than produce new traumatic experiences.

Training needed on traumatic experiences and processing them

Training and the knowledge it brings is also needed to enable employees to understand their own and their colleagues' reactions in traumatic situations and afterwards. Only knowledge and training can change the damaging atmosphere in organizations, enabling them to view traumatic stress and experiences in such a way that their consequences are reduced instead of their having an attitude that adds to them.

Thus, supervisory staff in organizations are in a particularly responsible position in identifying traumatic stress and incidents and organizing help for employees. To enable them to fulfil this duty, they must be given the necessary training. The objectives of the training should be the ability to recognize traumatic situations that necessitate psychological aftercare for employees, the ability to motivate employees to process their traumatic experiences, and care for their own psychological well-being, as well as the ability to organize expert services for the employees.

The support person system

Positive results have been achieved also by creating a support person system within organizations. Support persons must be selected with care. They should have experience of being on call at short notice, emotional maturity, capacity for team work, knowledge of processing of traumatic experiences and psychosocial methods. They must enjoy high regard and acceptance by their work communities, as well as being trustworthy, empathetic and in possession of high stress tolerance thresholds.

The duties of support persons are:

- supporting colleagues who have been involved in special incidents and are showing signs of psychological stress
- helping assess the need for further treatment for stress sufferers
- organizing psychological defusing and debriefing sessions and motivating employees to attend
- acting as contact person between crisis workers and the organization
- acting as intermediary with management.

Support persons require special training to fulfil these duties.

Finnair, the Finnish airline, has created a particularly good support person system. The support persons are carefully selected, they are appointed by the organization, and are provided with training to equip them for their task. Finnair has many positive experiences of the support person system in connection with traumatic incidents that its employees have encountered.

It is important that there are trained people within the organization, and that they understand critical incidents and crisis work. That way, crisis counsellors who come from outside the organization have a better chance of making a positive impact. Traumatic incidents that happen within the organization are also more astutely identified, if the organization contains trained staff.

The social services office of a small town was the target of an armed robbery. Two of the staff members were also members of the crisis group attached to the local health centre. They attended to their colleagues' psychological first aid immediately after the robbery.

They asked their superior to contact the crisis response group in order to arrange a PD session for the employees, and advised him on the required action. They also motivated their colleagues to participate in the session which they themselves attended as victims.

The psycho-social support and services received by frontline emergency staff after dealing with traumatic situations and tasks is far from comprehensive and sufficiently well organized; much work remains to be done. Organizations still do not appreciate what an important resource they have in personnel who are working at full capacity and enjoying well-being. Nor do they still clearly appreciate what a great risk unprocessed traumatic experiences pose to employees' endurance and well-being. Not enough attention is paid to prevention of consequences from traumatic situations, and those consequences manifest as absenteeism, sickness, medication and nursing costs and early retirement due to incapacity.

Occupational health services play an important role in the aftercare of traumatic situations. However, their resources are often inadequate in addressing acute traumatic critical incidents quickly and comprehensively enough. That is why organizations where employees deal with frequent traumatic situations should organize a specific system, to ensure sufficiently wide-ranging and expert help.

Tampere University Hospital in Finland is a suitable example. The occupational healthcare department for hospital employees has the support of about 60 trained and committed crisis counsellors. They have organized themselves into groups of three and have a weekly duty roster. Superiors, colleagues and traumatized employees themselves can contact the occupational health unit and request a PD session for their unit or working community. The occupational health unit passes on the request to the threesome on duty, and they implement the debriefing.

To date, this system is unique. Its operation is now in its third year, and the results are positive. The problems are similar to those in any other crisis work. Not all traumatic events encountered by hospital employees are passed on to the counsellors, and consequently some employees do not receive the support they need.

15

Organizing Crisis Services in Acute Traumatic Situations

Everyday traumatic incidents and situations

The basic operational principles and models for modern acute crisis work came to Finland from Norway. The first local crisis group was set up in 1990.

Large cities were the last to set up organized crisis groups. More traumatic incidents take place in cities than in small municipalities, and consequently the need for crisis work was desperate.

There are two possible reasons for the slow uptake. The large number of traumatic incidents was frightening. It appeared to be beyond control, and it seemed impossible to respond to the need it created. The second reason was sheer bureaucracy. Crisis work needs co-operation between various administrative bodies and local government. Sometimes, the organization of such co-operation tends to be ground up in the wheels of bureaucracy. Problems of power and jealousy hinder planning of the work.

Acute crisis work has been demanding, pioneering work. It cannot carry a cumbersome organization, and bureaucracy kills off the pioneering spirit. This spirit has been particularly necessary for those who have set out to organize crisis work in large cities.

The Finnish acute crisis care service is unique in the world. No other method has broken through even in Finland with such force and coverage as crisis work. In less than ten years, a comprehensive system was created to serve citizens affected by traumatic incidents and situations.

At least four factors influenced the above development:

1. The foundations, principles and methods of modern crisis care have inspired workers in various fields, so that they have enthusiastically trained for these tasks and set about creating a service system. Some

crisis groups have operated for almost ten years, but the enthusiasm has not waned. The majority of the first pioneering workers are still actively involved. The reason for their commitment is the experiences they have gained from crisis work. On the one hand, they have seen the anxiety and pain produced by traumatic experiences, and on the other, people coping with most difficult situations and the vital role of crisis work in that coping process. The meaningful and rewarding work is self-motivating.

2. Decision-makers and politicians have understood the importance of crisis care. Without their positive input, it would not have been possible to start and maintain the operation. The foundations and principles of modern crisis care are such that a layman can easily understand and accept them. Everybody has sufficient personal experience clearly and in a concrete way to appreciate the need of psycho-social support and services.

3. The people have embraced crisis work. Ordinary citizens, too, have gratefully embraced the new service. Along with spreading of the crisis network, people's knowledge of the consequences of traumatic experiences has also increased. They are motivated to seek help in processing their difficult experience, and know how to request and demand services. The idea of immediate crisis care as a national right, proposed by the Ministry of Social Affairs and Health in its memorandum, is being implemented.

4. The media have a positive attitude to crisis work. The Finnish media have throughout taken a very positive view of modern acute crisis care. They have well assumed their role as disseminators of information in catastrophes and major accidents, where one of the focal points of media interest has been people's reactions in traumatic situations, and how victims may be helped. The media have in an exemplary manner emphasized the importance of crisis work in all major traumatic events, and minor ones, too, that have befallen our country.

Local crisis groups
Structure and operational principles of crisis groups

Finland has a comprehensive network of local crisis groups. Every municipality either has its own crisis group, or several municipalities have organized a shared crisis group. The groups are usually led by the health centre psychologist, but in some cases also by, for example, a social worker, parish pastoral worker, doctor, nurse or community nurse.

The crisis group is a multidisciplinary specialist group, with members who are mostly appointed. The required qualifications are the employer's permission, basic training in a human relationships discipline, and specialist training in reactions caused by traumatic events and in acute crisis care. Thus, crisis group members are professionals who are involved in crisis care as a specialist task related to their own work. Legislation applicable to healthcare professionals is in most cases extended to cover crisis care.

Thus, operation of the crisis group is professional work that has been prioritized over other functions in municipalities. Members carry out crisis work during their normal working hours. If a crisis group assignment falls outside normal working hours, the employee is either entitled to special remuneration or time off in lieu.

Local crisis groups are usually attached to health centres. The services of crisis groups are free to clients.

Contacting the crisis group

The main prerequisite of successful acute crisis care is that the so-called frontline emergency services alert the crisis group to the traumatic incident. In this respect, the system is a departure from other healthcare, where the convention is that the person concerned himself seeks help. If this practice were followed in acute crisis care, the services would be timed too late. A crisis care worker who herself experienced a traumatic incident said: "At first there was no need, and then I was so confused and exhausted that I was incapable of contacting the services." This is why it is absolutely vital to apply a procedure where the service is alerted by an outsider, preferably an official.

Some crisis groups operate a 24-hour service, but the cell phone dedicated to the service is often turned off overnight. During that time, the caller can leave a voice message, and the duty crisis worker contacts him in the morning.

The contact numbers of crisis groups are not made public. The officials at the scene, for example the police, rescue personnel and hospital emergency room personnel, recognize the traumatic event and ask victims' permission to pass their contact details to the crisis group which then contacts them. Thus, the alert should come to crisis groups through frontline emergency personnel.

The manner in which frontline helpers tell victims about crisis care is important. An example of a recommended line is: "We have a local crisis group, and it's customary always to inform them when someone is involved in an incident like this. You don't have any objection if we pass your contact details to the duty crisis workers? They will get in touch with you. Of course, giving your contact details does not mean that you are obliged to accept their support, but you can discuss it directly with them."

It is important that crisis groups are informed about all traumatic incidents in the area. To this end, frontline helpers must recognize a traumatic incident and have the skill to motivate victims to give permission to pass on their details. It also means that frontline helpers should not assess the need for psychological support on the basis of victims' behaviour, as this is often misleading owing to the shock reaction.

Emergency call centres have the central role in organizing assistance in emergencies. Alerting the crisis group in certain clear-cut situations (serious accidents, sudden deaths, fires, serious incidents involving violence) could take place directly through the emergency centre. In this way, the crisis group would be informed at least about all serious incidents by the emergency centre, leaving the frontline staff to notify about other incidents at their discretion.

However, identification of all incidents where crisis care is necessary is not always possible. Here, it is important to stress the role of citizens' duty. Supervisors in working communities, principals and teachers in schools, coaches in sports activities have a duty to recognize the need for psychological help and to request it. Every friend, relative, neighbour or colleague can ask for help.

Local crisis work is carried out by officials, and it demands seamless co-operation and communication with other officials. The duty of confidentiality is often used as an excuse for inaction to the point of preventing co-operation. I would stress that it is a lesser misdemeanour to impart too much information than it is to neglect to do so and thus prevent citizens' access to assistance.

Operational preconditions for local crisis groups

The crisis group activity originated at grass roots level, from local needs and initiatives. It was considered so important that crisis group members devoted great personal effort to setting up and standardizing the work, without reward. They committed themselves to the cause with their hearts and souls, and fought many battles to win basic operational conditions for the group.

Today, we have clearly arrived at the stage of transition from pioneering work to making the activity official and uniform, and creating sufficient operational preconditions for crisis care work. This is important, in order to retain and attract the most qualified, able and responsible workers.

Establishing local crisis work includes:

- acknowledging the official status of crisis groups with their own place in the organization
- appointment of crisis group members
- financial provision – sufficient funds allocated for training, supervision and practical operation of crisis groups
- providing for the fact that crisis workers must receive a financial reward for work that is particularly demanding, difficult and requires enormous commitment
- recognising that duty rosters of crisis groups must be standardized and remunerated under employees' contractual terms and conditions.

The above recommendations were made by the Ministry to ensure establishment of crisis groups. The operational model of acute crisis care in Finland is extremely cost-effective. Its success is based on good organization of preparedness, built into customary jobs, and therefore generates very little extra cost. Yet the benefits gained from the operation are maximal, even if only the above minimal requirements are fulfilled.

The foundation of local acute crisis work is formed by municipal crisis groups operating within health centres. They fulfil the population's needs in cases of everyday traumatic experiences. The group members continually gain experience in crisis care and accumulate preparedness and know-how; it is essential that members are committed to long-term and continuous involvement.

Some hospitals and other organizations (military establishments, large companies, schools and colleges) have their own crisis groups. Usually, they work in close co-operation with the local crisis group.

Hospital crisis groups

Some large hospitals have their own crisis groups with the remit of providing aftercare for patients and their families who have endured a traumatic incident. At Etelä-Pohjanmaan keskussairaala hospital in northern Finland, the specific task of the crisis group is to provide help in traumatic situations immediately after the incident, or in the shock stage. The hospital crisis unit is prepared for attending the scene of the incident and staying long enough for the acute need for support to lessen.

However, in many municipalities, shock stage support is entirely neglected. The government recommendations oblige them to address the shock stage, too, and provide professional psychological help. This function could be added to the duties of local crisis groups, but it would mean replacing the present duty rosters with an on-call system, which would add to running costs.

Victims in the shock stage often become deeply attached to crisis workers. It would be beneficial if crisis work were started as early as possible, and also if the same people were involved from the beginning of the acute stage to the end.

The model implemented at the above hospital is currently unique, and the experiences gained from it are positive. If a large hospital decides to set up its own crisis group, there must be a clear demarcation of duties with the local crisis group, in cases of both everyday traumatic events and major accidents.

Major accidents

The need for psycho-social support and services is well recognized in Finland also with regard to major accidents. Today, one of the first actions is almost always organizing psychological support for the victims.

The credit for bringing this need into public awareness belongs to the national Psychologists' Major Accident Preparedness Group, originally set up in partnership by the Finnish Psychological Association and the Finnish Red Cross, later to be operated solely by the latter.

The group began its operation in 1993. Its members are about 15 of the most experienced crisis psychologists all around Finland. Their employers have signed an agreement allowing them to be released for crisis work in case of a major accident, within 24 hours of the incident. The group also contains about 15 'reservists', who are available within three days of the accident.

Members of the Psychologists' Preparedness Group have undergone specialist training in co-ordinating psychological services in major accident situations. The group has proved well prepared and functional in exercises and also in real-life situations.

The FRC Psychologists' Preparedness Group invites as its members experienced and distinguished crisis psychologists. The FRC signs a contract with the psychologists and appoints them. The majority of group members have been involved in the scheme from the start.

The psychologists carry a pager at all times; they are always on call. They receive no pay for being on call, but the actual work they are called to do is remunerated by the FRC.

The Psychologists' Preparedness Group has carried out psychological crisis care in every major accident in Finland since its inception. The first major accident it was involved in was the Sally Albatross shipwreck in 1994, followed six months later by the Estonia disaster, the group's greatest challenge to date.

The group was in charge of most psycho-social services in Finland after the Estonia disaster. The work went on for two weeks. In that time, the response group psychologists put in about 2400 hours of crisis work, which equals almost

300 eight-hour working days. Between them, they organized and led almost 250 psychological debriefing sessions, most of them with groups.

The largest target group was personnel of the car ferries, which took up the equivalent of 180 working days. Other clients were rescue workers, passengers, rescued accident victims and to some degree also families of those deceased in the accident.

Immediately after the disaster, representatives of the FRC Preparedness Group travelled to Estonia to set up crisis care services there. In collaboration with Estonian healthcare workers, they created a crisis organization and trained staff in crisis care. This co-operative work with Estonia continued actively through the year.

In most subsequent major accidents, local crisis groups have dealt with the majority of acute crisis work. The role of the Psychologists' Preparedness Group has evolved to consist mainly of co-ordination of national crisis care and acting as consultants for local groups. It forms a specialist resource, available when local resources are insufficient.

In recent years, the preparedness for organizing psycho-social support services after major accidents in Finland, both at local and national levels, has substantially improved. Operation of local crisis groups is now included in general emergency preparedness plans of municipalities and counties, resulting in clarification and establishment of the status of crisis care.

Today, it is impossible to imagine a major disaster without immediate psychological crisis care for the victims being set in motion. In fact, at times of catastrophes and major accidents, psychological crisis care is now the most extensive area of operation in terms of input, the reason being the large numbers of psychological victims. Medical treatment of accident victims is much less extensive in scale compared to the extent and scope of psychological work.

16

Impacts of Interventions Designed to Prevent Traumatization

Critical research

The value of psychological debriefing has been the subject of lively debate. Much has been made of the Cochrane Review which concluded that there is no evidence of any beneficial effects from single-session, preventive defusing. The method has even been suspected to cause harm (Wahlbeck 1998).

The Cochrane Review advocates medicine and healthcare based on scientific evidence. Thus, the fundamental premise is that only methods scientifically proven to be effective should be approved for use in healthcare services. However, we should bear in mind that the *British Medical Journal*, a staunch supporter of evidence-based medicine, admits that only 15 per cent of methods used in somatic medicine actually fulfil this criterion. In mental healthcare, there are probably no methods that would fulfil the criterion.

For a research study to be accepted by the Cochrane Review, the research design must fulfil certain conditions. The study must have an experimental group that is subjected to an intervention, and a control group that is not. The subjects must be allocated randomly into experimental and control groups, and the experimenter must not know which group each subject is in. This kind of double-blind study is generally used in pharmaceutical research, where the control group, too, is given 'medication' (usually chalk), so the subjects themselves do not know which group they are in. Only studies based on such a research design are noteworthy under the Cochrane criteria.

The Cochrane Review reported that the writers found six trials that fulfilled the above criteria. There was no follow-up information on one, and another study compared debriefing sessions of different durations. Thus, the measures of impact were obtained from four studies.

The review results showed that single-session debriefing does not reduce post-traumatic symptoms or prevent PTSD. It is particularly worrying that the subjects who participated in debriefing had an increased risk of developing PTSD compared to the control group that received no debriefing. Three months later, the risk was already higher, but after a year the increase was statistically significant. However, the last observation is based on a single study. (Rose, Bisson and Wessley 2002)

Let us take a closer look at the four studies accepted for the review. The study that found that the group subjected to debriefing had an increased risk of developing PTSD was by Bisson, Jenkins, Alexander and Bannister (1997). The subjects were hospital patients with serious burns, who were randomly divided into the debriefing group and the control group. The intervention was administered individually to each patient or couple, its mean duration was 44 minutes, and it was given by a nurse or a research psychiatrist. The results showed that 16 patients (26%) were suffering from PTSD after 13 months, whereas of the control group, 9 per cent were diagnosed with PTSD.

Even before the intervention, the PD group had twice as many significant prior traumas as the control group. In addition, the experimental group had more serious burns and were hospitalized for longer than the control group. These factors alone are sufficient to explain the result.

The intervention was implemented within 24–72 hours of the traumatic event. The experimenters themselves reported that the subjects' coping was worse, the sooner after the incident the intervention took place. It is well known that physical injury slows down psychological processing, so the timing of the interventions was incorrect. Furthermore, the report does not disclose the quantity of analgesics administered to the patients, but during the first days after serious burns it must have been considerable. It is quite possible that the subjects in the intervention group remembered nothing about the intervention.

It is also worth noting that the intervention was executed singly or in couples, when PD is first and foremost a group method. The duration of the intervention also indicates that the discussion and processing of the traumatic experience was very superficial. It is simply not possible to run through an adequate PD in that time.

Let us look at the other studies included in the Cochrane Review. In the UK, Lee, Slade and Lygo (1996) conducted a study where an intervention they called 'psychological debriefing' was applied to women who had suffered a miscarriage. The women were randomly split into two groups, one of which was offered a one-hour consultation at home two weeks after the miscarriage. The researchers had clearly stressed a formal method, going through the stages of debriefing.

The women were tested at a week and four weeks post-intervention for anxiety, depression, intrusive memories and avoidance reactions. No differences between the groups were found. The intervention employed in the study was a psychiatric consultation rather than PD. Its timing was faulty. The quantification of crisis intervention was also incorrect. It would have been a miracle if differences had been observed between the groups.

Hobbs, Mayou, Harrison and Worlock (1996) studied road accident casualties. The victims were randomly allocated into intervention and control groups. The one-hour intervention was implemented individually 24–48 hours after the accident. Before the intervention, the groups had seemed comparable in terms of severity of their physical injuries, but afterwards it transpired that the intervention group had more serious injuries and stayed in hospital longer than the control group. Four months post-intervention, the researchers found no significant reduction in the symptoms of either group.

This study was continued by extending the follow-up period to three years (Mayou, Ehlers and Hobbs 2000). The results found after four months were reinforced. The group that had received an individual, hour-long 'debriefing' session had more psychiatric symptoms (anxiety, depression, compulsive symptoms and anger). They also reported more pain than the control group. Their quality of life and capacity was poorer, so that it was apparent at home, leisure activities, work and with friends. They also suffered more financial hardship.

The researchers concluded that all this resulted from the one-hour discussion immediately after the accident. They did also report that the intervention subjects had more permanent injuries, and that 20 per cent of them suffered severe chronic disability as the result of the accident, while the corresponding figure with the control group was 3 per cent, but they attach no significance to this in interpreting their results. A good indication of the researchers' knowledge of debriefing is that they reject the criticism that debriefing is a group method and they have used it individually by asking how it is possible to form groups of traffic accident victims, when accidents happen randomly, the injuries vary, etc. (Mayou *et al.* 2000, p.593). This comment shows that the researchers have no understanding of how the debriefing method should be applied. In Finland, the debriefing would be conducted for victims' families along with the victims themselves, and it would be taken for granted that it is not a sufficient method of psychological support for someone who is seriously injured.

Before moving on to studies that have found results contrary to the above, I want to look at some fundamental principles in acute crisis care and PD research.

Fundamental principles in researching the impact of crisis care

Importance of clinical experience

The debate on the impact of psychological debriefing is very reminiscent of that conducted in the past on psychotherapy. The first round of studies unequivocally showed that psychotherapy brought no benefit; on the contrary, they showed that it might be harmful. But practising psychotherapists saw the benefits of their work daily and doggedly continued developing the methods regardless of criticism.

Only after several decades of development of research traditions, design and methods was it possible to study psychotherapy in such a way that its core phenomena were captured. As this research tradition developed, studies were carried out that indisputably showed the effectiveness of psychotherapy. But this demanded development of new research strategies, since the object of the research was new, and old strategies were clearly incapable of capturing its reality. Clinical experience did that much better.

In acute crisis care and also in PD, clinical experience shows indisputably that the methods are effective and produce impressive results. Every crisis worker who has led a successful debriefing session and witnessed the immediate effect on the participants, heard their feedback after a few weeks, and with his own eyes seen them coping and recovering, cannot but be convinced of the efficacy of the method, however sceptical a person he may be.

Acute crisis care and the PD method have been in wider use and under development for only a decade or so. Creation of a research tradition capable of capturing the core phenomena of such a difficult object of research takes at least as long, usually longer. Clinical experience captures these core phenomena much more effectively than statistical research can ever do.

Crisis work at its best is social work

When acute crisis care is most effective, the social aspect of the phenomenon is recognized in its implementation. A traumatic event impacts widely on many social groups, and at its best crisis care is social work.

There are very few studies that take the social aspect of crisis work into consideration. They should look at impacts of the intervention at societal level, or rather that in spite of the traumatic event, no changes at community level have taken place.

Studies of the impact of crisis work on social groups concerned situations that arose largely by chance, where one group underwent a great deal of crisis care, and another group subjected to the same traumatic event received none. I will address these studies later, as many other issues in this chapter touch on them.

Psychological debriefing is only one method

Finnish acute crisis work always consists of a number of contacts. Before the actual debriefing session, the crisis worker is in contact with the victims and their representatives several times. These early contacts always include guidance, counselling and support in crisis situations. It is recommended that this shock stage support should be further improved.

Shock stage support creates the foundation for a successful PD session. Whenever possible, the session is organized in group format, allowing the intervention to best achieve its objectives: facing and accepting reality, processing psychological reactions, normalization of reactions and preparation for future reactions, as well as reinforcing social support.

At the PD session, follow-up arrangements are made. They may take the form of a follow-up session attended by all the participants, or a telephone call on an appointed date. The purpose is to ensure that people are coping. An essential part of debriefing or follow-up is directing people into further therapy, if it transpires that debriefing is an insufficient support form for their needs.

All of the above studies were based on one-off individual interventions; their results cannot be generalized to crisis work as implemented in Finland.

The group format of debriefing sets its own parameters on a research study on the method. It is generally agreed that only randomized studies yield reliable data on the impact of debriefing. Because PD is most effective when administered in groups, the object of research should be these groups; the unit for randomization should be, for example, a group or a family. This in turn places considerable demands on the research both in terms of funding and time. The number of randomized groups should be sufficiently large for statistically significant differences to emerge.

Psychological debriefing is based on interaction

PD is not like a pill that can be administered uniformly to everyone in the experimental group. It is a method based on complex interaction. Thus, the intervention and its impact are influenced by numerous factors. Atle Dyregrov (1998) identified seven groups of factors, each with numerous subgroups, which affect the process and efficacy of PD: intensity of the traumatic experience, structure and course of the PD session, group cohesiveness, the organization to which the group belongs, participants' personal backgrounds, the leaders and their expertise, and the environment of the PD session.

Research studies should include as intervening variables details of the debriefing session, because it is never possible to achieve a standardized session, the same for everyone, and this should not indeed be an objective. On the contrary, intuition and an ability to apply his expertise in new, challenging situations, to adapt the method to suit each group and situation, are qualities required of a debriefing leader, where his professional skills come into their own.

In Finland, PD sessions are led only by human relations professionals. Crisis group members receive training for the job. Outside the Nordic countries, PD is often implemented by volunteers.

PD can take a variety of formats, depending on the leaders' professional skills. In the Nordic countries, it has developed more in the direction of a process, precisely because of the leaders' high professional skills. This method may be applied relatively mechanically, going through the various stages, but its efficacy may be substantially increased by paying attention to the group's psychological processes. By directing them, the participants are helped to process their own difficult issues and feelings, and therefore move the process forward. Leading process debriefing is a special skill that requires special know-how, but it also produces better results. None of the usually quoted studies employed this process-like debriefing leadership technique.

Finnish acute crisis care has reached the stage where it is time to establish quality criteria for crisis work and psychological debriefing. Then we would also acquire more systematic data on its impact.

Objectives and results of crisis work

In most studies, impact of PD was measured by indicators of PTSD or the number of various stress symptoms after a traumatic incident. Typical tools were various symptom indicators and the Impact of Event Scale, which measures recurring intrusive memories, avoidance tendency and emotional responses indicative of agitation.

According to current knowledge, customary, successful psychological processing of a serious traumatic experience takes several months, even a year or more. During most of this time, while the psychological processing is ongoing, an individual can be diagnosed with PTSD.

The objective of PD is that the victim of a traumatic experience should recognize his own reactions, feelings and thoughts, be able to accept them, work through them and live with them. This naturally shows in studies in the quantity of symptoms and difficult feelings, if the objectives have been successfully fulfilled. Similarly, many of the measures used in follow-up studies identify those very factors that people have been trained to recognize and accept during debriefing.

The aim of acute crisis work is prevention of psychological trauma. Better indicators of the desired effect than psychological or somatic symptoms or PTSD and associated phenomena would be, for example, whether sickness absences, use of healthcare services, medication or alcohol have increased after the traumatic event. Important criteria are also people's ability to continue in their former line of work and that changes of job and early retirement through incapacity are prevented.

In many studies, the follow-up periods are sufficiently short for diagnosis of PTSD, but far too short for all the effects of psychological trauma to manifest. Furthermore, the follow-up methods fail to capture all the consequences that result from psychological trauma.

Appropriate targets of psychological debriefing

Most of the studies that conclude that PD is of no benefit focus on traumatic events of the kind where this intervention would not be applied in Finland, or it would be applied differently.

It is important that PD is employed when the situation or event that caused the stress is over. Most of the studies focused on traumatic events where the victims were physically injured (burns patients, hospitalized traffic accident victims, women who had miscarried, etc). An essential part of clinical know-how is selection of appropriate interventions for the target. The studies betray the authors' poor clinical judgement in selecting interventions.

In Finland, a PD session would be organized for the family of a burn victim, a person injured in a traffic accident or a victim of violence resulting in serious physical injury, and the injured victim would be one of the participants. However, no experienced crisis worker would consider this intervention to be adequate psychological support for the injured victim.

Small samples

One of the crucial factors determining research results is sample size. Interpretation of individual studies – even those that are randomized and otherwise well controlled – is impaired by small sample sizes.

Importance of victims' perceptions

The Cochrane Review, in common with other critical research summaries, attaches no value whatsoever to the perceptions of the subjects themselves of whether or not PD was helpful to them. Yet, all the impact criteria used are in effect based on self-assessments by the subjects. Surprisingly, the subjects' responses become valuable when they are filling in questionnaires and subjectively assessing whether or not they have this or that symptom, or when responding to researchers' questions in psychiatric interviews. It seems to me that when responses are given to a researcher in an interview and recorded, they miraculously become valuable research data. For example in pharmaceutical research, recorded results consist of patients' perceptions of whether the symptoms were alleviated and whether there were side effects.

Why, then, are people's perceptions of crisis work and PD not valuable and suitable as data of impact research studies? As a matter of fact, the foundation of modern healthcare development is deemed to be the end user's experiences and opinions. In crisis work, too, perceptions and assessments of users of the service should be valued.

There are hundreds of studies that have found that PD sessions are of significant benefit. Usually, 75–90 per cent of participants have found them helpful. Very few other healthcare methods are able to show equivalent results.

Research results on the impact of crisis work

I would like to summarize some research findings on the impact of acute crisis work. They were gleaned from studies that captured at least some of its basic principles. The most impressive concerns two air disasters in the USA and personnel involved in the rescue effort. Mitchell and Everly (1993) compared the impacts of two similar air disasters. In the San Diego disaster in 1978, 125 people were killed, and in the Cerritos crash in 1986, the number of dead was 82. The rescue personnel at San Diego received no crisis care, whereas Mitchell's Critical Incident Stress Debriefing (CISD) programme was implemented among the rescuers at Cerritos.

In a year, use of mental health services increased by 31 per cent among the San Diego rescuers, and by 1 per cent among those at Cerritos. Of the San Diego rescuers, five police officers, seven firemen and seventeen medical professionals changed jobs. After the Cerritos accident, only one person from each professional group changed jobs.

The framework of this study came about by chance. In conjunction with one disaster, comprehensive crisis work was undertaken among the rescuers; with the other, none was undertaken. The results are impressive and reliable.

A similar situation occurred at the Estonia disaster between crews of different ferries. Unfortunately, in spite of energetic efforts, collecting data from the crew of a ferry where no crisis work was conducted failed, and a great opportunity was lost (Saari et al. 1996).

It is possible to form a good impression of the impact of crisis work by comparing the results of several studies. In 1987, the Herald of Free Enterprise was shipwrecked and 196 of the 545 people on board died. Forty-two crew members were saved, of whom only two are reported to have returned to work at sea (Johnston 1993; Yule, Williams and Joseph 1997).

In 1990, there was a fire on the car ferry Scandinavian Star, and 159 people lost their lives. A study found that after three and a half years, 43 per cent of those saved had changed jobs and 39 per cent were experiencing serious problems at work or within their families (Elklit, Andersen and Aretander 1995). At the time of both disasters, there was no preparedness to respond to the psychological needs of those involved in the disasters and their close social groups.

After the Estonia disaster, no problems of this kind were observed in Finland. This is shown by studies of the ships' personnel (Minkkinen 1999; Palosaari 1999) and also by data acquired from the shipping companies. After the Estonia disaster, no increase in staff sickness absences, typical after a traumatic event, was discernible, but absences remained at normal level. Neither has staff turnover increased after the accident. These results show the importance of disaster-psychological work.

Leeman-Conley (1990) documented the impact of the Critical Incident Stress Management (CISM) programme in an Australian bank. The programme was applied after an armed robbery that had shocked the working community. The study found that sickness absences and sick pay and compensation costs were reduced by 60 per cent compared to the previous year. This was the case in spite of the robbery.

Bohl (1991) provided data on more detailed effects of crisis work. He studied the perceptions of the CISM programme of rescue workers at the Delta 191 plane crash. He found positive results in six areas:

1. Workers who had participated in debriefing were better able to face their stress symptoms.

2. Debriefing helped participants accept their symptoms and understand that they were not going mad.

3. The participants were supported and strengthened by other participants.

4. Solutions were found to some problems.

5. The participants felt that it was safe to talk about feelings. There was no need to hide them.

6. Debriefing was mandatory, and the participants did not need to assess their own need for help.

Hanneman's (1994) thesis looked at the impact of debriefing on volunteer firemen in Nova Scotia. She found effects in seven areas:

1. Debriefing had a positive effect on the whole atmosphere of the department.

2. Debriefing had a positive effect on individuals' trauma processing.

3. The firemen acknowledged the importance of airing and expressing feelings.

4. The firemen acknowledged the importance of forming an overview of the whole incident.

5. The firemen understood that they had done their best.

6. The firemen became aware that other people have similar feelings.

7. The sense of cohesion and belonging increased.

Campbell (1992) studied the impact of PD on the perceptions of FBI agents in processing traumatic events. The results were statistically significant in five areas:

1. Colleagues were no longer used as scapegoats.

2. Use of alcohol after shooting incidents decreased.

3. Their attitudes to the job became more positive.

4. Severe counter-reactions decreased in other FBI agents.

5. Isolation and loneliness reduced.

Eränen, Paavola and Kajanne (1999) studied the open-ended responses of ships' personnel after the Estonia disaster, using the Content Analysis method. They split the respondents into two groups: those who had undergone PD and those who had not. They found that the PD group had a much more organized overview of the course of the event and related factors. The non-PD group gave responses that consisted of disjointed descriptions of detail. They were not in possession of the whole picture. The result is important and interesting as creation of the whole picture is one of the aims of debriefing.

Research results clearly show that the factors that most affect the benefit gained from debriefing are the leaders' training and experience. The result is the same in studies of psychotherapy. This was the conclusion of, for example, Atle Dyregrov (1998) when he summarized experiences gained from a number of traumatic experiences.

I will illustrate the phenomenon using material on two different traumatic events. One was a bus accident when a number of people were killed and injured.

The other data was collected from a series of dramatic bank robberies. After both events, very experienced debriefing leaders were used.

This material was compared to an air disaster when over a hundred people died. The victims of this disaster underwent debriefing where the leaders were employed in the mental health sector, but received only a few hours' training on debriefing.

Nobody in the experienced leaders' groups reported that they had not benefited from the sessions, but 3 per cent of the participants in the inexperienced leaders' groups felt that they had gained no benefit. Forty-four per cent of the bus accident victims and 56 per cent of robbery victims reported that debriefing had helped them, and 21 per cent of the bus accident victims and 40 per cent of the robbery victims felt that debriefing had helped a great deal. The corresponding figures of the groups led by inexperienced leaders for the air accident victims were only 31 per cent and 14 per cent. Thus, the experience and expertise of leaders has a significant effect on the impact of debriefing.

Conclusions on efficacy of crisis work

Already, barely a decade after modern crisis work began, we have clear evidence, both research and clinical, of its efficacy. The results are often very dramatic, and they can also be quantified in terms of economic gain. Consequently, the arguments posed by some psychiatrists in many countries seem very loaded. It is particularly astonishing that although many well-conducted studies show, contrary to expectation, that initiating early use of tranquillizing medication has no effect on later post-traumatic symptoms and disorders, no attention is paid to these results.

It is rather the case of an argument running within the psychiatric profession. It is founded on different concepts of human beings. The opponents of crisis work and debriefing are representatives of the biological view of psychiatry. All psychological phenomena, too, are biological, and they should be treated by biological means.

Crisis work is based on phenomenological psychological thinking. Human beings are psycho-physical entities and traumatic experiences produce psychological, somatic and social consequences. By addressing the psychological meanings of traumatic experiences it is often possible to influence the whole personality, its psychological, biological and social aspects.

References

Alavuotunki, R. and E. (1995) *Miksi? Olli uuvutettiin hengiltä Suomen armeijassa vuonna 1995.* Hankasalmi: Havusalmen kirjapaino.

Alexander, D. and Wells, A. (1991) 'Reactions of police officers to body-handling after a major disaster.' *British Journal of Psychiatry 159,* 547–555.

American Psychiatric Association (1987) *Diagnostic and Statistical Manual for Mental Disorders.* 3rd edn, revised. Washington DC: American Psychiatric Association.

Bisson, J.I., Jenkins, P.L., Alexander, J. and Bannister, C. (1997) 'Randomized controlled trial of psychological debriefing for victims of acute burn trauma.' *British Journal of Psychiatry 171,* 78–81.

Bohl, N. (1991) 'The effectiveness of brief psychological interventions in police officers after critical incidents.' In J. Reese, J. Horn, and C. Dunning (eds) *Critical Incidents in Policing.* Washington DC: US Government Printing Office.

Campbell, J.H. (1992) 'A Comparative Analysis of the Effects of Post Shooting Trauma on Special Agents of Federal Bureau of Investigation.' (Dissertation) Michigan State University.

Cullberg, J. (1991) *Tasapainon järkkyessä – psykoanalyyttinen ja sosiaalipsykiatrinen tutkielma.* Helsinki: Otava.

Dyregrov, A. (1994) *Katastrofipsykologian perusteet.* Tampere: Vastapaino.

Dyregrov, A. (1996) Training seminar for journalists organised by the Finnish Psychological Association and Finnish Association of Journalists, Helsinki.

Dyregrov, A. (1998) 'Psychological Debriefing – an effective method?' *Traumatology 4,* 2, 1.

Dyregrov, A. and Matthiesen, S. B. (1991) 'Parental grief following the death of an infant. A follow-up over one year.' *Scandinavian Journal of Psychology 32,* 193–207.

Elklit, A., Andersen, L.B. and Aretander, T. (1995) 'Scandinavian Star. Anden Del. En opfölgende undersögelse af de fysiske, psykologiske og sociale eftervirkninger 3,5 år efter katastrofen.' *Psykologisk Skriftserie 20,* 2. Aarhus Universitet.

Eränen, L., Paavola, J. and Kajanne, A. (1999) 'Psykologinen jälkipuinti ja traumaattisten muistojen jäsentyminen kertomuksiksi.' *Suomen Lääkärilehti 7,* 99, 54, 763–769.

Finnish Ministry of Justice (1992) *Tutkintaselostus Taipalsaarella 14.6.1991 tapahtuneesta miehistönkuljetusvaunun uppoamisesta.* Finnish Ministry of Justice report: Suuronnettomuuden tutkintaselostus No. 2/1991. Helsinki.

Finnish Ministry of Social Affairs and Health (1998a) *Psykososiaaliset tukipalvelut traumaattisen kriisin kohdanneille. Ohjeisto hätäkeskuspäivystäjille.* Finnish Ministry of Social Affairs and Health 28.

Finnish Ministry of Social Affairs and Health (1998b) *Traumaattisten tilanteiden psykososiaalinen tuki ja palvelut.* Finnish Ministry of Social Affairs and Health.

Finnish Red Cross (1994) *Suomen punaisen ristin avustustoimenpiteet Estoniaonnettomuudessa.* Report 30 November.

Freud, S. and Strachey, J. (Tr) (1989) [First published1920] *Introductory Lectures on Psychoanalysis*. New York: Liveright Publishing Corporation.

Freud, S. (1990) [First published 1920] *Beyond the Pleasure Principle*. New York: W.W. Norton & Company.

Gleser, G.C., Green, B.L. and Winget, C. (1981) *Prolonged Psychosocial Effects of Disaster. A Study of Buffalo Creek*. New York: Academic Press.

Green, B.L., Grace, M.C., Lindy, J.D., Gleser, G.C., Leonard, A.C. and Kramer, T.L. (1990) 'Buffalo Creek survivors in the second decade: Comparison with unexposed and nonlitigant groups.' *Journal of Applied Social Psychology 20*, 1033–1050.

Hanneman, M.F. (1994) 'Evaluation of Critical Incident Stress Debriefing as Perceived by Volunteer Firefighters in Nova Scotia.' Ann Arber, MI: UMI Dissertation Service.

Hersberger, P.J. and Walsh, W.B. (1990) 'Multiple role involvements and the adjustment to conjugal bereavement: An exploratory study.' *Omega 21*, 91–102.

Hobbs, M., Mayou, R., Harrison, B. and Worlock, P. (1996) 'A randomised controlled trial of psychological debriefing for victims of road traffic accidents.' *British Medical Journal 313*, 1438–1439.

Holen, A. (1990) *A Long-Term Outcome Study of Survivors from a Disaster*. University of Oslo.

Johnston, S.J. (1993) 'Traumatic stress reactions in the crew of the Herald of Free Enterprise.' In J.P. Wilson and P. Raphael (eds) *International Handbook of Traumatic Stress Syndromes*. New York: Plenum Press.

Jokinen, J-V. (1999) *Raiteilta*. Helsinki: Kirjapaja.

Lee, C., Slade, P. and Lygo, V. (1996) 'The influence of psychological debriefing on emotional adaptation in women following early miscarriage: A preliminary study.' *British Journal of Medical Psychology 69*, 47–58.

Leeman-Conley, M.M. (1990) 'After a violent robbery.' *Criminology Australia*, April/May, 4–6.

Lindeman, M., Saari, S., Verkasalo, M. and Prytz, H. (1996) 'Traumatic stress and its risk factors among peripheral victims of the MS Estonia Disaster.' *European Psychologists Vol. 1*, No. 4, 2–17.

Mayou, R.A., Ehlers, A. and Hobbs, M. (2000) 'Psychological debriefing for road traffic accident victims.' *The British Journal of Psychiatry 176*, 589–593.

Mitchell, J.T. and Everly, G.S. (1993) *Critical Incident Stress Debriefing (CISD)*. Ellicot City: Chevron Publishing Corp.

McFarlane, A.C. (1990) 'An Australian Disaster. The 1983 bushfires.' *International Journal of Mental Health 19*, 36–47.

Minkkinen, T. (1999) 'M/S Estonian haveri ja pelastustyö.' *Acta Universitatis Tamperensis 662*.

Palosaari, E. (1999) 'Coping merikatastrofin yhteydessä suomalaisten laivatyöntekijöiden kertomana.' *Acta Universitatis Tamperensis 661*.

Parkes, C.M. (1990) 'Risk factors in bereavement; implications for the prevention and treatment of pathologic grief.' *Psychiatric Annals 20*, 308–313.

Pöyhönen, T. (1987) 'Työ, toiminta stressitilanteissa ja mielenterveys – tutkimus psykiatrisen sairaalan henkilökunnasta.' *Työ ja ihminen. Työympäristötutkimuksen aikakausikirja.* Supplement 2/87, Part 2.

Raittila, P. (1996) *Mediernas Estonia. Myndigheter och massmedier som informatörer i Finland.* Stockholm: Rapport.

Raphael, B. (1986) *When Disaster Strikes.* New York: Basic Books.

Rose, S., Bisson, J. and Wessley, S. 'Psychological debriefing for preventing post-traumatic stress disorder (PTSD).' *Cochrane Review,* The Cochrane Library, Issue 2, Oxford.

Saari, S., Lindeman, M., Verkasalo, M. and Prytz, H. (1996) 'The Estonia Disaster: A description of the crisis intervention in Finland.' *European Psychologists 1,* 2, 135–139.

Theorell, T., Leymann, H., Jodko, M., Konarski, K., Norbeck, H.E. and Eneroth, P. (1992) '"Person under train" incidents: Medical consequences for subway drivers.' *Psychosomatic Medicine 54,* 480–488.

Wahlbeck, K. (1998) 'Onko jälkipuinti ehkäisevänä toimintana haitallista?' *Impakti 3,* 98, 7–8.

Winje, D. (1996) 'Foreldres og barns traumereaksjoner over tid.' Paper, XIX Nordiska Psykologkongressen, Sollentune.

Yule, W., Williams, R. and Joseph, S. (1997) 'The Herald of Free Enterprise Disaster.' In D. Black, M. Newman, J. Harris-Hendriks and G. Mezey (eds) *Psychological Trauma. A Developmental Approach.* London: Gaskell.

Subject Index

Author Index